Integrated Chinese

中文聽說讀寫

Traditional and Simplified Characters
Teacher's Manual

Yuehua Liu, Tao-Chung Yao
Nyan-ping Bi and Yaohua Shi

Cheng & Tsui Company

First edition 1997
1998 Printing

Cheng & Tsui Company
25 West Street
Boston, MA 02111-1213 USA

Traditional and Simplified Character Edition
ISBN 0-88727-277-0

Companion textbooks, workbooks, character workbooks and audio tapes are also available from the publisher.

PUBLISHER'S NOTE

The Cheng & Tsui Company is pleased to announce the most recent addition to its Asian Language Series, *Integrated Chinese*. This entirely new course program for the beginning to advanced student of Mandarin Chinese will incorporate textbooks, workbooks, character workbooks, teaching aids, audio tapes, video tapes, CD-ROM computer programs and interactive multimedia programs. Field-tested since 1994, this series has been very well received. It is our intention to keep it a dynamic product by continuing to add, revise and refine the content as we get your valuable feedback.

This series seeks to train students in all four language skills: listening, speaking, reading and writing. It utilizes a variety of pedagogical approaches—grammar translation, audio-lingual, direct method, total physical response—to achieve the desired results. Because no two Chinese language programs are the same, *Integrated Chinese* provides those classes that cover the lessons more speedily with additional material in the form of Supplementary Vocabulary. The Supplementary Vocabulary section, however, is purely optional.

The *C&T Asian Language Series* is designed to publish and widely distribute quality language texts as they are completed by such leading institutions as the Beijing Language Institute, as well as other significant works in the field of Asian languages developed in the United States and elsewhere.

We welcome readers' comments and suggestions concerning the publications in this series. Please contact the following members of the Editorial Board:

Professor Shou-hsin Teng, Chief Editor
3 Coach Lane, Amherst, MA 01002

Professor Dana Scott Bourgerie
Asian and Near Eastern Languages, Brigham Young University, Provo, UT 84602

Professor Samuel Cheung
Dept. of Oriental Languages, University of California, Berkeley, CA 94720

Professor Ying-che Li
Dept. of East Asian Languages, University of Hawaii, Honolulu, HI 96822

Professor Timothy Light
Office of the Provost, Western Michigan University, Kalamazoo, MI 49008

PREFACE

We named this set of instructional materials *Integrated Chinese* out of the belief that a holistic approach is the best way to develop students' listening, speaking, reading, and writing skills. The textbooks, their companion workbooks and teacher's manuals are all designed to achieve that purpose.

The ultimate goal of learning a new language is to develop the ability to communicate in that language. Without neglecting basic structures, we strive to develop students' communicative skills by incorporating topics that are of interest to them: campus and family life, social issues, aspects of Chinese culture, etc. The hope is that students will be sufficiently engaged by the subjects and be motivated to quickly apply their newly-acquired vocabulary and grammatical structures in conversation. The workbooks provide many such topics for oral practice.

While we emphasize the communicative functions, we attempt to give equal weight to linguistic structures. We believe that to master a foreign language one must study phonetics and grammar as well as vocabulary. Therefore, we devote much attention to teaching grammar, sentence patterns, and important phrases and expressions. Our grammar notes go beyond merely describing discrete grammatical phenomena; instead, we try to situate them in their appropriate contexts and emphasize their usage. In *Integrated Chinese, Level Two*, we try to expand the student's understanding of Chinese grammar further by highlighting similar or easily confused structures.

To teach Chinese language is also to teach Chinese culture. Because most of the dialogues in *Integrated Chinese* are set in the United States, we use the listening and reading exercises to acquaint students with aspects of Chinese culture. In the second half of *Integrated Chinese, Level Two*, for example, we include a paragraph about contemporary China after each dialogue.

The workbooks are an essential part of *Integrated Chinese*. A great variety of materials designed to develop students' listening, speaking, reading, and writing skills are included: pattern drills, grammar and translation exercises, oral practice, writing practice, reading exercises, etc. Because no two language programs are alike, instructors need not assign all the exercises, nor use them in the same order as they appear in the books. There is flexibility in their application.

At present, the teacher's manual contain all the exercises in the student workbooks, workbook answer keys and grammar notes in Chinese. In time, we plan to add pedagogical suggestions, classroom activities and a test bank.

Despite our best intentions and efforts, we realize that there is room for improvement. The sheer scale of the project also means that mistakes are occasionally overlooked. Feedback on any aspect of *Integrated Chinese* will be much appreciated.

ABOUT THE WORKBOOK

In designing *Integrated Chinese, Level Two* workbook exercises, we strove to give equal emphasis to the students' listening, speaking, reading and writing skills. There are different difficulty levels in order to provide variety and flexibility to suit different curriculum needs. Teachers should assign the exercises at their discretion; they should not feel pressured into using all of them and should feel free to use them out of sequence if appropriate. Moreover, they can complement this workbook with their own exercises.

I. Listening Comprehension

All too often listening comprehension is sacrificed in a formal classroom setting because of time constraint. Students tend to focus their time and energies on the the mastery of a few grammar points. This workbook tries to remedy this imbalance by including a substantial number of listening comprehension exercises.

There are two categories of listening exercises, both of which can be done on the students' own time or in the classroom. In either case, it is important to have the instructor review the students' answers for accuracy.

The first category of listening exercises consists of a tape recording of each lesson. For the exercises to be meaningful, students should *first* study the vocabulary list, *then* listen to the recordings *before* attempting to read the texts. The questions are provided to help students' aural understanding of the texts and to test their reading comprehension.

The second category of listening exercises consists of a tape recording of three or more mini-dialogues or solo narrations. These exercises are designed to recycle the vocabulary and grammar points introduced in the new lesson. Some of the exercises are significantly more difficult since students are asked to choose among several possible answers. These exercises, therefore, should be assigned towards the end of a lesson, when the students have become familiar with the content of the texts.

II. Speaking Exercises

Here, too, there are two types of exercises. However, they are designed for different levels of proficiency within each lesson and should be assigned at the appropriate time. In the first type, to help students apply their newly-acquired vocabulary and grammatical understanding to meaningful communication, we ask concrete, personal questions related to their daily lives. These questions require a one or two-sentence answer. By stringing together short questions and answers, students can construct their own mini-dialogues, practice in pairs or take turns asking or answering the questions.

Once they have gained some confidence, the students can progress to more difficult questions where they are invited to express their opinions on a number of topics. Typically, the questions are more abstract, so the students will gradually learn to express their opinions and give their answers in paragraph-length discourse. As the school year progresses, these types of questions should take up more class discussion time. Because this second type of speaking exercise is quite challenging, it should be attempted only *after* students are well-grounded in the grammar and vocabulary of a particular lesson. This is usually *not immediately* after completing the first part of the speaking exercises.

III. *Reading Comprehension*

There are three to four passages for reading comprehension in each leasson. The first passage, usually short and related in content to the lesson at hand, recycles vocabulary and grammar points.

The second passage consists of slightly modified authentic materials, such as print advertisements, announcements, school diplomas, newspaper articles, etc. This passage may contain some unfamiliar vocabulary. The purpose of these materials is to train students to scan for useful information and not to let the appearance of a few new words distract them from comprehending the "big picture". Here, the teacher has a particularly important role to play in easing the students' anxiety about unfamiliar vocabulary. Teachers should encourage the student to ask: What do I really need to look for in a job announcement, a personal ad, or movie listings? Students should refer frequently to the questions to help them decipher these materials and should resist looking up every new word in their dictionary.

The third passage has to do with an aspect of Chinese culture. It might be a short folk tale, or it might explain the origin of a literary or historical allusion. By adding these passages to a textbook whose lessons are set in America, we hope to expose the students to a little bit of Chinese culture as well.

IV. *Grammar and Usage*

These drills and exercises are designed to solidify the students' grasp of important grammar points. Through brief exchanges, students answer questions using specific grammatical forms or are given sentences to complete. By providing context for these exercises, students gain a clearer understanding of the grammar points and will not treat them as simple mechanical repetition drills.

Towards the last quarter of the lessons, students are introduced to increasingly sophisticated and abstract vocabulary. Corresponding exercises help them to grasp the nuances of new words. For example, synonyms are a source of great difficulty, so exercises are provided to help students distinguish among them.

V. *Translation*

Translation has been a tool for language teaching throughout the ages, and positive student feedback confirms our belief that it continues to play an important role. The exercises we have devised serve to reinforce two primary areas: one, to get students to apply specific grammatical structures; two, to allow students to build on their ever-increasing vocabulary. Ultimately, our hope is that this dual-pronged approach will enable students to understand that it takes more than just literal translation to convey an idea in a foreign language.

VI. *Composition*

This is the culmination of the written exercises and is where students learn to express themselves in writing. Many of the topics overlap with those used in oral practice. We expect that students will find it easier to put in writing what they have already learned to express orally.

Table of Contents

Appendix: Teacher's Grammar Notes

第一課　　開　學

第一部分：聽力練習 Listening Comprehension

A: Listen to the tape recording of *Lesson One* and answer the following questions.

1. What year is Zhang Tianming?

    (He is a freshman.)

2. How did Zhang Tianming get to the campus?

    (He flew.)

3. Who is Ke Lin?

    (He is a returning student who helps freshmen move into dorms.)

4. Where does Ke Lin live?

    (He lives off campus.)

5. What does Ke Lin offer to do for Zhang Tianming?

    (He will help Zhang find a place to live next semester if he decides to move out.)

6. What did Zhang's mother tell him right before he left for college?

    (You can rely on your parents while you are at home, but when you are away from home, you will have to rely on your friends.)

B: Listen to the following passage.

1. Please answer the following questions on the basis of the recording.

    （在中國大陸或台灣，也有很多大學生住校。"住校"的意思
    就是在學校的宿舍裏住。宿舍的一個房間常常兩三個人合
    住，"合住"就是幾個人住在一起的意思。住在一個房間的
    人，在台灣叫"室友"，在中國大陸叫"同屋"。）

問題：

1) " 住校 " 是什麼意思？

2) 什麼是 " 室友 " ？什麼是 " 同屋 " ？

2. Please answer the following questions on the basis of the recording.

（上個學期小王住校，但是宿舍裏人太多，他不能好好念書，所以
決定搬出去。小王沒有車，只能在學校附近找房子。小王找
的地方離學校很近，走路只要五分鐘。這個地方很好，但是太
貴。爲了省錢，小王想找一個同學跟他一起住。）

Questions:

1) Why does Xiao Wang want to move out of his dorm?

   (He cannot study in the dorm.)

2) What is good about Xiao Wang's new place?

   (It's very good except for the rent. It's close to school, etc.)

3) Do you think Xiao Wang will live at his new place alone?

   Why or why not?

   (No, he cannot afford it.)

3. After listening to the recording, please fill out Mr. Zhang's daily schedule, and answer the following questions.

（小張每天早上起床以後，都要到外邊跑步。他覺得早上空氣好，
學校裏人不太多，這個時候跑步最好了。跑完步以後，他回宿舍
洗了澡才到餐廳吃早飯。吃了早飯以後，小張先去語言教室聽半
個鐘頭錄音再去上課。小張上午有三堂課，下課以後，他常常先
去圖書館看報紙再去吃午飯。吃完了飯，小張還得上兩門課。
上完了那兩門課，小張先去找小柯練習說漢語，練習完了才回宿
舍吃晚飯。）

起床
跑步
洗澡
吃早飯
聽錄音
上課
上課
上課
看報
吃午飯
上課
上課
練習漢語
吃晚飯

問題：

1）小張每天聽多長時間錄音？

2）小張每天有幾節課？

3）小張在哪兒吃晚飯？

4. Do you know how to write my friend's name in Chinese characters after you
   listen to the following short passage?

   （我有一個朋友，他姓張，叫念祖，弓長張，念書的念，祖籍的祖。
   請你把他的名字寫出來。）

5. Please write the name in characters on the basis of the recording.

   （我有一個老師，姓謝，謝謝的謝，他的名字叫適全，適應的適，安
   全的全。請你把他的名字寫出來。）

第二部分：口語練習 Speaking Exercises

A: Please practice asking and answering the following questions with a partner before class.

1. 你是在什麼地方出生的？
2. 你是在什麼地方長大的？
3. 你的暑假是怎麼過的？
4. 你今天是幾點來的學校？
5. 你今天是怎麼來的學校？
6. 你們學校是幾號開的學？
7. 你住校內還是住校外？
8. 要是你有錢，你想搬到什麼地方去住？為什麼？

B: Please practice speaking on the following topics.

1. 請你做一個簡單的自我介紹。
2. 請你談一談你上大學的第一天是怎麼過的。
3. 你認為住在學校宿舍好，還是住在校外好？為什麼？

第三部分：閱讀練習 Reading Comprehension

A: Please answer the questions after you have read the following passage.

(Traditional Characters)

　　張天明的家在波士頓，他們已經在那兒住了十多年了。張天明的父母都工作，每天早出晚歸(1)，只有晚上下班以後，一家人才能在一起，一邊吃飯，一邊聊天。張天明排行老三，上邊有一個哥哥，一個姐姐，下邊還有一個妹妹。張天明上大學以前從來沒離開過家，到學校才一天，他已經非常想家了。

(1)歸　guī　回來

(Simplified Characters)

　　张天明的家在波士顿，他们已经在那儿住了十多年了。张天明的父母都工作，每天早出晚归(1)，只有晚上下班以后，一家人才能在一起，一边吃饭，一边聊天。张天明排行老三，上边有一个哥哥，一个姐姐，下边还有一个妹妹。张天明上大学以前从来没离过家，到学校才一天，他已经非常想家了。

(1)归　guī　回来

問題：
1) 張天明的父母為什麼只有晚上才有時間？
　　（他們白天工作。）
2) 張天明一共有幾個兄弟姐妹？
　　（三個）
3) 張天明為什麼很想家？
　　（因為他從來沒離開過家。）

B: Take a look at the following business card and see if what you can make of it.

北京文化学院中国文学系

张百华　教授

地址：

北京文化学院19楼5门502

100083

电话：2017531-480（办公室）

問題：

1) 請問這個人在什麼地方工作？

    （北京文化學院）

2) 他是做什麼的？

    （他是老師）

3) 他家在哪兒？

    （北京文化學院19樓5門502）

4) 這上邊有沒有他家的電話？

    （沒有）

C: 請讀故事回答問題

Please answer the questions after reading the following story.

$$\frac{1 \mid 2}{3 \mid 4}$$

(Traditional Characters)

從前，有一個人，姓張，叫張文，他很有錢。可是他的兒子很不聰明，已經十幾歲了，連一個字都不認識。張文想，他已經六十多歲了，兒子不認識字，他死了以後，不會寫信，不會記賬(1)，怎麼辦？所以他就請了一位老師來教他兒子念書，識字。老師先教他"一"字，他覺得很容易，又教他"二"字，他也覺得很容易，等老師教完"三"字，他就說："寫字太容易了！"老師走了以後，他對爸爸說："爸爸，明天不用請老師了，我把中國字都學會了。"爸爸聽了很高興地說："過幾天是我的生日，我要請很多客人，你趕快寫一些請柬(2)吧。我的好朋友叫萬千，你先給他寫吧。"兒子說："沒問題。"張文給兒子準備了很多紙，兒子寫了十幾張紙，還沒寫完。爸爸過來問他："快寫完了嗎？"兒子說："沒有，才寫了三百多筆，還有很多很多呢。"

(1) 記賬 (jì zhàng): keep accounts   (2) 請柬 (qǐngjiǎn): invitation

(Simplified Characters)

从前，有一个人，姓张，叫张文，他很有钱。可是他的儿子很不聪明，已经十几岁了，连一个字都不认识。张文想，他已经六十多岁了，儿子不认识字，他死了以后，不会写信，不会记账(1)，怎么办？所以他就请了一位老师来教他儿子念书，识字。老师先教他"一"字，他觉得很容易，又教他"二"字，他也觉得很容易，等老师教完"三"字，他就说："写字太容易了！"老师走了以后，他对爸爸说："爸爸，明天不用请老师了，我把中国字都学会了。"爸爸听了很高兴地说："过几天是我的生日，我要请很多客人，你赶快写一些请柬(2)吧。我的好朋友叫万千，你先给他写吧。"儿子说："没问题。"张文给儿子准备了很多纸，儿子写了十几张纸，还没写完。爸爸过来问他："快写完了吗？"儿子说："没有，才写了三百多笔，还有很多很多呢。"

(1) 记账 (jì zhàng): keep accounts   (2) 请柬 (qǐngjiǎn): invitation letter

Questions:

1) Why is Zhang Wen worried about his son?

   (Because he doesn't know how to read and write. / He is not very bright.)

2) What does Zhang Wen do to help his son?

   (He asks a teacher to come and teach his son to read and write.)

3) Why does the son say that he does not need help any more?

   (Because he has learned how to write "one", "two", "three" and thinks that he has mastered all the Chinese characters.)

4) Does the son learn to write Chinese? How do you know?

   (No. His father asks him to write an invitation to "Wan Qian", a name meaning ten thousand and one thousand literally. The son begins to write 10,000 strokes and 1,000 strokes, thinking this is the way to write these numbers.)

第四部分：句型與詞語練習 Grammar & Usage

A: 請按自己的情況回答下面問題。

Answer the following questions on the basis of your personal experience.

1. A: 學校開學幾天了？

    B:_____。

2. A: 你學中文學了幾個學期了？

    B:_____。

3. A: 每天吃了晚飯以後，你做些什麼事情？

    B:_____。

B: 請根據張天明的作息時間表填空。

Complete the following passage, based on the information given in Zhang Tianming's schedule.

	起床
	吃早飯
早上	上漢語課
	上化學課
	聽錄音

	吃午飯
下午	上歷史課
	打球
	回宿舍

	吃晚飯
晚上	做功課
	看電視
	睡覺

　　張天明今天早晨<u>起床</u>以後，很快地吃了點早飯，就去上課。<u>上完漢語課</u>以後，沒能休息，就去上化學課。<u>下了化學課(上完化學課)</u>，他到語言實驗室去<u>聽錄音</u>。吃午飯的時候，柯林坐在他的旁邊。柯林說：＂我今天有四節課，已經上了三節了，你呢？＂小張回答說：＂我<u>上了兩節課了</u>，還有一節歷史課。＂下午回宿舍前，張天明跟朋友去<u>打球</u>。<u>打完球</u>，才回宿舍吃晚飯。張天明今天的功課不多，<u>做了</u>一個鐘頭就<u>做完了</u>。然後，<u>看了</u>半個鐘頭的電視，就上床<u>睡覺</u>了。

C: 請用 " 是...的 " 完成下面對話。

Please use "是...的" to complete the following dialogues.

1. A: 你今天是幾點起的床？

   B:＿＿＿＿＿＿＿＿＿＿＿＿＿＿＿＿＿＿＿＿＿＿＿＿＿ 。

2. A:＿＿＿＿＿＿＿＿＿＿＿＿＿＿＿＿＿＿＿＿＿＿＿＿＿ ？

   B: 我今天是走路去的學校 。

3. A: 你身上穿的衣服是在哪兒買的？

   B:＿＿＿＿＿＿＿＿＿＿＿＿＿＿＿＿＿＿＿＿＿＿＿＿＿ 。

4. A: 你是從哪兒來的？

   B:＿＿＿＿＿＿＿＿＿＿＿＿＿＿＿＿＿＿＿＿＿＿＿＿＿ 。

5. A: 你是什麼時候開始學的漢語？

   B:＿＿＿＿＿＿＿＿＿＿＿＿＿＿＿＿＿＿＿＿＿＿＿＿＿ ？

D: 請用 "除了...以外，還..." 改寫下面句子。

Please rewrite the following sentences using "除了...以外，還..." .

1. 這個學校開的語言課很多，有中文，日文，法文和德文。

   --->這個學校開的語言課很多，＿＿＿＿＿＿＿＿＿＿＿＿ 。

2. 我覺得住校很方便，也很安全。

   --->我覺得住校，＿＿＿＿＿＿＿＿＿＿＿＿＿＿＿＿＿＿ 。

3. 學校剛開學，人很多，有新生，老生和新生的父母。

   --->學校剛開學，人很多，＿＿＿＿＿＿＿＿＿＿＿＿＿ 。

E: 請用 "除了...以外，都..." 改寫下面句子。

Please rewrite the following sentences using "除了...以外，都..." .

1. 大學二，三，四年級的學生都不用住校，只有一年級的新生得住校。

   --->＿＿＿＿＿＿＿＿＿＿＿＿＿＿＿＿＿＿＿＿＿＿＿ 。

2. 每到週末，學校裏只有圖書館沒人，別的地方人都很多。

   --->＿＿＿＿＿＿＿＿＿＿＿＿＿＿＿＿＿＿＿＿＿＿＿ 。

3. 新生只有小張還沒辦註冊手續，別的人都辦好了。

   --->_____。

F:請用＂再說＂回答下面的問題。

Please use "再說" to answer the following questions.

例: A: 你為什麼今天沒去註冊？

B: <u>因為我爸爸的錢還沒到，再說註冊的人也太多</u>。

1. A: 你為什麼學中文？

   B: _____ ，_____ 。

2. A: 你為什麼上這個學校？

   B: _____ ，_____ 。

3. A: 你為什麼喜歡住校？

   B: _____ ，_____ 。

G:請用＂不見得＂回答下面的對話。

Please use "不見得" to answer the following questions.

例: A: 你的父母是中國人，你學中文很容易吧？

B: 在美國長大的中國孩子，<u>學中文也不見得容易</u>。

1. A: 這個宿舍又小又不貴。我真想搬出去住。 （有好處）

   B: 很多校外的房子也很小很貴，_____。

2. A: 下個學期我打算搬到你們這個宿舍來，我已經辦了手續了。（搬得進來）

   B: 很多人都想搬進來，你_____。

3. A: 他是老生，聽他的話，沒錯。 （有道理）

   B: 他只比我們早來一年，他說的話_____。

第五部分：翻譯 Translation

A: Translate the following dialogues into Chinese.

1. A: When will the new semester begin?
    B: Next Wednesday.

    （A: 什麼時候開學？）

    （B: 下個星期三。）

2. A: Why did a lot of people arrive on the campus?
    B: You didn't know? They were new students. They came to register.

    （A: 爲什麼校園裏來了這麼多人？）

    （B: 你不知道？他們是新生，是來學校辦註冊手續的。）

3. A: Did you come here by plane or by car?
    B: I came by car.

    （A: 你是坐飛機來的還是開車來的？）

    （B: 我是開車來的。）

4. Living in the dormitory is very convenient. However, it does not save you money.

    （住在學校宿舍裏/住在校內很方便。但是不省錢。）

B:
That first year student was born in China, but raised in America. I helped her register.
Her parents wanted her to live in the dorm to get used to college life. She felt that living
in the dorm was too restricted. She said that she wanted to live off-campus next semester.

（　那個新生是在中國出生，在美國長大的。昨天我幫她辦註冊手續。她的父母
要她住校，適應一下大學生活。可是她自己覺得住校太不自由了。她說她下
個學期要搬到校外去住。）

C:

Zhang Tianming met a new friend this morning. His name was Ke Lin. Zhang Tianming met Ke Lin in the dorm. There were many people in the dorm. Except for Ke Lin, Zhang Tianming didn't know anyone else. Ke Lin helped Zhang Tianming move, and also helped other new students move. After finishing moving, Ke Lin said to Zhang Tianming, "If you need my help, please don't hesitate to call me."

（　今天早上張天明認識了一個新朋友，他叫柯林。張天明是在宿舍裏
　　遇見柯林的。宿舍裏人很多，除了柯林以外，別的人張天明都不認
　　識。柯林幫張天明搬東西，也幫別的新生搬東西。搬完東西以後，
　　柯林對張天明說：「如果你需要我幫忙的話，就給我打電話。」）

第六部分：寫作練習 Composition

作文：

《開學的第一天》

Please describe your first day in college.

第二課　　宿　舍

第一部分：聽力練習 Listening Comprehension

A: Listen to the tape recording of *Lesson Two* and answer the following questions.

1. Who moved in first? Zhang Tianming or John?

   (John did.)

2. What furniture do Zhang Tianming and John both have?

   (A chair, a desk, a bed, a closet, and a bookshelf.)

3. Is their dorm close to the main street?

   (No.)

4. What are the advantages things of living in this dorm?

   (The dorm is close to classrooms and a mini-mart. Very convenient for doing laundry)

5. What are the disadvantages of living in this dorm?

   (Dorm food is bad, no air-conditioning.)

B: Listen to the following short passages.

1. Please transcribe the character on the basis of the recording.

   （上邊一個告訴的告，下邊一個非常的非。請問這是什麼字？）
   （靠）

2. Please transcribe the character on the basis of the recording.

   （左邊一個木字旁，右邊一個東南西北的東。請問這是什麼字？）
   （棟）

3. Listen to the recording and answer the following questions.

   （柯林今年大三，他對學外語很有興趣。念高中的時候，他學過三
   年法語。現在他學的是中文。他說他的很多同學都是從中國來
   的，他常常跟他們練習說中文。）

   問題：
   1) 柯林會哪些外語？   （法語，漢語）
   2) 他什麼時候學過法語？   （上高中的時候）
   3) 他跟什麼人練習說漢語？   （他的從中國來的同學）

4. Listen to the recording and answer the following questions.

   （我的房間裏邊家俱很少，除了一個書桌，一個衣櫃和一張床以
   外，只有一個書架和兩把椅子。我的房間離教室很近，洗衣服吃
   飯也很方便，要是有一個窗戶就更好了。）

   問題：
   1) 房間裏有幾件傢俱？（6）
   2) 這個房間什麼都好，就是哪一點不好？（沒有窗戶）

5. Please draw a picture of Xiao Li's room based on the recording and answer the
   question you hear at the end of the recording.

   （ 李家剛搬家，房子大多了。小李自己有一個房間，不必跟哥哥睡一
   個房間了。小李的屋子裏有一個窗戶。窗戶的前邊擺著一張書桌，
   桌子的左邊是一張新床，桌子的右邊是衣櫃，衣櫃的門是開著的，
   裏邊沒掛衣服。李媽媽覺得小李需要一個書架，打算明天幫他買一
   個好的，但是小李還少一樣傢俱，你知道是什麼嗎？）（椅子）

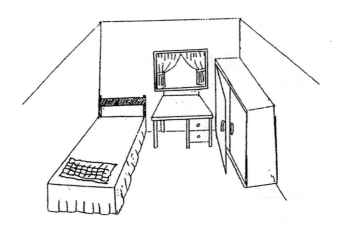

第二部分：口語練習 Speaking Exercises

A: Please practice asking and answering the following questions with a partner before class.

1. 你的房間有什麼家俱？

2. 你的書桌上擺著一些什麼東西？

3. 你住的地方離學校哪一棟樓最近？

4. 你去過的中國餐館，哪一家的菜最地道？

B: Please practice speaking on the following topics.

1. 請你用中文描述一下自己的房間。（我現在住在...）

2. 你喜歡什麼樣的房間？

C: Please choose one of the six rooms and describe the room in detail.

第三部分：閱讀練習 Reading Comprehension

A: Please answer the questions after reading the following passage.

(Traditional Characters)

在中國，學生高中畢業以後都需要考試才能上大學。考試考得好，就上好一點的大學，考得不好，就上差一點的大學。每個新生一進大學，就已經知道自己的專業(1)是什麼了，要是不喜歡，也可以轉系或者轉學。但是轉系，轉學還是得考試。

(1)專業 (zhuānyè): major

(Simplified Characters)

在中国，学生高中毕业以后都需要考试才能上大学。考试考得好，就上好一点的大学，考得不好，就上差一点的大学。每个新生一进大学，就已经知道自己的专业(1)是什么了，要是不喜欢，也可以转系或者转学。但是转系，转学还是得考试。

(1)专业 (zhuānyè): major

問題：
1) 在美國上大學跟在中國上大學有什麼不一樣？
2) 請問 " 轉系 " 和 " 轉學 " 英文怎麼說？

B: Please draw a picture and answer the questions after reading the following passage.

(Traditional Characters)

小高的新家有兩層樓，樓上有三個房間，樓下有客廳，餐廳和洗衣房。樓上左邊的房間是小高的書房。房間的中間是一張很大的書桌，書桌的後邊是兩個又高又大的書架。中間的房間是廁所。右邊的房間是小高的臥房，中間放著一張床，床的旁邊擺著一個衣櫃。樓下右邊的房間是洗衣房，裏邊有烘乾機和洗衣機。洗衣房的隔壁是餐廳，再過去才是客廳。客廳的外邊是車庫，裏邊停著兩輛車，一輛大的，一輛小的。小高非常喜歡他的新家。

(Simplified Characters)

小高的新家有两层楼，楼上有三个房间，楼下有客厅，餐厅和洗衣房。楼上左边的房间是小高的书房。房间的中间是一张很大的书桌，书桌的后边是两个又高又大的书架。中间的房间是厕所。右边的房间是小高的卧房，中间放着一张床，床的旁边摆着一个衣柜。楼下右边的房间是洗衣房，里边有烘乾机和洗衣机。洗衣房的隔壁是餐厅，再过去才是客厅。客厅的外边是车库，里边停着两辆车，一辆大的，一辆小的。小高非常喜欢他的新家。

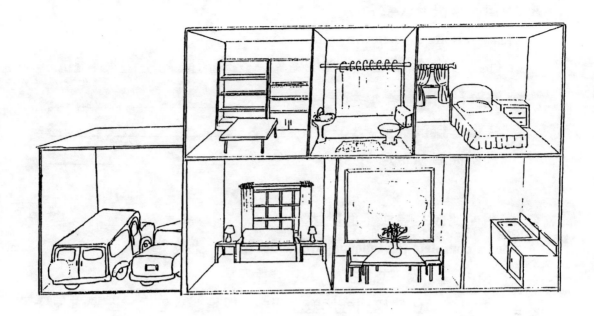

是非題：

1) <u>F</u> 這個房子有五個房間。

2) <u>T</u> 小高不再到外邊洗衣服了。

3) <u>F</u> 要是小高的朋友來家裏聊天、吃飯，他們應該上二樓。

第四部分：句型與詞語練習 Grammar & Usage

A: 請用 " 比較 " 完成下面對話。

Please complete the following dialogues using "比較".

1. A: 一年有四季。你喜歡哪一個季節？

    B:＿＿＿＿＿＿＿＿＿＿＿＿＿＿＿＿＿＿＿＿＿＿＿＿＿＿。

2. A: 你覺得住校內比較省錢，還是住校外比較省錢？

    B:＿＿＿＿＿＿＿＿＿＿＿＿＿＿＿＿＿＿＿＿＿＿＿＿＿＿。

3. A: 你家誰的胃口好？

    B:＿＿＿＿＿＿＿＿＿＿＿＿＿＿＿＿＿＿＿＿＿＿＿＿＿＿。

B: 請用「得很」改寫句子。

Please rewrite the following sentences using "得很".

例：那家飯館的菜非常地道。----> <u>那家飯館的菜地道得很</u>。

1. 他住的那棟宿舍很安靜。----->_____。
2. 這個學校很安全。----->_____。
3. 那家商店非常遠。----->_____。

C: 請用「比較」完成下面對話。

Please complete the following dialogues using "比較".

例：　A: 我不想住校，太不自由了。

　　　B: <u>住學校宿舍比較不自由</u>，但是離教室近，上課方便多了。

1. A: 這個店的傢俱很貴，我想看一看別的店怎麼樣。
   B:_____，但是比別的店都好得多。
2. A: 這個洗衣機和烘乾機太吵了，應該買新的。
   B:_____，但是還可以用。
3. A: 你怎麼帶我來這家餐館，你看他們的設備那麼舊。
   B:_____，但是菜又好吃又地道。

D: 請用「恐怕」完成下面對話。

Please complete the following dialogues using "恐怕".

例：　A: 哎，你的房間怎麼這麼熱？

　　　B: 我也不知道，<u>恐怕是空調壞了</u>。

1. A: 我剛下課，肚子餓得很。今天宿舍餐廳的晚飯怎麼樣？
   B: 還不錯。可是現在已經快九點了。這麼晚了，_____。
2. A: 都已經十二點半了，他怎麼還沒來？　（迷路）
   B: 波士頓的路不好找，_____。

3. A: 你覺得我應該買些什麼樣兒的家俱？

　　B: 你的新家不大，家俱太多，＿＿＿＿＿＿＿＿，最好少買一些。

E: Translate the following sentences into Chinese. Pay attention to word order.

1. I read a book in the library yesterday afternoon.

    (我昨天在圖書館看了一本書。)

2. My brother drove from Boston to Washington D.C. last weekend to visit a friend.

    (我哥哥上個週末開車從波士頓到華盛頓去看朋友。)

3. He was doing laundry on the second floor when his father called.

    (他父親打電話來的時候，他正在二樓洗衣服。)

4. Xiao Zhang is going to play basketball with his friends after class.

    (小張下了課以後要跟朋友一起打籃球。)

5. This is the restaurant that my roommate mentioned.

    (這就是我同屋說的那家餐館。)

6. The dorm where I used to live was small and old.

    (我以前住的宿舍又小又舊。)

7. The food that your mom made last night was delicious.

    (你母親昨天晚上做的菜好吃極了。)

8. The store we went to this morning also sells stationery.

    (我們今天早上去的那家商店也賣文具。)

F: " 著 "

Describe the following photograph: What are the two people wearing?, What is on the table?, etc. Don't forget to include the background scenery and the restaurant setting. Remember to use "著" in your description.

抽煙 (chōu yān): smoke (a cigarette)	手提箱 (shǒutíxiāng): purse; brief case
抽煙斗 (chōu yāndǒu): smoke (a cigar)	戴眼鏡 (dài yǎnjìng): wear glasses
火柴 (huǒchái): matches	手錶 (shǒubiǎo): watch
掛 (guà): hang	畫 (huà): picture; painting

第五部分：翻譯 Translation

A: Translate the following dialogues into Chinese.

1. A: Where is your roommate from?
   B: He's from Washington.

   （ A: 你的同屋是從哪兒來的？ ）

   （ B: 他是從華盛頓來的。 ）

2. A: I am starving.
   B: Then let's go eat.

   （ A: 我餓得很。 ）

   （ B: 那麼我們去吃飯吧。 ）

3. A: Does the store on campus sell furniture?
   B: No, the store on campus only sells daily necessities and stationery.

（ A: 我們學校的商店賣不賣家俱？）

（ B: 不賣，我們學校的商店只賣日用品和文具，學校裏的商店
一般都不賣家具。）

B: Translate the following passages into Chinese using the grammar points and vocabulary items from this lesson.

1. Near the campus there is a Chinese restaurant and a Japanese restaurant. The Japanese restaurant is relatively more expensive. The Chinese restaurant is much cheaper than the Japanese restaurant. The restaurants are very close to the campus. That's really convenient.

（ 學校附近有一家中國餐館和一家日本餐館。日本餐館比較貴，中
國餐館比日本餐館便宜得多。餐館離校園很近，方便得很。 ）

2. This is Zhang Tianming's room. In the middle of the room, there is a bed. There is a blanket and a comforter on the bed. There is a wardrobe on the right side of the room. However, the wardrobe is empty. There is a picture hanging on the door, and there's a bookcase below the picture. There are some books on the shelf.

（ 這是張天明的房間。房間的中間有一張床，床上有毯子和被子。房
間的右邊是一個衣櫃，可是衣櫃是空的。門上掛著一張照片，照片
下邊是一個書架，書架上有一些書。 ）

3. I am moving into the dorm in a few days. The facilities of the dorm are relatively new. My room is close to the bathroom. There are washers and driers on my floor. It's really convenient to live there. However, I'm afraid it will be a bit noisy.

（ 我過幾天要搬到宿舍去。那棟宿舍的設備比較新。我的房間離廁所
很近。我住的那層樓有洗衣機和烘乾機，很方便。但是恐怕有點兒
吵。 ）

第六部分：寫作練習 Composition

Please describe your ideal living quarters. Start with "要是我有錢的話 …"

第三課　在飯館

第一部分：聽力練習 Listening Comprehension

A: Listen to the tape recording of *Lesson Three* and answer the following questions.

1. Why does Zhang Tianming want to go to Chinatown?

    (He wants to have some Chinese food.)

2. Who goes to Chinatown with Zhang Tianming?

    (Ke Lin and his girlfriend.)

3. Who is a frequent patron of the restaurant?

    (Ke Lin.)

4. What do they order?

    (They order "steamed fish", "beef broccoli", "spinach and tofu soup", and "small Chinese cabbage.")

5. Do they agree with the reporter?

    (All three of them disagreed.)

B: Listen to the tape for the workbook.

1. Listen to the passage and answer the following multiple-choice question.

    （小陳工作的餐館生意不錯，每天都有很多客人。小陳的老板
    對他很好，客人給的錢也不少，但是小陳決定不做了。老
    板問他爲什麼不做了，小陳回答說，因爲他最近開始吃素，
    餐館裏的菜都不是素菜，所以他覺得不太習慣，再說，有
    些客人吸煙吸得太多，他也受不了。）

Question:

Why did Xiao Chen decide to quit?

      a. He was not allowed to smoke in the restaurant.

      b. The boss didn't like him.

      c. His customers didn't tip him well.

      d. Xiao Chen became a vegetarian.

2. Listen to the passage and answer the following question in English.

（中國人跟美國人到中國飯館吃飯是很有意思的事。中國人是點了菜以後，大家一起吃。美國人總是自己吃自己點的菜。中國人習慣吃了飯再喝湯，美國人是先喝湯再吃飯。中國人常叫熱茶喝，美國人叫的是冰茶或是可樂。中國人常用飯碗吃飯，但是美國人把飯放在盤子裏吃。）

New Vocabulary:

飯碗 (fànwǎn): rice bowl   盤子 (pánzi): plate

Question:

In which four ways do Chinese and American differ when it comes to eating and drinking?

    a. Unlike Americans who order separately, Chinese order together and share their food.

    b. Chinese serve soup last unlike Americans.

    c. Chinese drink hot tea whereas Americans drink iced tea or coke.

    d. Chinese eat rice from bowls whereas Americans put their food on a plate.

3. Listen to the passage and answer the following questions in English.

（小張是大學一年級的新生，對校內校外還不太熟悉。有一天他想
到校外的中國餐館吃飯。以前都是同學開車帶他去，這一次他想
自己去。他記得那家餐館不太遠，走一刻鐘應該可以走到。小張
走了半天，過了好幾條馬路，經過了好幾家美國餐館，但是沒找
到他要去的那家中國餐館。小張餓極了，不想再找了，正好前邊
有一家賣素菜的餐館，小張決定就在那家餐館吃飯。）

Questions:

1) What was Xiao Zhang's adventure about?

   (He tried to find the Chinese restaurant on his own.)

2) Was his adventure a successful one? Why or why not?

   (No, he didn't find the place.)

3) What did Xiao Zhang finally do?

   (He went to a vegetarian restaurant..)

第二部分：口語練習 Speaking Exercises

A: Please practice asking and answering the following questions with a partner before class.

1. 開學已經多長時間了？

2. 你多長時間沒吃中國飯了？

3. 你媽媽做什麼菜最拿手？

B: Please practice speaking on the following topics.

1. 請你談一下你一般都到什麼樣的餐館吃飯？為什麼？

2. 你覺得吃什麼東西對身體健康有好處？

3. Find a partner and make up a dialogue about eating out. One of you could be a customer, the other a waiter. Or one could invite the other to eat at a restaurant.

第三部分：閱讀練習 Reading Comprehension

A: Please answer the questions after reading the following passage.

(Traditional Characters)

　　法國人跟美國人對吃的看法好像很不同。法國人認爲應該是想吃什麼就吃什麼，不要怕油多，卡路里高，但是最重要的是每天一定要喝些紅酒。法國人認爲喝葡萄酒對身體有好處。美國人認爲吃得越清淡越好，少吃肉，尤其是牛肉，多吃青菜，做菜的時候，要少放油，少放鹽。如果你問我這兩種看法哪一種對？我想這就要看每個人的情況了。每個人應該根據自己的身體情況，生活習慣來決定自己應該吃什麼，不應該吃什麼。

　　　　葡萄 (pútao): grapes

(Simplified Characters)

　　法国人跟美国人对吃的看法好像很不同。法国人认为应该是想吃什么就吃什么，不要怕油多，卡路里高，但是最重要的是每天一定要喝些红酒。法国人认为喝葡萄酒对身体有好处。美国人认为吃得越清淡越好，少吃肉，尤其是牛肉，多吃青菜，做菜的时候，要少放油，少放盐。如果你问我这两种看法哪一种对？我想这就要看每个人的情况了。每个人应该根据自己的身体情况，生活习惯来决定自己应该吃什么，不应该吃什么。

　　　　葡萄 (pútao): grapes

Questions:

1) Does the author prefer the American or the French diet? How do you know?

　　(Neither. The author says it is up to each individual to decide.)

2) Why do the French drink red wine every day?

　　(It's good for your health.)

3) How do you think the French diet differs from the American diet according to this passage?

   (The French diet is greasier and higher in calories.)

4) Is one diet better than the other according to the author?

   (No, not necessarily.)

B: Please answer the questions after reading the following passage.

(Traditional Characters)

　　小柯到學校附近的一家中國餐館吃飯。那家飯館的菜又便宜又地道。小柯是那兒的常客，老闆，服務員都認識他。但是今天一進門，小柯就覺得跟以前不一樣了。原來飯館裏是不讓人吸煙的，怎麼今天那麼多人吸煙？那些服務員小柯也從來沒見過。菜單上的菜也比以前貴多了。除了這些以外，小柯點的菜裏還放了很多味精。小柯決定下次再也不到這家餐館來吃飯了。

(Simplified Characters)

　　小柯到学校附近的一家中国餐馆吃饭。那家饭馆的菜又便宜又地道。小柯是那儿的常客，老板，服务员都认识他。但是一进门，小柯就觉得不对。原来饭馆里是不让人吸烟的，怎麼今天那麼多人吸烟？服务员小柯也从来没见过。菜单上的菜也比以前贵多了。除了这些以外，小柯的菜里还放了很多味精。小柯决定下次再也不到这家餐馆来吃饭了。

Questions:

1) What attracts Xiao Ke to the restaurant?

   (The food is good and inexpensive.)

2) What four changes did Xiao Ke notice on this visit?

   (Price has gone up, people smoke, a lot of MSG, and he didn't recognize the waiters.)

3) Did he eat? How do you know?

   (Yes, he did. Because he complained about the MSG in his food.)

4) Will he eat there again?

   (Never.)

C: Please glance over the following menu and circle the (all) seafood category.

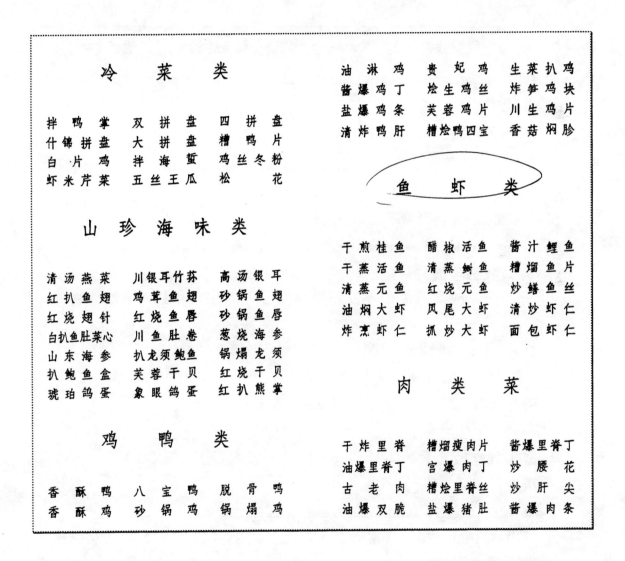

第四部分：句型與詞語練習 Grammer & Usage

A: 話題：Topics

Please rewrite the following sentences using the words in the parentheses.

> 例： A: 學校附近有很多飯館，還有一家中國餐館。 （那家餐館）
>
> B: <u>那家餐館我去過。菜做得很地道。</u>

1. A: 我聽說小柯剛交了一個女朋友。你認識嗎？ （那個女孩）

   B: _____。

2. A: 這個餐館我第一次來，想吃他們的清蒸魚。你說呢？（他們的 清蒸魚）

   B: _____。

3. A: 你昨天買什麼了？

   B: 我昨天買了一本書。（那本書）

   A: _____。

B: 請用「原來」(1)改寫下面的句子。

Please rewrite the following sentences by using "原來(1)".

> 例：我三年前見到他的時候，他在學日文。昨天我在商店裏遇見
> 他。他跟我說他早就不學日文了，他一年半以前開始學中文
> 了。
>
> ---> 他原來學日文，後來改學中文了。

1. 約翰想買一台空調。到店裏看了看，沒有好的。但是天氣實在太熱，
   所以他買了一台電扇 (diànshàn: electric fan)。

   --->_____。

2. 他請我吃飯。我想叫清蒸魚，但是一看太貴了，結果叫了一盤炒青
   菜。

   --->_____。

3. 他上高中的時候，常常喝酒，但是聽說上大學，有了女朋友以後，
   就不喝酒了。

   --->_____。

C: 請用 « 原來 » (2)完成下面的句子。

Please complete the following sentences by using "原來(2)".

1. 屋子裏怎麼這麼熱，噢 ＿＿＿＿＿＿＿＿＿＿＿＿＿＿＿＿＿ 。（空調）

2. 小張晚飯沒吃什麼，我以爲他不喜歡吃我做的牛肉，後來才知道 ＿＿＿＿＿＿＿＿＿＿＿＿＿＿＿＿＿＿＿＿＿＿＿ 。（吃素）

3. 我找了你半天，找不到你，＿＿＿＿＿＿＿＿＿＿＿＿＿＿ 。

D: 請用 « ...又...又... » 改寫下面的句子。

Please rewrite the following sentences using "...又...又...".

例：那棟宿舍很新，也很漂亮。---->那棟宿舍又新又漂亮。

1. 我媽媽做的牛肉很嫩，而且很好吃。

    ---->＿＿＿＿＿＿＿＿＿＿＿＿＿＿＿＿＿＿＿＿＿ 。

2. 有些記者寫文章寫得很長，而且沒有意思。

    ---->＿＿＿＿＿＿＿＿＿＿＿＿＿＿＿＿＿＿＿＿＿ 。

3. 聽說那家商店的青菜水果非常新鮮，而且很便宜。

    ---->＿＿＿＿＿＿＿＿＿＿＿＿＿＿＿＿＿＿＿＿＿ 。

E: 請用 « 這就要看 » 回答下面的問題。

Please answer the following questions using "這就要看".

例：A: 你今天想點什麼菜呢？

B: 這就要看這家餐館什麼菜好吃了。

1. A: 你下個學期還要學中文嗎？

   B:＿＿＿＿＿＿＿＿＿＿＿＿＿＿＿＿＿＿＿＿＿ 。

2. A: 你這個週末打算做什麼？

   B:＿＿＿＿＿＿＿＿＿＿＿＿＿＿＿＿＿＿＿＿＿ 。

3. A: 你明年還要住校嗎？

   B:＿＿＿＿＿＿＿＿＿＿＿＿＿＿＿＿＿＿＿＿＿ 。

F: 請用「其實」完成下面的句子。

Please complete the following sentences using "其實".

例：我的同學都認爲這次考試有一點兒難，<u>其實這次考試不太難</u>。

1. 大家都覺得那個女孩長得很漂亮，＿＿＿＿＿＿＿＿＿＿＿＿＿。

2. 很多人都覺得住在校外比較好，＿＿＿＿＿＿＿＿＿＿＿＿＿。

3. 最近有一些文章說中國菜太油，＿＿＿＿＿＿＿＿＿＿＿＿＿。

G: 請用「特別是」完成下面的句子。

Please complete the following sentences using "特別是".

例：開學大家都很忙，<u>特別是新生</u>。

1. 小林非常喜歡吃中國菜，＿＿＿＿＿＿＿＿＿＿＿＿＿。

2. 那個記者寫的很多文章沒有什麼道理，＿＿＿＿＿＿＿＿＿。

3. 小張這學期每門課的功課都很多，＿＿＿＿＿＿＿＿＿＿。

H: 請用「要不然」完成下面的句子：

Please complete the following sentences using "要不然".

例：租房子最好租帶家俱的，<u>要不然得花很多錢買家俱</u>。

1. 學中文最好天天聽錄音復習課文，＿＿＿＿＿＿＿＿＿＿。

2. 在中國飯館吃飯，常常得告訴老板少放點兒鹽和味精，

＿＿＿＿＿＿＿＿＿＿＿＿＿＿＿＿＿＿＿。

3. 找房子最好不要找在大馬路旁邊的，＿＿＿＿＿＿＿＿＿。

I: 請用「的」，「地」，「得」填空。

Please fill in the blanks with "的", "地", or "得".

(Traditional Characters)

　　前些日子，校園報紙做了一個調查，看看附近哪一家餐館<u>的</u>菜做<u>得</u>最好吃。結果，是城裏一家中國飯館<u>的</u>菜最受歡迎。聽說，那家餐館上菜上<u>得</u>快，菜也做<u>得</u>地道。地方又大又安靜，客人雖多，

但是不怕沒有坐的地方。大家都喜歡坐在那兒慢慢兒地吃，邊吃飯，邊聊天。

(Simplified Characters)

前些日子，校园报纸做了一个调查，看看附近哪一家餐馆的菜做得最好吃。结果，是城里一家中国饭馆的菜最受欢迎。听说，那家餐馆上菜上得快，菜也做得地道。地方又大又安静，客人虽多，但是不怕没有坐的地方。大家都喜欢坐在那儿慢慢儿地吃，边吃饭，边聊天。

J: Please fill in the blanks with the words and phrases provided.

(Traditional Characters)

要不然，..又...又...，這就要看你，非常，比較，特別是

這家餐館的菜做得<u>非常</u>不錯，<u>特別</u>是他們的炒青菜，<u>又</u>新鮮<u>又</u>好吃。不過，有的人覺得他們的菜太清淡。但是，我覺得<u>這就要看</u>你平常吃的菜油不油了。我自己吃的<u>比較</u>清淡，<u>要不然</u>，我就不會說這家餐館的菜好吃了。

(Simplified Characters)

要不然，..又...又...，这就要看你，非常，比较，特别是

这家餐馆的菜做得<u>非常</u>不错，<u>特别</u>是他们的炒青菜，<u>又</u>新鲜<u>又</u>好吃。不过，有的人觉得他们的菜太清淡。但是，我觉得<u>这就要看</u>你平常吃的菜油不油了。我自己吃的<u>比较</u>清淡，<u>要不然</u>，我就不会说这家餐馆的菜好吃了。

第五部分：翻譯 Translation

A: Translate the following sentences into Chinese.

1. I finished reading the book I bought yesterday. **(topic-comment)**

   （昨天買的那本書我已經看完了。）

2. Your younger sister is very pretty. （長得）

   （你的妹妹長得很漂亮。）

3. The steamed fish tastes excellent.

   （清蒸魚的味道好極了。）

4. The "beef and broccoli" in this restaurant is superb. The beef is tender and smells good wonderful. （又...又...）

   （這家飯館的芥蘭牛肉好極了，牛肉又嫩又香。）

5. Could I trouble you to tell the boss not to put MSG in the dishes?

   （能不能麻煩你告訴老板[菜裏]不要放味精？）

B: Translate the following passage into Chinese.

Ke Lin and Zhang Tianming went out to eat last night. Ke Lin drove very fast. They got to Chinatown very quickly. Originally they wanted to order four dishes. In the end they only ordered three. The dishes that they ordered were all very delicious. As soon as they finished eating, they went back to school. On their way home(在回家的路上), they alked and laughed. They were very happy.

（　柯林和張天明昨天晚上出去吃飯。柯林開車開得很快，他們很快就到了中國城。原來他們想點四個菜，後來只點了三個。他們點的菜都很好吃。他們一吃完飯就回學校了。在回家的路上，他們又說又笑，很高興。）

第六部分：寫作練習 Composition

作文：《我最喜歡的飯館》

第四課　買東西

第一部分：聽力練習 Listening Comprehension

A: Listen to the tape recording of *Lesson Four* and answer the following questions.

1. Why doesn't Zhang Tianming like the clothes that his mother bought for him?

   (He doesn't like the color, the style, and the brand of the clothes.)

2. What does Zhang Tianming say about his philosophy on shopping for clothes?

   (It has to be good quality, brand name. Price is no object.)

3. What are Ke Lin's criteria for buying clothes?

   (It has to be comfortable to wear, good quality, and inexpensive.)

4. Whom does Lin Xuemei agree with?

   (She agrees with Zhang Tianming.)

B: Listen to the tape for the workbook.

1. Listen to the passage and answer the following questions in Chinese.

   （在中國，大家出門的時候都帶著現金，買東西不用支票。付錢的
   　時候，也不需要付稅。）

   Questions:

   1) Will you write a check to pay for your purchases in China? Why or why not?

      (No, because most people pay in cash.)

   2) In which two ways do Chinese and American differ when it comes to shopping?

      (In China there is no sales tax. Besides, people don't write checks.)

2. Listen to the passage and answer the following questions in English.

（小林每次出門總是穿一件T恤衫，一條褲子。他覺得穿衣服只要是純棉的，穿起來舒服就好。無論樣子好不好，價錢貴不貴，他都不在乎。但是他的好朋友小王覺得，穿什麼衣服得看去什麼地方。光圖穿得舒服是不行的。所以每次他們一起逛街買衣服，一定會有爭論。）

Questions:

1) What does Xiao Lin look for when buying clothes?

   (They have to be made of cotton and comfortable to wear.)

2) What does Xiao Wang think about Xiao Lin's criteria in choosing what to wear?

   (Wang thinks Lin should also take one more thing into consideration: occasion.)

3) Would you go shopping with Lin and Wang together? Why or why not?

3. Listen to the passage and answer the following questions in English.

（" 親愛的顧客，歡迎您來大大購物中心。為了慶祝本中心開業三週年，我們中心的商品大減價，打七五折。要是您買的東西超過1000元，我們還會送您一個大大購物中心的杯子。本中心一樓專賣男女服裝，二樓專賣兒童服裝，三樓專賣傢俱和日用品。要是您有問題，請您上四樓，我們會有服務員為您服務，解決問題。謝謝！"）

Questions:

1) What is the name of the shopping center?

   （大大）

2) How many floors are there?

   (four)

3) If you want to buy some clothes for your kids, which floor should you go to?
   (second)

4) Why is there a sale at the shopping center? How big is the discount?

(It's the third anniversary of the store.) *(25% discount)*

5) What extra incentive is the shopping center offering to lure customers to spend more money?

(If the merchandise that you purchase is worth more than 1000 dollars, they will give you a cup as a gift.)

4. Listen to the passage and answer the question.

（小張穿衣服很挑剔，不是名牌的不穿，不是純棉的不穿，顏色太花也不穿，要替他買衣服實在太難了！）

Question:

If you have to buy a T-shirt for Xiao Zhang, which of the following three will you choose?

5. Listen to the passage and answer the following questions in English.

（大家出門旅行都得住旅館。大部分美國旅館的服務和設備都很不錯，你不必帶杯子，毯子，和香皂、浴巾什麼的，每個房間都有空調，還有電視，什麼都很方便，也很舒服。付錢的時候也不必付現金，用信用卡就可以了。只是旅館稅太高，有的地方住旅館要付百分之十的稅。）

Questions:

1) What would an American hotel prepare for the staying guest?

   (Cup, blanket, soap, bath towel)

2) How could the guest pay the bill?

   (With a credit card.)

3) What is the disadvantage of staying at a hotel?

   (You have to pay a high tax.)

4) How high could the hotel tax be?

   (10%)

第二部分：口語練習 Speaking Exercises

A: Please practice asking and answering the following questions with a partner before class.

1. 你差不多多長時間買一次衣服？

2. 你身上穿的衣服/襯衫/褲子是什麼顏色的？

3. 你買衣服的標準是什麼？

4. 一般來說，買完東西以後，你付現金，開支票還是用信用卡？

5. 這一州買衣服需要付稅嗎？

B: Please practice speaking on the following topics.

1. 你跟你的朋友一起去逛街，他看到什麼東西都要買，你怎麼讓他少買一些？

2. 請你說說你對名牌衣服的看法。你買衣服一定要買名牌的嗎？為什麼？

3. 編對話：買東西（兩個人或三個人，有的人是顧客，有的人是售貨員。也可以是兩個人在討論買東西的事）

第三部分：閱讀練習 Reading Comprehension

A: Please answer the questions after reading the following passage.

(Traditional Characters)

　　在美國，上餐館吃飯跟在中國有很多不一樣的地方。比方說，中國人吃完飯，常常得爭論誰付錢。美國人一般不會有這樣的情況。付錢的時候，在美國可以用現金，支票，或者信用卡，但是在中國，一般來說都付現金。在美國吃完飯以後得給服務員小費，但是在中國不用付小費。還有一點就是，中國人一般不要收據。

(Simplified Characters)

　　在美国，上餐馆吃饭跟在中国有很多不一样的地方。比方说，中国人吃完饭，常常得争论谁付钱。美国人一般不会有这样的情况。付钱的时候，在美国可以用现金，支票，或者信用卡，但是在中国，一般来说都付现金。在美国吃完饭以后得给服务员小费，但是在中国不用付小费。还有一点就是，中国人一般不要收据。

Question:

What are the four major differences between eating out in America and in China?

> *(Chinese people argue who will pay for the meal; Chinese people pay cash; They don't tip the waiter; Chinese people generally don't ask for receipts.)*

B: Since the mid-nineties retailers from overseas have been setting up camps in coastal cities in mainland China. Upscale boutiques and department stores are now becoming quite commonplace in Shanghai, Guangzhou and Shenzhen. The following advertisement appeared in a Shanghai-based evening paper. Skim through it and answer the following questions.

Questions:

1) Please circle the Chinese name of this store.

2) Please circle the address of the store.

3) Please circle the description that is used to persuade the Chinese customer of the prestige of the store.

4) What will the 60 lucky customers receive?

第四部分：句型與詞語練習 Grammar & Usage

A: The position of time phrases.

Please answer the following questions in Chinese.

1. A: 今天是幾月幾號星期幾？

   B: _____ 。

2. A: 開學多久了？

   B: _____ 。

3. A: 你一個星期上幾次中文課？什麼時候上？

   B: _____ 。

4. A: 你昨天做功課做了多長時間？

   B: _____ 。

5. A: 你多長時間沒聽錄音了？

   B: _____ 。

6. A: 你一天吃幾頓飯？

   B: _____ 。

7. A: 你多長時間沒給你父母打電話了？

   B: _____ 。

8. A: 你多長時間洗一次衣服？

   B: _____ 。

9. A: 從你住的地方開車到最近的購物中心要多長時間？

   B: _____ 。

B: 請用 " 什麼的 " 完成下面的句子。

Please complete the following sentences using "什麼的".

例：這個購物中心真大，<u>吃的、穿的、用的什麼的</u>，你都買得到。

1. 這家飯館的菜真多，_____，你都吃得到。

2. 他買衣服非常挑剔。_____，他都得考慮。

3. 跟他一起找房子真不容易，房子的_____，他都得問
   清楚。

C: 請用 " 無論...都/也 " 改寫下面句子。

Please rewrite the following sentences using "無論...都/也".

例： 這兩天他沒什麼胃口，清蒸魚、芥蘭牛肉、菠菜豆腐什麼的他
   都不想吃。

   ---> <u>這兩天他沒什麼胃口，無論什麼菜，他都不想吃。</u>

1. 他吸煙吸得真多，上班也吸，上課也吸，在家也吸。

   --->_____。

2. 美國的稅很重。買吃的要稅，買穿的要稅，買用的也要稅。

   --->_____。

3. 我家附近新開的購物中心非常大。衣服、日用品、文具，他們都有。

   --->_____。

D: 請用 “ 無論...都... ” 完成下面句子。

Please complete the following sentences using "無論...都...".

例：英文真难，<u>無論我怎麼學都學不好</u>。

1. 昨天我們想去一家新的購物中心買東西，但是路不熟，

   _____。(找)

2. 小林的父母不同意小林和她的男朋友在一起，但是_____，

   小林還是覺得他們倆挺合適的。(說：persuade)

3. 這個問題難極了，_____。（想）

E: 請用 “ ...adj./V+是+adj./V，可是... ” 完成對話。

Please complete the following sentences use "...adj./V+是+adj./V，可是...".

例：A: 你為什麼不喜歡去那家餐館吃飯？他們的菜做得很地道。

   B: <u>他們的菜地道是地道，可是對我來說，有點太油</u>。

1. A: 住校很好，你為什麼要搬出去？

   B: _____。

2. A: 這個宿舍的設備那麼舊，你為什麼不搬到別的地方去？

   B: _____。

3. A: 這條褲子你穿起來挺好看的，為什麼不買？

   B: _____。

F: 請用 " 非...不可... " 改寫下面句子。

Please rewrite the following sentences using "非...不可...".

> 例： 柯老板這個人壞得很。跟他做生意一定會有問題。
>
> --->柯老板這個人壞得很。<u>跟他做生意非有問題不可</u>。

1. 每次出去吃飯，他一定點清蒸魚。

   --->_____。

2. 小林逛街一定買化妝品。

   --->_____。

3. 我母親買衣服，一定買純棉的。

   --->_____。

第五部分 ： 翻譯 Translation

A: 中翻英。

Please translate the following into English.

(Traditional Characters)

　　小張買東西的標準是只要名牌的，不管樣子好不好，價錢貴不貴，只要是名牌的，他就買。小林買東西又在乎質量，又要價錢便宜。他們兩個一起出門買東西，常會有爭論。小張認為小林光圖便宜，小林批評小張只看名牌，不管衣服穿著合適不合適。所以他們常常很高興地出去，很不高興地回來。

(Simplified Characters)

　　小张买东西的标准是只要名牌的，不管样子好不好，价钱贵不贵，只要是名牌的，他就买。小林买东西又在乎质量，又要价钱便宜。他们两个一起出门买东西，常会有争论。小张认为小林光图便宜，小林批评小张只看名牌，不管衣服穿着合适不合适。所以他们常常很高兴地出去，很不高兴地回来。

(Xiao Zhang looks for brand names when he shops. Style and prices don't really matter. As long as it's a brand name, he will buy it. Xiao Lin pays attention to quality and price when she goes shopping. They always get into arguments when they go shopping together. Xiao Zhang thinks Xiao Lin only looks for cheaper prices, whereas Xiao Lin criticizes Xiao Zhang for being blinded with brand names and not caring about whether the clothes fit or not. They often go out shopping in high spirits, and end up coming back home in a very bad mood.)

B: 中翻英。

Please translate the following into English.

(Traditional Characters)

　　小李只有在打折的時候才買衣服，一聽說哪家商店打折，就去買。打折的東西雖然比較便宜一些，但是質量也差一些。小李的看法是衣服便宜可以多買幾件，質量差一點也沒關係，穿壞了再買新的。

(Simplified Characters)

　　小李只有在打折的时候才买衣服，一听说哪家商店打折，就去买。打折的东西虽然比较便宜一些，但是质量也差一些。小李的看法是衣服便宜可以多买几件，质量差一点也没关系，穿坏了再买新的。

(Xiao Li goes shopping only when there's a sale. As soon as she hears a store is having a sale, she will go shopping. Things on sale are cheaper. However, their quality is bit poorer, too. However, Xiao Li thinks one can buy more clothes when they are cheap; it doesn't matter if the quality of the clothes is poorer. One can buy more new ones when the old ones are worn out.)

C: 英翻中。

Please translate the following into Chinese.

1. Zhang Tianming doesn't have a car. He has to depend on Ke Lin wherever he wants to go.

　　（張天明沒有車，無論到什麼地方他都要靠柯林。）

2. They had dinner at a restaurant in Chinatown. The dishes that they ordered, such as Chinese broccoli, steamed fish, etc., were all very delicious.

（他們在中國城的一家餐館裏吃晚飯。他們點的菜，像芥蘭，清蒸魚什麼的，都很好吃。）

3. Although it is convenient to live on-campus, it is very expensive.

（住在校內方便是方便，可是太貴。）

4. This place is not suitable for driving, but it suits you. You like walking.

（這個地方開車很難，對你倒很合適，因爲你喜歡走路。）

5. Would you please sign your name on the receipt?

（請你在收據上簽字。）

6. Can you accompany me to the shopping center to buy a pair of athletic shoes?

（你能不能陪我到購物中心去買一雙運動鞋？）

D: 英翻中

Please translate the following into Chinese and pay attention to the position of time phrases.

1. A: How long has your teacher been teaching?

（你的老師教中文教了多久了？）

   B: My teacher has been teaching Chinese for five years.

（我的老師教中文教了五年了。）

2. A: How long have you not had any Chinese food?

（你多長時間沒吃中國飯了？）

   B: I haven't had any Chinese food for two weeks.

（我兩個星期沒吃中國飯了。）

3. A: How often does your sister shop?

（你姐姐多久買一次東西？）

   B: My sister goes shopping once a week.

（我姐姐每個星期買一次東西。）

4. A: How many hours did your roommate sleep last night?

（你的同屋昨晚睡覺睡了幾個鐘頭？）

   B: My roommate slept for three hours last night.

（我同屋昨天晚上(睡覺)睡了三個鐘頭。）

5. A: How long do you work everyday?

（你每天工作多長時間？）

   B: I have to work two hours a day.

（我每天工作兩個小時。）

6. The doctor said that you have to drink water ten times a day.

（醫生說你每天得喝十次水。）

7. Xiao Zhang writes to his parents every other month.

（小張(每)兩個月給他爸爸媽媽寫一次信。）

8. He moved three times last year.

（他去年搬了三次家。）

9. My brother hasn't talked to me for four days.

（我弟弟四天沒跟我說話了。）

10. He lived in the dorm for six months and moved off campus last week.

（他在宿舍住了六個月，上個星期搬到校外去了。）

第六部分：寫作練習 Composition

作文：《我對名牌的看法》

第五課　選專業

A: Listen to the tape recording of *Lesson Five* and answer the following questions.

1. What is Zhang Tianming taking this semester?

   (East Asian History, Statistics, American Literature, and Chinese.)

2. What do Zhang's parents want him to do after he graduates from college?

   (They want him to go to medical school.)

3. What does Li Zhe plan to do after he graduates from college?

   (He plans to go to graduate school.)

4. What does Zhang think that Li should do after he graduates from college?

   (Find a job first.)

B: Listen to the tape for the workbook.

1. Listen to the passage and answer the following questions in English.

   （這個大學有文學院，工學院，管理學院和醫學院。其中醫學院學費最貴，工學院的學生最多，管理學院的老師最有名，文學院的圖書館最好。這所大學很大，有大學部也有研究所。研究生百分之八十五都能從學校得到錢。除了醫學院的學生外，其他的學生都得上一門外語，而且得上兩年。有些學生認為自己的專業課已經夠重的了，沒有時間再去學外語，但是學校認為多懂一種外語，對學生只有好處，沒有壞處。）

   Question:

   1) How many schools does the university have?

      (four)

2) What are they?

(College of Humanities, Engineering School, Medical School, and School of Management)

3) Which school is the most expensive?

(Medical School)

4) Which school has the most students?

(Engineering School)

5) Which school has the best library?

(College of Humanities)

6) Which school has the most famous teachers?

(School of Management)

7) What is the percentage of graduate students on scholarships?

(85%)

8) What was the controversy about?

(The foreign language requirement)

9) What were the two opposing positions?

(The students complained it would be too much work, and they wouldn't have time for it. The school felt it would be beneficial for the students.)

2. Listen to the passage and answer the following questions in English.

（最近幾年大學畢業生找工作很難，所以有些人為了將來吃飯的問題，念大學的時候，同時念兩個專業。比方說，越來越多的學生念電腦系和東亞系的雙學位，也有很多人念管理學系和東亞系的雙學位。念雙學位，雖然課很多，很忙，但是可能對將來申請工作有很大的幫助。）

Questions:

1) Why are more and more students interested in having double majors?

(To prepare themselves for the job market.)

2) What examples of double majors are mentioned in the passage?

(Computer Science and East Asian Studies; Business & Management and East Asian Studies)

3. Listen to the passage and answer the following questions in English.

(許多學生發現上大學交了那麼多學費，卻學不到他們想學的。比方說，很多指導教授太忙，抽不出時間和每個學生好好談話。另外，還有很多教授，因為太有名了，常常到校外演講，不能給學生上課。這些情況使學生覺得上課沒有什麼意思。有些學生給學校提意見，但是由於教授需要有時間做自己的研究，寫文章，學校也沒有辦法。）

Questions:

1) What are the two things that many college students complain about?

(They pay too much tuition and do not get too much out of it. Many professors are so famous that they are always away giving lectures. They don't have time for their students.)

2) What's the reaction from the school?

(They can't do anything about it.)

第二部分：口語練習 Speaking Exercises

A: Please practice asking and answering the following questions with a partner before class.

1. 你這學期選了幾門課？

2. 你最喜歡哪一門課？為什麼？

3. 哪門課最讓你受不了？為什麼？

4. 中文聽說讀寫，哪一方面最難？為什麼？

5. 你下個學期有什麼打算？

B: Please practice speaking on the following topics.

1. 請談一談你的專業及畢業以後的打算。

2. 你父母對你選專業有影響嗎？

3. 請談一談你跟指導教授之間的關係怎麼樣。

第三部分：閱讀練習 Reading Comprehension

A: Please answer the questions after reading the following passage.

(Traditional Characters)

　　大學生每個學期都得註冊。在註冊前，每個學生都會和指導教授討論選哪些課。新生常常不知道應該選什麼課，指導教授就會給他們一些建議。可是因為有些課是必修課(1)，很多學生都得選，所以這些課有時可能選不上，這對新生來說是個大問題。

　　(1)必修課(bìxiūkè): required courses

(Simplified Characters)

　　大学生每个学期都得注册。在注册前，每个学生都会和指导教授讨论选哪些课。新生常常不知道应该选什么课，指导教授就会给他们一些建议。可是因为有些课是必修课(1)，很多学生都得选，所以这些课有时可能选不上，这对新生来说是个大问题。

　　(1)必修课(bìxiūkè): required courses

Questions:

1) According to the passage, why do freshmen have to talk to their advisors?

   (To get advice on what courses to take.)

2) What kind of problem do freshmen face when they try to take courses?

   (Sometimes it is hard for them to get into required courses.)

B: The following is a degree certificate issued by a mainland Chinese college. What information can you glean from it? Skim through it and try to answer the following questions.

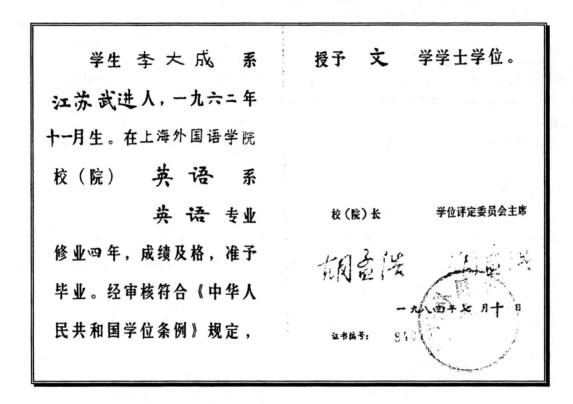

Note: This is an authentic certificate. Only the name has been changed in order to protect the privacy of the individual.

Questions:

1) What is the degree recipient's name?

(李大成)

2) What is his date of birth?

(November, 1962)

3) What is the name of the college?

(Shanghai Foreign Language Institute)

4) What is the degree recipient's major?

   (English)

5) How long is the degree program?

   (Four years)

6) What degree do you think was awarded?

   (Bachelor)

7) Can you locate the college president's name?

   (胡孟浩)

8) When was the degree awarded?

   (July 10, 1984)

C: 成語故事

Please answer the questions after reading the following story.

$$\begin{array}{c|c} 1 & 2 \\ \hline 3 & 4 \end{array}$$

(Traditional Characters)

名落孫山 (1)

中國宋朝（960-1279）的時候，有一個叫孫山的人，他很會說笑話。

有一年，他離開家到外地參加考試，結果考上了，可是發榜(2)時，他的名字在最後。孫山回到家裏以後，很多人來看他。孫山的一個朋友的兒子也參加考試了，就來問孫山，他兒子考上了沒有，孫山沒有直接回答。他說："我的名字在榜上是最後一個，你兒子的名字在我的後面。"

(1)孫山 (Sūn Shān): a person's name

(2)發榜 (fābǎng): to publish a list of successful candidates or applicants

(Simplified Characters)

名落孙山 (1)

中国宋朝（960-1279）的时候，有一个叫孙山的人，他很会说笑话。

有一年，他离开家到外地参加考试，结果考上了，可是发榜(2)时，他的名字在最后。孙山回到家里以后，很多人来看他。孙山的一个朋友的儿子也参加考试了，就来问孙山，他儿子考上了没有，孙山没有直接回答。他说，"我的名字在榜上是最后一个，你儿子的名字在我的后面。"

(1)孙山 (Sūn Shān): a person's name

(2)发榜(fābǎng): to publish a list of successful candidates or applicants

Questions:

1) What was Sun Shan good at?

    (Telling jokes.)

2) Why did he leave home?

    (To take an exam.)

3) Did he pass the examination?

    (Yes, but his name was last on the list of those passed the exam.)

4) What did his friend want to know?

(If his son had passed the exam or not.)

5) Why didn't Sun Shan answer his friend directly?

(Because his son hadn't passed.)

6) What did Sun Shan tell his friend? What was he really saying?

(That Sun Shan's own name was last on the list and the neighbor's son's name was behind that. His son didn't pass.)

第四部分：句型與詞語練習 Grammar & Usage

A: 請用 " 就是 " 完成下面的句子。

Please complete the following sentences using "就是".

例：這條運動褲質量好，價錢便宜，... 。（不好看）

--->這條運動褲質量好，價錢便宜，就是穿起來不好看。

1. 中國歷史很有意思，_____。（人的名字）

2. 在波士頓找工作比較容易，_____。（房租）

3. 他做的菜好吃是好吃，_____。（油）

B: 請用 " 至於 " 改寫下面的句子。

Please rewrite the following sentences using "至於".

例：有些人找工作就要找賺錢多的，不在乎工作有沒有意思。

--->有些人找工作就要找賺錢多的，至於工作有沒有意思，他們不在乎。

1. 很多人買衣服，只看牌子，不在乎價錢貴不貴。

---> _____ 。

2. 老高明年上半年想去中國學中文，下半年做什麼，他還不知道。

---> _____ 。

3. 告訴你們一個好消息，明天有一個大家都很喜歡的客人要來，我現在先不告訴你們他是誰。

    --->_____。

C: 請完成下面的對話。

Please fill in blanks with the correct resultative complements and answer the questions.

1. A: 第四課的漢字你都記<u>住</u>了嗎？

    B: _____。

2. A: 昨天老師給你的功課你都做<u>完</u>了嗎

    B: _____。

3. A: 張天明買<u>到</u>他要的運動服了嗎?

    B: _____。

4. A: 李哲下學期的課選<u>好</u>了嗎?

    B: _____。

D: 請用 "另外(1)" 完成下面的對話。

Please complete the following dialogues using "另外(1)".

    例： A: 你的同屋都是美國人嗎？

           B: 我有三個同屋，兩個美國人，<u>另外一個是日本人</u>。

1. A: 這附近有幾家購物中心？ 離這兒遠嗎？

    B: 有兩家。一家很近，_____。

2. A: 我們放三天假，你打算做什麼？

    B: 我打算一天洗衣服，_____。

3. A: 你的三個弟弟都大學畢業了吧？

    B: 我大弟弟已經畢業了，_____。

E: 請用「另外(2)」完成下面的對話。

Please complete the following dialogues using "另外(2)".

  例：A: 學校宿舍裏有什麼設備？

    B: 每層樓都有洗衣機和烘乾機，<u>另外每棟樓都有電腦</u>。

 1. A: 你這學期上什麼課？

  B: 中文，_____。

 2. A: 張天明，柯林和林雪梅三個人去中國飯館吃飯，點了些什麼菜？

  B: 他們點了芥蘭牛肉，_____。

 3. A: 張天明去購物中心買買了些什麼東西？

  B: 他買了一套運動服，_____。

F: 請用「要麼...要麼...」完成下面的對話。

Please use "要麼...要麼..." to complete the following dialogues.

  例：A: 學什麼畢業以後好找工作？（醫/商）

    B: <u>要麼學醫，要麼學商</u>，不要學文。

 1. A: 你這個暑假打算到哪兒去旅行？（中國/法國）

  B: _____。

 2. A: 你學習上有困難的時候找誰幫忙？（教授/同學）

  B: _____。

 3. A: 你常常穿什麼衣服逛街？（T恤衫/運動服）

  B: _____。

G: 請用「跟...打交道」完成下面的對話。

Please complete the following dialogues using "跟...打交道".

  例：A: 你爲什麼不念醫學院？（patients）

    B: <u>我不願意跟病人打交道</u>。

 1. A: 你爲什麼不當售貨員了？（money, customers, etc.）

  B: _____。

2. A: 你的房子這麼大，房間這麼多，為什麼不出租？（tenants）

   B: _____。

3. A: 快開學了，學校需要一些老生幫新生辦註冊手續，你願意不願意
     去幫忙？（freshmen）

   B: _____。

H: 請用「肯定」完成下面的對話。

   Please complete the following dialogues using "肯定".

     例：A: 都這麼晚了，他還會來嗎？

       B: <u>他肯定不會來了，我們別等了</u>。

1. A: 他下個學期會搬到校外去嗎？

   B: _____，他已經找好房子了。

2. A: 小張大學畢業以後，打算工作還是念研究所？

   B: _____，他早就找到工作了。

3. A: 他五月畢得了業嗎？

   B: 他還少三個學分，今年五月_____。

第五部分：翻譯 Translation

A: Please translate the following dialogue into Chinese.

Zhang Tianming:	This sports jacket is really nice.
Ke Lin:	Adidas sportswear *is* very nice, but it is just too expensive.（運動服）
Zhang Tianming:	It's not that I don't want to save money, it is just that other sportswear is too poorly-made. (質量)
Ke Lin:	As long as something is well-made, no matter how expensive it is, you'll get it? (無論...都)
Zhang Tianming:	To me the most important thing is quality, not price.
Lin Xuemei:	I agree. Either you buy good quality or you don't buy. The Chinese say, "There are no good cheap things. Good things don't come cheap." (要麼 ...，要麼 ...)

Ke Lin: That's not necessarily true. You can find good things at good prices. The two of you really know how to spend money. You must have very rich parents. (找到，會花錢)

Zhang Tianming: I don't ask my parents for money to get clothes. (要錢買衣服)

Lin Xuemei: Neither do I.

（　張天明：這件運動服真不錯。

　柯　林：阿迪達斯運動服好是好，就是太貴了。

　張天明：不是我不想省錢，只是別的運動服質量太不好了。

　柯　林：所以只要東西做得好，無論多貴你都買？

　張天明：對我來說，最重要的是質量，而不是價錢。

　林雪梅：我同意。你要麼買質量好的，要麼別買。中國人說，

　　　　　　"便宜沒好貨，好貨不便宜。"

　柯　林：那也不一定。（你）能找到價廉物美的東西。你們兩個人

　　　　　　那麼會花錢，你們的父母肯定很有錢。

　張天明：我不跟我父母要錢買衣服。

　林雪梅：我也不跟他們要錢。 ）

B: Please translate the following passage into Chinese.

My younger brother plans to go to graduate school after he graduates next semester. He will either study engineering or medicine. He hasn't decided yet. My parents hope that he will study engineering and make a lot of money in the future. They know that my brother might make even more money by going to medical school. However, they don't want him to deal with patients all day long. (決定，學工賺很多錢，打交道)

（ 我弟弟下個學期畢業以後要上研究所。他要麼上工學院，要麼上醫學院，還沒

　有決定。我父母希望他念工科賺很多錢。他們知道學醫將來賺的錢更多，但是

　他們不願意讓我弟弟整天跟病人打交道。 ）

C: Please translate the following passage into Chinese.

Xiao Lin wanted to take Chinese next year. She thought learning Chinese would be helpful for her future study and career. She went to talk to her advisor and hoped to get some advice from her. Her advisor told her that as long as she did her homework, listens to the tapes, and practiced writing characters repeatedly everyday, Xiao Lin would definitely learn a lot.

（小林明年想選中文。她覺得學中文對將來申請學校，找工作都很有好處。她去找
她的指導教授，聽聽她的意見。指導教授告訴她，只要她每天做功課，聽錄音，
反復練習寫漢字，她肯定能學到不少東西。）

第六部分：寫作練習 Composition

1. 請你介紹一下你的專業。

What is your major? Why did you choose it as your major? If you do not have a major yet, what do you hope to major in? Why?

2. 你父母對你選專業有什麼影響？

第六課　租房子

第一部分：聽力練習 Listening Comprehension

A: Listen to the tape recording of *Lesson Six* and answer the following questions.

   1. What were the reasons that made Zhang Tianming move out?

      (The hallway was too noisy. His neighbor was noisy, too.)

   2. Why didn't Zhang Tianming go to check out the first place he called?

      (The rent was a little over his budget.)

   3. Why wasn't Zhang Tianming interested in the second place?

      (It was too close to the stadium.)

   4. What was good about the third place?

      (Reasonable rent, spacious rooms, quiet neighborhood.)

B: Listen to the tape for the workbook.

   1. Listen to the passage and answer the following questions.

（ 很多人認為買房子比租房子麻煩。但是也有很多人覺得買房子比租
房子省錢。認為租房子好的人覺得買房子是件大事，需要考慮的事
情太多：房子價錢貴不貴，附近環境怎麼樣，安靜不安靜，安全不
安全，離學校近不近什麼的都得考慮。買了房子以後，又擔心房子
會不會出什麼問題；要是換工作，房子怎麼辦？認為買房子好的人
的想法是，租房子得天天跟房東打交道，每個月的租金也不便宜，
不如買一個房子，每個月花的錢差不多，可是最後房子是自己
的。 ）

Questions:

1) According to the passage, what are the things that you need to consider when you plan to buy a house?

   (Is the price expensive? Are the surroundings quiet? Is the neighborhood safe? Is it close to school?)

2) According to the passage, what are the advantages of renting a place vs. buying a house?

   (You don't need to worry about whether or not the house has problems or what will happen if you change jobs and need to move.)

2. Listen to the passage and answer the following questions.

（大學生常常需要找房子。找到一套好的公寓非常不容易，除了要考慮房租合適不合適，離學校和圖書館近不近，房間大不大以外，還要考慮同屋好不好。有時候，好的同屋比好的公寓還要難找。去年夏天，約翰想搬到校外住，因為他覺得住在校內不自由。他在報上看到一個廣告，給房東打電話約好時間，看了那個公寓以後，非常滿意，所以他馬上搬了進去。他有三個同屋，一個怕熱，整天開空調，每天一回家就把空調開到最大，屋子冷得像冰箱一樣。第二個同屋怕冷，一回來就把空調關了。屋子裏一會兒冷，一會兒熱，沒過幾天約翰就病了。第三個同屋，像貓一樣，晚上不睡覺，白天睡覺，睡覺的時候，不讓別人打電話，也不讓接電話。約翰想和醫生約時間看病，可是不能在公寓裏打電話，只好用公用電話。一個星期後，約翰決定還是搬回學校宿舍住。）

問題：
1）找房子的時候需要考慮什麼？
2）好的同屋容易不容易找？
3）約翰為什麼搬到校外去住？
4）他有幾個同屋？
5）約翰為什麼生病了？
6）他為什麼不能在家裏打電話？
7）他為什麼決定搬回學校住？

第二部分：口語練習 Speaking Exercises

A: Please practice asking and answering the following questions with a partner.

1. 你每個月的房租多少錢？包不包水電？

2. 如果你想出租房子，廣告應該寫什麼？

3. 如果你的同屋或者你隔壁的同學吵得你不能學習，你怎麼辦？

B: Please practice speaking on the following topics.

1. 請你談一談找什麼樣的人做同屋最理想。

2. 請你談一談租什麼樣的房子最理想。

3. Find a partner and make up a dialogue about renting an apartment. One of you could be the landlord and the other the tenant.

第三部分：閱讀練習 Reading Comprehension

A: Please answer the questions after reading the following ad.

> 有公寓一套，三房一廳，不帶家俱，有地毯，洗碗機和有線電視。
> 月租$500。房客不可以吸煙或養狗，最好是女生，研究生更好。有
> 興趣者，請電：555-2456（日）；555-3654（夜）。

Questions:

1) How many bedrooms are there?

   (Three)

2) What is the day time phone number?

   (555-2456)

3) Who will be an ideal tenant?

    (A female graduate student who doesn't smoke and doesn't have a dog.)

4) What are provided in the apartment?

    (It's carpeted. It has cable and a dish washer.)

B: If you were looking for an apartment in the Boston area, which of the following two ads would you be interested in? Why?

公寓出租

東波士頓一房一廳

交通購物方便

安全安靜。月租$400。

請電：(617)338-7548

晚11時前

房屋出租

房間大而明亮，近BU、

BC及Harvard，近公共汽

車，包水電，暖氣，帶家

具，供晚餐。兩人合住一房

月租$190。請電：

(617)868-9736

C: 成語故事

Please answer the questions after reading the following story.

(Traditional Characters)

孟母三遷

　　孟子是中國歷史上影響最大的思想家之一。他很小的時候，父親就去世了，孟子是他的母親帶大的。

　　孟子的家附近是一塊墓地(1)，他經常去那兒玩，跟著別人學挖墓(2)。孟子的母親看見了就說：「這地方對小孩不好。」所以她就把家搬到別的地方去了。新家在一個市場旁邊，孟子常常去市場玩。孟子的母親又說：「這地方對小孩也不好。」就把家搬到了一個學校旁邊。孟子看到學校裏的學生都念書，也跟著念書。孟子的母親高興地說：「這才是小孩子應該住的地方。」所以孟子的母親跟孟子就在那兒住下來了。孟子後來成了一個很有學問的人。

(1) 思想家(sīxiǎngjiā): philosopher

(2) 墓地(mùdì): graveyard; cemetery

(3) 挖墓(wā mù): dig grave

(Simplified Characters)

孟母三迁

    孟子是中国历史上影响最大的思想家之一。他很小的时候，父亲就去世了，孟子是他的母亲带大的。

    孟子的家附近是一块墓地(1)，他经常去那儿玩，跟着别人学挖墓(2)。孟子的母亲看见了就说："这地方对小孩不好。"所以她就把家搬到别的地方去了。新家在一个市场旁边，孟子常常去市场玩。孟子的母亲又说："这地方对小孩也不好。"就把家搬到了一个学校旁边。孟子看到学校里的学生都念书，也跟着念书。孟子的母亲高兴地说："这才是小孩子应该住的地方。"所以孟子的母亲跟孟子就在那儿住下来了。孟子后来成了一个很有学问的人。

(1) 思想家(sīxiǎngjiā): philosopher

(2) 墓地(mùdì): graveyard; cemetery

(3) 挖墓(wā mù): dig grave

Questions:

1) When did Mencius lose his father?

    (When he was very young.)

2) Why did Mencius' mother decide to move?

    (Because they lived near a cemetary.)

3) Where did they move?

    (Next to a market.)

4) What did Mencius take up playing?

    (He played a banker.)

5) Where was their next home?

(Next to a school.)

6) Why did Mencius' mother decide to settle there?

(Because Mencius saw other kits study and began to study as well.)

第四部分：句型與詞語練習 Grammar & Usage

A: 請用 "一直" 改寫下面句子。

Please rewrite the following sentences using "一直".

例：他上次嘗過那家素菜館的菜以後，就老想再去吃一頓。

--->他上次嘗過那家素菜館的菜以後，就一直想再去吃一頓。

1. 小李的父母從他上大學以來總是反對小李從家裏搬出去。

--->_____ 。

2. 安德森上了中學以後，就對打籃球很有興趣。

--->_____ 。

3. 他的房子的地點不太理想，在報上登了廣告以後也租不出去。

--->_____ 。

B: 請用 "最好" 完成下面對話。

Please complete the following dialogues using "最好".

例：A: 我想學哲學。

B: 你最好選別的專業，學哲學找工作不容易。

1. A: 住我隔壁的天天吵得我念不下書。

B: _____ 。

2. A: 這雙運動鞋是我媽媽昨天給我買的，稍微小了點兒。

B: _____ 。

3. A: 我的專業是統計學，但是我實在沒什麼興趣。

B: _____ 。

C: 請用 "...的話" 回答下面問題。

Please answer the following questions using "...的話".

例：A: 要是走在路上有人跟你打招呼，但是你想不起來那個人是
誰，怎麼辦？

B: <u>要是走在路上有人跟我打招呼，但是我想不起來他叫什麼的</u>
<u>話，我一定會問他姓什麼，叫什麼。</u>

1. A: 如果你喜歡的球隊正在打球，但是你的電視壞了，你怎麼辦？

B: _____ 。

2. A: 要是住你隔壁的同學天天吵你，怎麼辦？

B: _____ 。

3. A: 要是你父母要你上醫學院，但是你不願意將來整天跟病人打交道。
你怎麼辦？

B: _____ 。

D: 請用 "再...不過了" 完成下面對話。

Please complete the following dialogues using "再...不過了".

例：A: 你說我買房子應該在什麼地方買才理想？（河邊）

B: <u>你那麼喜歡釣魚，要是能住在河邊，那再好不過了。</u>

1. A: 我不知道選什麼做我的專業才合適？（歷史）

B: _____ ，_____ 。

2. A: 小梅快要過生日了，送什麼禮物給她才好呢？（名牌化妝品）

B: _____ ，_____ 。

3. A: 我這個週末得請我老闆吃飯，你說上哪一家餐館好呢？

（中國餐館）

B: _____ ，_____ 。

E: 請用「稍微」完成下面對話。

Please complete the following dialogues using "稍微".

例： A: 聽說你病了？

B: 我昨天肚子不舒服，<u>今天稍微好了點兒</u>，但是還得吃藥。

1. A: 這個房子有三個臥室，離學校又近，我覺得很理想。

B: 但是每個月的租金$850，＿＿＿＿＿＿＿＿＿＿＿＿。我們再多看兩家吧。

2. A: 這條褲子樣子好，價錢也不貴，買了吧？！

B: 我也覺得不錯，但是＿＿＿＿＿＿＿＿＿＿＿＿。放洗衣機一洗，烘乾機一烘，肯定更小。

3. A: 張太太做的菜真地道，好吃極了。

B: 她做的菜好吃是好吃，只是＿＿＿＿＿＿＿＿＿＿＿。我喜歡吃清淡一點兒的。

F: 請用「以後」或者「的時候」填空。

Please fill in the blanks with either "以後" or "的時候".

1. 他每次看球賽<u>的時候</u>，都會激動地大喊大叫。
2. 小林從購物中心出來了<u>以後</u>，才想起來忘了買衛生紙。
3. 小張打算大學畢業<u>以後</u>到日本去旅行。
4. 選專業<u>的時候</u>，一定要考慮自己的興趣。
5. 我每次在中國餐館叫菜<u>的時候</u>，都得告訴服務員別放味精。
6. 老李每天回宿舍<u>以後</u>，第一件事情就是給小柯打電話。

G: 請用趨向補語完成下面的對話。

Please complete the following dialogues with appropriate verbs and directional complements

1. A: 明天小王過生日開舞會，你打算帶什麼東西去？（帶）

B: ＿＿＿＿＿＿＿＿＿＿＿＿＿＿＿＿＿＿＿＿＿＿＿。

2. A: 你一上課就從書包裏拿出什麼東西來？　（拿）

   B: _____ 。

3. A: 要是教室裏的椅子不夠，你怎麼辦？　　（搬）

   B: _____ 。

4. A: 要是你的宿舍吵得你受不了，你怎麼辦?　（搬）

   B: _____ 。

5. A: 你去找朋友。他住在九樓，但是電梯(diàntī: elevator)壞了，
   你怎麼辦？（走）

   B: _____ 。

第五部分：翻譯　Translation

A: 中翻英 ： Please translate the following passage into English.

(Traditional Characters)

　　每天翻開報紙都有體育新聞。記者把前一天各隊比賽的情況都寫出來。除此之外，還介紹當天有什麼好看的球賽。

(Simplified Characters)

　　每天翻开报纸都有体育新闻。记者把前一天各队比赛的情况都写出来。除此之外，还介绍当天有什么好看的球赛。

(Everyday when you flip through the newspaper, you'll find sports news. Sports writers report on the previous day's games. Besides they preview what games of the day will be worth watching.)

B: 英翻中 ： Please translate the following passage into Chinese.

My advisor lived very close to the stadium. Whenever there was a basketball game, there were a lot of fans yelling and screaming in front of his house. His studies were affected.

He could not stand to deal with the fans all day long, and decided to move. The place he rented was behind the woods. It was furnished. The rent included utilities. He felt the place was most ideal for him.

（我的指導教授住的地方離體育場很近，一有籃球比賽，就有很多球迷在他家前面大喊大叫，他的研究很受影響。他想，住在這兒得整天跟球迷打交道，真受不了，所以決定搬家。他租的房子在一片樹林後頭，而且帶家俱，房租包水電，他覺得這個地方對他來說再合適不過了。）

C: 英翻中： Please translate the following passage into Chinese using appropriate directional complements.

I went to the shopping center to get my sister a birthday gift. Right after I walked into the house, my sister ran down from the stairs and wanted to see what I had brought home. She pulled over a chair and sat down. I took out a pair of jeans and a T-shirt to show her. She picked them up, took a look, and said, "Please take them back(退) to the store. I don't like them." I was really angry at her.

（昨天我去購物中心給我妹妹買生日禮物。我回家一走進屋子，我妹妹就跑下樓來，想看看我買回來了什麼。她搬了一把椅子過來，然後坐了下來。我拿出一條牛仔褲和一件 T恤衫給她看。她把衣服拿起來，看了看，然後說：" 請把這些衣服退回店裏去，我不喜歡。" 我很生氣。）

第六部分：寫作練習 Composition

請寫一個租房子的廣告。

You plan to find a roommate to share your apartment. Please write a flyer briefly describing your place, and explaining specifically what kind of roommate you are looking for.

第七課 男朋友

第一部分：聽力練習 Listening Comprehension

A: Listen to the tape recording of *Lesson Seven* and answer the following questions.

1. What are Tom and Tianhua's hobbies?

   (Tom likes sports and rock 'n' roll music, whereas Tianhua likes theater and classical music.)

2. What is the major reason for their fights?

   (Tom drinks too much.)

3. Will Tianming be the mediator?

   (No, Tianhua asks him to stay out of it.)

4. What will Tianming do this coming weekend?

   (He will go visit Tianhua with his girlfriend Lisa.)

B: Listen to the tape for the workbook.

1. Listen to the passage and answer the following questions in English.

   (小王心情不好的時候有兩個辦法讓自己高興。一個是一邊聽搖滾樂一邊對著鏡子唱歌跳舞，看到自己在鏡子裏的樣子，他就會覺得高興一些。另一個辦法是到房間外邊的走廊上跟來往認識的人大聲打招呼。這樣大喊大叫了以後，小王的心情就不那麼糟糕了。這兩個方法聽起來有一點特別，但是對小王來說非常有用。)

   Questions:

   1) What are Xiao Wang's two ways to cheer himself up?

      (He plays rock 'n' roll music, and sings and dances in front of the mirror; He gets outside of his building and says "Hi" to people passing by.)

   2) Which of the two methods do you prefer? Why?

2. Listen to the passage and answer the following questions in English.

（小張以前喝酒喝得很厲害，不但在家裏喝，而且還到酒吧去喝。有一次他跟指導教授去開會，吃晚飯的時候，他喝醉了，說了一些很難聽的話，把指導教授氣壞了。小張酒醒了以後，非常後悔。 從那以後，他再也不喝酒了。）

Questions:

1) How do we know Xiao Zhang used to drink a lot?

   (He drank at home and in bars.)

2) What incident made him quit drinking?

   (Once he got drunk and said some awful things in front of his advisor. His advisor was really angry at him.)

3. Listen to the passage and answer the following questions in English.

（高中畢業生申請學校的時候，除了要了解各個學校的教學情況以外，也要打聽學校附近的環境怎麼樣。有的人覺得小地方的環境好，有山有水，有樹有河，能讓人安安靜靜地學習。有的人對到大城市去念書更有興趣。他們覺得大城市文化活動多，可以看表演，聽音樂會什麼的，跟文化背景不同的人交往的機會也比較多。要是叫他們這些人待在小地方，會把他們憋死的。 ）

Questions:

1) According to the passage, what are some of the things that people consider when they choose a college?

   (The teaching and learning and the larger community surrounding the school.)

2) What attracts people to small towns or big cities to study?

   (In small towns, the natural environment is good and students can study peacefully. In big cities, there are more cultural activities and more opportunities to meet with people of different cultural backgrounds.)

3) Which part of the passage do you disagree with? Why?

第二部分：口語練習 Speaking Exercises

A: Please practice asking and answering the following questions with a partner before class.

1. 你對什麼有興趣？
2. 班上同學誰的性格比較開朗？
3. 你家裏誰的脾氣比較急躁？
4. 你心情不好的時候做什麼？
5. 你每天晚上回家以後先做什麼再做什麼？

B: Please practice speaking on the following topics.

1. 請談一談自己的愛好與興趣。
2. 請談一談你選擇男/女朋友的標準。

第三部分：閱讀練習 Reading Comprehension

A: Please answer the questions in English after reading the following passage.

(Traditional Characters)

　　張天明的父母結婚已經二十八年了，這麼多年他們一直相處得很好，從來沒爭吵過。他們倆的性格和愛好有很多相同的地方，比如他們都很開朗，都很愛交朋友，也都愛吃中國菜，差不多每個週末都要找一家中國餐館吃上一頓。還有，他們都愛旅行，最近幾年他們一起去過世界各地不少的國家。可是他們也有不一樣的地方：張先生是個籃球迷，而張太太對體育不感興趣，卻特別喜歡看喜劇，晚上的電視如果又有籃球比賽又有喜劇的話，張太太就只好把電視機讓給張先生，自己給朋友打電話聊天。可是有的時候張先生為了讓太太高興，也只好不看球賽，陪太太一起看喜劇。

(Simplified Characters)

张天明的父母结婚已经二十八年了，这么多年他们一直相处得很好，从来没争吵过。他们俩的性格和爱好有很多相同的地方，比如他们都很开朗，都很爱交朋友，也都爱吃中国菜，差不多每个週末都要找一家中国餐馆吃上一顿。还有，他们都爱旅行，最近几年他们一起去过世界各地不少的国家。可是他们也有不一样的地方：张先生是个篮球迷，而张太太对体育不感兴趣，却特别喜欢看喜剧，晚上的电视如果又有篮球比赛又有喜剧的话，张太太就只好把电视机让给张先生，自己给朋友打电话聊天。可是有的时候张先生为了让太太高兴，也只好不看球赛，陪太太一起看喜剧。

問題：

1) 張天明的父母為什麼一直相處得很好？

2) 張天明的父母在哪些方面有相同的興趣？

3) 張太太為什麼在電視上又有喜劇又有球賽的時候，和朋友打電話聊天？

B: Please read the passage and answer the question in English.

(Traditional Characters)

我的情緒常會受音樂的影響。聽古典音樂時，心情特別平靜；聽搖滾樂時，就感覺比較激動。但是我的同屋跟我不一樣，覺得聽古典音樂很沒意思，搖滾樂又太吵。你呢？

(Simplified Characters)

我的情绪常会受音乐的影响。听古典音乐时，心情特别平静；听搖滾乐时，就感觉比较激动。但是我的同屋跟我不一样，觉得听古典音乐很没意思，搖滾乐又太吵。你呢？

C: As in the U.S., newspapers and magazines in the PRC and Taiwan carry personal advertisements. The following is taken from a mainland Chinese magazine. Please read the advertisement and answer the following questions.

> **安琪小姐**　大专学历，24 岁，未婚，出身于北京一高知家庭，身高 1.67 米，知书达理，端庄美丽，温柔善良，聪慧能干，身材健美。爱好体育，擅长烹调及室内设计。能说一口流利地道的英语（托福成绩 617 分），现在国内一家外商独资公司工作。欲寻一位有事业心，真诚善良，品德高尚，具有硕士以上学历的海外男士为侣（以在美加为宜）。有意者请寄简历、全身近照、电话号码及婚姻状况证明。来信请寄：100083　中国北京市海淀区暂安处一号魏淑珍转安琪小姐收。

Questions:

1) Please circle the name of the person advertising.

   (安琪)

2) How old is she?

   (24.)

3) Where is she from?

   (Beijing.)

4) What are some of her attributes?

   (Educated, beautiful, smart, capable, healthy...)

5) What education does she have?

   (College education.)

6) Where does she work?

   (At a foreign company in China.)

7) What kind of person is she looking for?

   (A honest man with career ambition. He has to have a master's degree or a Ph.D. He has to reside in the U.S. or Canada.)

D: Suppose you want to place a personal ad in a magazine. The following is a personal information form that you need to fill out for that purpose. Please fill in the blanks.

留学人员征婚需填表格

姓名		性别		出生日期		民族	
籍贯		身高		相貌		学历	
爱好		职业		护照号		所在国	
居留身份				婚姻状况			
有无子女				身体状况			
通讯地址						电话	
其它情况							
要求对方							

E: 成語故事

Please read the story and answer the following questions.

1	2
3	4

(Traditional Characters)

東床快婿

　　中國東晉（344-405）有個叫郗(1)太傅(2)的官(3)，有一天叫他的學生給當時的宰相(4)送一封信，請宰相幫他選一個女婿(5)。宰相回答說，"我有很多學生住在我家東邊的屋子裏，您去選吧。"郗太傅的學生去東邊的屋子看了以後回來報告說，"王先生的學生都很不錯，聽說我來為您選女婿，個個都很客氣，站起來打招呼，只有一個年輕人躺在東邊的一張床上，好像沒看見我似的。"郗太傅說，"這個人好！"於是他去看那個年輕人。原來他就是有名的書法家(6)王羲之(7)，後來郗太傅就把女兒嫁給了王羲之。現在中國人把女婿也叫做"東床"，就是從這個故事來的。

(1) 郗 (Xī)：a Chinese surname

(2) 太傅 (tàifù)：Grand Master; tutor to the crown prince

(3) 官 (guān)：official

(4) 宰相 (zǎixiàng)：prime minister

(5) 女婿 (nǚxù)：son-in-law

(6) 書法家 (shūfǎjiā)：calligrapher

(7) 王羲之 (Wáng Xīzhī)：a person's name

(Simplified Characters)

东床快婿

　　中国东晋（344-405）有个叫郗(1)太傅(2)的官(3)，有一天叫他的学生给当时的宰相(4)送一封信，请宰相帮他选一个女婿(5)。宰相回答说，"我有很多学生住在我家东边的屋子里，您去选吧。"郗太傅的学生去东边的屋子看了以后回来报告说，"王先生的学生都很不错，听说我来为您选女婿，个个都很客气，站起来打招呼，只有一个年轻人躺在东边的一张床上，好像没看见我似的。"郗太傅说，"这个人好！"于是他去看那个年轻人。原来他就是有名的书法家(6)王羲之(7)，后来郗太傅就把女儿嫁给了王羲之。现在中国人把女婿也叫做"东床"，就是从这个故事来的。

(1) 郗 (Xī)：a Chinese surname

(2) 太傅 (tàifù)：Grand Master; tutor to the crown prince

(3) 官 (guān)：official

(4) 宰相 (zǎixiàng)：prime minister

(5) 女婿 (nǚxù)：son-in-law

(6) 书法家 (shūfǎjiā)：calligrapher

(7) 王羲之 (Wáng Xīzhī)：a person's name

Questions:

1) Why did Xi Taifu send his student to Wang Dao?

   (To ask him help find a husband for his daughter.)

2) What did Wang Dao tell Xi's student?

   (He could go choose one of his students who lived in the room to the east of his house.)

3) What did Xi's student tell Xi about one particular young man?

   (This young man was lying on his back on a bed and seemed not to have seen him.)

4) Why do you think Xi picked Wang Xizhi?

第四部分：句型與詞語練習 Grammar & Usage

A: 請用 “聽起來好像” 完成下面的對話：

Please complete the following dialogues using “聽起來好像”.

   例：　A: 你不是說想找同學教你怎麼做功課嗎？

   　　　B: 我跟他提了一下，<u>聽起來他好像不太願意幫忙</u>。

1. A: 球賽快要開始了，小張到底來不來？

   B: 我剛打電話給他，＿＿＿＿＿＿＿＿＿＿＿＿＿＿＿＿＿＿。

2. A: 我剛跟小林在門口說了幾句話，＿＿＿＿＿＿＿＿＿＿＿，
   你知道不知道他最近怎麼了？

   B: 我聽說他跟他女朋友鬧翻了。詳細情況怎麼樣，我也不太清楚。

3. A: 那個人說話＿＿＿＿＿＿＿＿＿＿＿＿＿＿＿，她們是姐妹嗎？

   B: 對，她是小梅的妹妹。

B: 請用 " 才 " 完成下面的對話。

Please complete the following dialogues using "才".

例：A: 請你把事情的經過說給我聽聽。（不生氣）

B: 你要答應我你聽了不生氣，我才說給你聽。

1. A: 我們一起去聽音樂會，好嗎？（你請客）

   B: ＿＿＿＿＿＿＿＿＿＿＿＿＿＿＿＿＿＿＿＿＿。

2. A: 你打算申請州立大學嗎？（給錢）

   B: ＿＿＿＿＿＿＿＿＿＿＿＿＿＿＿＿＿＿＿＿＿。

3. A: 小姐，你想租什麼樣兒的房子？（有空調）

   B: ＿＿＿＿＿＿＿＿＿＿＿＿＿＿＿＿＿＿＿＿＿。

C: 請用 " 先…再… " 完成下面的對話。

Please complete the following dialogues using "先…再…".

例：A: 你現在去餐廳吃飯嗎？（做完功課／去吃飯）

B: 我先做完功課，再去吃飯。

1. A: 你明年暑假打算做什麼？（打工賺錢／去亞洲旅行）

   B: ＿＿＿＿＿＿＿＿＿＿＿＿＿＿＿＿＿＿＿＿＿。

2. A: 你覺得這件事，我應該答應嗎？（看情況／決定）

   B: ＿＿＿＿＿＿＿＿＿＿＿＿＿＿＿＿＿＿＿＿＿。

3. A: 你大學畢業以後，打算念研究所還是找工作？

   （做兩年事／上研究所）

   B: ＿＿＿＿＿＿＿＿＿＿＿＿＿＿＿＿＿＿＿＿＿。

D: 請用 " V得／不＋出來 " 完成下面的對話。

Please complete the following dialogues using "V得／不＋出來".

例：A: 你覺得他生氣了嗎？

B: 我不知道，看不出來。

1. 這個問題非常難，我想了很久，<u>想不出來</u>。

2. A: 喂？

   B: 是小張吧？

   A: 哎，你怎麼知道是我？

   B: 你的聲音，<u>我聽得出來</u>。

3. A: 這肯定不是你做的菜。這麼好吃！

   B: 怎麼不是我做的？就是我做的。

   A: 你做的菜又油又鹹，<u>我吃得出來</u>。

E: 請用 " 以來 " 完成下面的對話。

   Please complete the following dialogues using "以來" .

   例：A: 他多久沒跟他的指導教授見面了？（鬧翻）

   B: <u>從鬧翻以來</u>，他們已經一個多月沒見面了。

   1. A: 你今年看了多少球賽了？（春天開始）

      B: ＿＿＿＿＿＿＿＿＿＿＿＿＿＿＿＿＿＿，我已經看了十二場了。

   2. A: 老張怎麼醉得這麼厲害？（跟女朋友吹了）

      B: ＿＿＿＿＿＿＿＿＿＿＿＿＿＿＿＿＿＿，他幾乎天天都喝醉酒。

   3. A: 聽說你又要搬家了。你好像常搬家。（上大學）

      B: ＿＿＿＿＿＿＿＿＿＿＿＿＿＿＿＿＿＿，這是第五次了。

F: 請用 " 從來 " 完成下面的對話。

   Please complete the following dialogues using "從來".

   例：A: 你吃過芥蘭牛肉嗎？

   B: <u>我從來沒吃過</u>，聽說很好吃。

   1. A: 你看過大學籃球比賽嗎？

      B: 我對球賽沒有興趣，＿＿＿＿＿＿＿＿＿＿＿＿＿＿＿＿＿＿。

   2. A: 聽說附近新開了一家購物中心，你知道不知道在什麼地方？

      B: 我不知道在哪兒。＿＿＿＿＿＿＿＿＿＿＿＿＿＿＿＿＿＿。

3. A: 大家都說會電腦對將來找工作很有幫助。你選過電腦課嗎？

   B: ＿＿＿＿＿＿＿＿＿＿＿＿＿。不過，下個學期我打算選一門電腦課。

第五部分：翻譯 Translation

A: Translate the following passage into English.

(Traditional Characters)

　　柯先生跟柯太太剛買了一棟三層樓房，裏面有四房兩廳、三個廁所。兩個人搬進去才住了一個月，就發現房子太大，電費特別貴。柯先生建議租出去一個房間，可以有一點租金。柯太太不同意，她覺得這樣問題太多，要是跟租房子的人相處得不好，那多讓人生氣。沒想到柯先生瞞著柯太太在報上登了一個出租廣告。後來柯太太知道了，非常不高興，兩個人差點鬧翻。柯先生非常後悔。

(Simplified Characters)

　　柯先生跟柯太太刚买了一栋三层楼房，里面有四房两厅、三个厕所。两个人搬进去才住了一个月，就发现房子太大，电费特别贵。柯先生建议租出去一个房间，可以有一点租金。柯太太不同意，她觉得这样问题太多，要是跟租房子的人相处得不好，那多让人生气。没想到柯先生瞒着柯太太在报上登了一个出租广告。后来柯太太知道了，非常不高兴，两个人差点闹翻。柯先生非常后悔。

(Mr. and Mrs. Ke just bought a three-level house with four bedrooms, a living room, and three baths. They had just moved in and lived there for a month, they discovered that it was a big house with extremely expensive electric bills. When Mr. Ke suggested renting out a room to collect a little rent. Mrs. Ke didn't agree. She thought this way they would have a lot of problems; if they didn't get along well with the tenants, and quarreled with them, that would be upsetting. Who would have thought Mr. Ke put in a "for rent" advertisement in the newspaper without telling Mrs. Ke. Later, Mrs. Ke found out about this and was extremely angry. The two of them almost had a falling out. Mr. Ke was really sorry.)

B: Translate the following sentences into Chinese.

1. Not until his roommate finished watching the basketball game did John fall asleep.
    （約翰在他的同屋看完了籃球賽以後才睡著。）

2. Anderson always watches TV before doing his homework.
    （安德森總是先看電視再做功課。）

3. Mr. Zhang and Mrs. Zhang have very different interests.
    （在興趣上，張先生和張太太很不一樣。）

C: Translate the following passage into Chinese.

Zhang Tianming thought for a long time. He decided to talk to his roommate and ask him not to make so much noise when he watches a ball game. If his roommate wouldn't listen, Zhang Tianming would move out right away.

（張天明想來想去決定跟他的同屋談談，叫他看球賽的時候別大聲喊
叫。如果他的同屋不聽的話，他就搬出宿舍去。）

D: Translate the following passage into Chinese.

No wonder she was in a very bad mood today. It turned out that she just broke up with her boyfriend. They've been dating since high school. Both of them are outgoing and are easy to get along with. After pondering, no one knows why they fell out with each other.

（難怪她今天心情那麼不好，原來她跟她男朋友吹了。他們從上高中就開始交
往。兩個人的性格都很開朗，也很容易跟人相處。大家想來想去，都不知道
他們為什麼鬧翻了。）

第六部分：寫作練習 (Composition)

What attributes do you look for in an ideal girlfriend or boyfriend?

第八課　電影和電視的影響

第一部分：聽力練習 Listening Comprehension

A: Listen to the tape recording of *Lesson Eight* and answer the following questions.

1. What was on TV while Zhang Tianming was waiting for Lisa?

    (News about MTV's bad influence on kids. A boy accidentally burned his little sister to death.)

2. Who should be responsible for children's behaviors according to Lisa?

    (TV and movies have to share some of the responsibilities.)

3. Did they go to see a movie? Why or why not?

    (No. The movie got canceled because of a bomb threat.)

4. Why did the woman shoot her boyfriend's daughter?

    (Because she thought the daughter was another girlfriend of his.)

B: Listen to the tape for the workbook.

1. Listen to the passage and answer the following questions.

    （很多孩子一放學回家就坐在沙發上看電視。卡通也看，廣告也看，什麼都看，慢慢兒地都成了電視兒童了。雖然家長有責任指導孩子，告訴他們什麼電視可以看，什麼不能看，但是現在的孩子越來越厲害，會用不吃飯，不做功課等各種辦法來威脅父母讓他們看電視，這種情況常常搞得父母親不知道怎麼辦才好。）

Questions:

1) What do we call kids who watch a lot of TV?

    (TV kids.)

2) What do kids do to make their parents give them more TV time?

    (They don't eat, and don't do homework.)

2. Listen to the passage and answer the following questions.

（最近電視裏有一個頻道播的節目很特別，不播新聞，也沒有廣告，所有的節目都不是演員演的。只要你有錢，有時間，就可以跟電視台買半個鐘頭的時間，自己上電視，想演什麼就演什麼。聽說自從播出以來很受歡迎，因為大部分節目都很新鮮，所以看的人不少。）

Questions:

1) Why is the programming on this one channel so different from others?

   (There's no news or commercials. There are no professional actors.)

2) Why has it become so popular?

   (Because it is very creative, and very novel.)

3) Who can take advantage of this kind of programming?

   (Anyone with time and money can buy half an hour of time to go on TV and perform what they want to.)

3. Listen to the passage and answer the following questions.

（今天報上有一則消息說，加州山上發生火災，燒死了三個人。據說本來以為是小孩玩火柴引起的，後來才知道是有人在樹林裏吸煙引起的。這種不負責任的行為，讓人感到非常生氣。）

Questions:

1) What was reported in the newspaper?

   (There was mountain fire in California. Three people died.)

2) What was responsible for it?

   (People smoking in the woods.)

第二部分：口語練習　Speaking Exercises

A: Please practice asking and answering the following questions with a partner before class.

1. 你最喜歡看什麼電視節目？為什麼？
2. 你常常一邊做功課一邊聽音樂嗎？為什麼？
3. 什麼情況常常會引起火災？
4. 美國晚上的電視新聞多半幾點播？

B: Please practice speaking on the following topics.

1. 請你談一談你最喜歡的電視節目。
2. 你覺得電視電影對人有沒有影響？為什麼？

第三部分：閱讀練習　Reading Comprehension

A: Please fill in the blanks with "的", "得", or "地".

(Traditional Characters)

　　今天電影院上演的是一部法國的藝術電影。電影演得很不錯，小張看得很高興。出了電影院，他慢慢地走回家。他一邊走，一邊模仿電影裏的人物。他越模仿，覺得越有意思，旁邊的人都覺得他很奇怪。他打算回家以後把電影給同屋小李詳細地說一說。

(Simplified Characters)

　　今天电影院上演的是一部法国的艺术电影。电影演得很不错，小张看得很高兴。出了电影院，他慢慢地走回家。他一边走，一边模仿电影里的人物。他越模仿，觉得越有意思，旁边的人都觉得他很奇怪。他打算回家以后把电影给同屋小李详细地说一说。

B: Please answer the questions after reading the following passage.

(Traditional Characters)

　　現在打開電視什麼節目都有，不過我覺得最有意思的是有許多電視台
只播一種節目。比如說，有的電視公司只播新聞，這種電視公司，只要是
新聞就播。有的電視台只播卡通片，除了卡通，還是卡通。另外還有的電
視台只播讓人看了笑，看了高興的喜劇片。但是不是每個人都可以看得到
這些電視台播的節目。因為這些都是有線電視台播出的，每個月得付點錢
才能看得到。

(Simplified Characters)

　　现在打开电视什么节目都有，不过我觉得最有意思的是有许多电视台
只播一种节目。比如说，有的电视公司只播新闻，这种电视公司，只要是
新闻就播。有的电视台只播卡通片，除了卡通，还是卡通。另外还有的电
视台只播让人看了笑，看了高兴的喜剧片。但是不是每个人都可以看得到
这些电视台播的节目。因为这些都是有线电视台播出的，每个月得付点钱
才能看得到。

Questions:

1) What three kinds of TV programming are mentioned in the passage?

　　(News only; cartoons only; comedies only.)

2) Who can enjoy these TV programs?

　　(People who pay money each month.)

C: Answer the following questions on the basis of the newspaper clipping.

立体电影　　独家放映
燎原电影院小厅
《驯狮三郎》
放映时间：1：30　3：00
4：30　6：00　7：30(双片)
长寿路600号　电话：2539254

問題：

1) 這家電影院叫什麼名字？

　　　（燎原）

2) 請你圈出 (quān chū: circle)這個電影的名字。

　　　（馴獅三郎）

3) 電影院的地址是什麼？

　　　（長壽路600號）

4) 這個電影上午演幾場？

　　　（上午不演）

D: As in the U.S., Chinese newspapers carry TV and movie listings, which are sometimes printed on the crease of the newspaper. The following is taken from a Shanghai-based newspaper.

今 明 电 视

4月11日　星期一
中央电视台·五频道
23:35 4集连续剧：特区警察
③④
上海电视台·八频道
10:17 包青天：真假状元(1)
23:01 故事片：风雨相思雁
上海电视台·十四频道
0:20 杨贵妃(28)
东方电视台·廿频道
21:54 台湾电视连续剧：末
代皇孙(54)
上海教育电视台(26频道)
19:59 音乐专题：军歌声声
4月12日　星期二
中央电视台·五频道
20:05 14集连续剧：还是那
条街⑤
上海电视台·八频道
20:10 包青天：真假状元(2)
上海电视台·十四频道
23:38 杨贵妃(29)
东方电视台·廿频道
21:53 末代皇孙(55)
上海教育电视台(26频道)
20:13 七彩讲坛 话剧《冰山
情》

Questions:

1) What dates are the viewing guide for?

   (April 11 and April 12.)

2) How many TV channels are available for the residents of Shanghai?

   (5.)

3) If you are interested in watching a music program, which channel should you watch?

   (26.)

E: 成語故事

Please answer the questions after reading the following story.

<u>1 | 2</u>
3 | 4

(Traditional Characters)

自相矛盾

  從前有個人在市場上賣矛(1)和盾(2)。他拿起他的盾對人說：「你們看我的盾！我的盾是世界上最好的，什麼矛都刺不穿(3)它。」然後，他又拿起他的矛說：「你們再來看我的矛！我的矛是世界上最厲害的，什麼盾它都能刺穿。」

  大家聽了他的話，都覺得十分好笑。有個人問他：「如果你說的都是真話，你的矛是世界上最厲害的，什麼盾都能刺穿，你的盾是世界上最好的，什麼矛都刺不穿它，那你用你的矛來刺你的盾，結果會怎麼樣呢？」那個人聽了，就很快地收起他的矛和盾，離開了。

(1)矛 (máo): spear (2)盾 (dùn): shield (3)刺穿(cì chuān): pierce through

(Simplified Characters)

自相矛盾

  从前有个人在市场上卖矛(1)和盾(2)。他拿起他的盾对人说："你们看我的盾！我的盾是世界上最好的，什麼矛都刺不穿(3)它。"然后，他又拿起他的矛说："你们再来看我的矛！我的矛是世界上最厉害的，什麼盾它都能刺穿。"

  大家听了他的话，都觉得十分好笑。有个人问他："如果你说的都是真话，你的矛是世界上最厉害的，什麼盾都能刺穿，你的盾是世界上最好的，什麼矛都刺不穿它，那你用你的矛来刺你的盾，结果会怎么样呢？"那个人听了，就很快地收起他的矛和盾，离开了。

(1)矛 (máo): spear (2)盾 (dùn): shield (3)刺穿 (cì chuān): pierce through

Questions:

1) What did the person say about his spear and shield?

   (No spear could pierce his shield. His spear could pierce any shield.)

2) Did people believe what he said? Why or why not?

> *(No, they wanted to know what would happen if he used his spear to pierce his shield.)*

3) What did the person do after hearing people's comments?

> *(He quickly gathered up his spear and shield and left.)*

4) What do you think the title means?

> *(Be self-contradictory.)*

第四部分：句型與詞語練習 Grammar & Usage

A: 請用 " 一邊...一邊... " 完成下面的句子。

Please complete the following sentences using "一邊...一邊...".

例：他喜歡一邊聽錄音，一邊唱歌。

1. 現在有許多研究生都是＿＿＿＿＿＿＿＿＿＿＿＿。（打工/做研究）

2. 我不像他那麼厲害，可以一心兩用，＿＿＿＿＿＿＿＿＿＿＿。

　　　　　　　　　　　　　　　　　　　　　　（看球賽/做功課）

3. 他每天早上都是＿＿＿＿＿＿＿＿＿＿＿。（上廁所/看報紙）

B: 請用 " 偶爾 " 回答下面的問題。

Please answer the following questions using "偶爾".

例：A: 你真的一點肉都不吃嗎？

　　B: 偶爾也吃一點兒。

1. A: 公共電視台播商業片嗎？

　 B: ＿＿＿＿＿＿＿＿＿＿＿＿＿＿＿＿＿。

2. A: 你常看 " 芝蔴街 " 嗎？

　 B: ＿＿＿＿＿＿＿＿＿＿＿＿＿＿＿＿＿。

3. A: 美國的電視常播紀錄片嗎？

B: _____ 。

C: 請用＂引起＂完成下面的句子。

Please complete the following sentences using "引起".

例：學校禮堂常演外國藝術片，爲了<u>引起學生看電影的興趣</u>，電影
票一張只要一塊錢。

1. 他們兩個人交往不到三個月就要結婚，_____ 。
（家長／反對）

2. 爲了_____，我們的漢語老師常常教我們唱中文歌。
（學生／興趣）

3. 上課的時候他對他的指導教授說了一些難聽的話，_____ 。
（大家／不滿）

D: 請用＂反而＂改寫下面的句子。

Please rewrite the following sentences using "反而".

例：他平常什麼都管，今天這麼重要的事，<u>沒想到他反而不管了</u>。

1. 這本來就是他的錯，_____ 。（怪別人）

2. 小王比我們晚半年上研究所，_____ 。（早畢業）

3. 電視新聞說加州今天天氣很好，_____ 。（下雨）

E: 請用＂難免＂完成下面的句子。

Please complete the following sentences using "難免".

例：夫妻兩個人生活在一起，<u>難免會吵架</u>。

1. 他第一次離開家，_____ 。（想家）

2. 看球賽看到好看的地方，_____ 。（大喊大叫）

3. 兒童看電視，_____ 。（模仿）

F: 請用 " 就是...也... " 完成下面的對話。

Please complete the following sentences using "就是...也...".

例：A: 今天天氣這麼冷，你就別去戲院看戲了。

B: 戲非看不可，<u>就是天氣再冷我也要去</u>。

1. A: 小梅的父母反對你們兩個交往，你就不要再去找她了。

   B: 我們兩個彼此相愛，＿＿＿＿＿＿＿＿＿＿＿＿＿＿＿＿。

2. A: 這個藝術片真的沒什麼意思。我看得有點兒受不了了。

   B: ＿＿＿＿＿＿＿＿＿＿＿＿＿。別忘了，看完了還得寫報告呢！

3. A: 這個人在那麼多人的面前說那麼難聽的話氣你，你怎麼受得了？

   B: ＿＿＿＿＿＿＿＿＿＿＿＿＿＿＿＿＿，因為他是我父親。

G: 請用 " 還是 " 完成下面的對話。

Please complete the following dialogues using "還是".

例：A: 這雙鞋子挺好的，買吧。

B: 稍微貴了一點兒，<u>還是等打折的時候買吧</u>。

1. A: 我有點兒不舒服，想先回家。

   B: 我看你病得挺厲害的，＿＿＿＿＿＿＿＿＿＿＿＿。（看大夫）

2. A: 媽，我看完這個卡通片再做功課，好嗎？

   B: 你今天的功課那麼多，＿＿＿＿＿＿＿＿＿＿＿＿＿＿。

3. A: 你們去看電影吧。別管我。

   B: 你別老在家憋著，憋久了對身體不好，＿＿＿＿＿＿＿＿＿。

第五部分：翻譯 Translation

A: Translate the following passage into English.

(Traditional Characters)

　　最近電視裏播的新聞沒有什麼好消息。不是誰開槍殺了人，就是哪兒有火災，看了讓人心情非常不好。難怪有些人不看電視，免得越看越生氣。

(Traditional Characters)

　　最近电视里播的新闻没有什麼好消息。不是谁开枪杀了人，就是哪儿有火灾。看了让人心情非常不好。难怪有些人不看电视，免得越看越生气。

(*Lately when one turns on the TV, it seems that there is no good news. If it's not someone is shooting and killing someone, then it's a fire somewhere. Watching it puts people in a bad mood. No wonder some people don't watch TV just so that they don't get angry.*)

B: Please translate the following sentences into Chinese.
The movies shown in the auditorium are almost all documentaries. Occasionally, the auditorium shows commercial movies.

（這個禮堂演的多半是紀錄片，偶爾也演商業片。）

C: Please translate the following passage into Chinese.
At college many students work (while studying) in order to make some money. Even rich people's kids are no exceptions. However, if students spend too much time working, their study inevitably suffer/are inevitably affected.

（在大學，很多學生一邊學習，一邊工作賺點兒錢。就是有錢人的孩子
　也一樣。但是如果他們工作的時間太多，他們的學習難免會受影響。）

第六部分：寫作練習 Composition

1. 請你談一談你最喜歡的電視節目。

   What is your favorite TV program? Why?

2. 談電視電影對人的影響

第九課　旅行

第一部分：聽力練習 (Listening Comprehension)

A: **Listen to the tape recording of *Lesson Nine* and answer the following questions.**

1. Why does Zhang Tianming want to go to China?

   (To see his parents' hometown and other places)

2. Will Zhang Tianming travel alone? How do you know?

   (No, he would like to have Lisa go with him.)

3. Will this be the first time for them to travel together? How do you know?

   (No, they've been to the east coast and the west coast.)

4. Which route will be Lisa's choice if they go to China?

   (She would like to go via Hong Kong.)

B: **Listen to the tape for the workbook.**

1. Listen to the passage and answer the following questions.

   （去年李先生和李太太出國到墨西哥去旅行。有一天他們在旅館吃完飯以後，李先生叫太太跟他到海邊去散步。可是李太太覺得外邊熱得像火爐，就先回房間了。李先生散完步回來，發現李太太坐在沙發上好像有什麼心事，就問她發生了什麼事。原來李太太從旅館房間的窗戶看見李先生跟一個女的在海邊聊天，就吃起醋來了。李先生趕緊說那個女的其實只是問他幾點鐘，順便聊了幾句。可是李太太聽了以後還是很生氣，搞得李先生不知道怎麼辦才好。）

   Questions:

   1) Why didn't Mrs. Li take a walk with Mr. Li?

      (She felt it was too hot to take a walk.)

2) Why did Mrs. Li quarrel with Mr. Li?

   (She saw Mr. Li chatting with a woman on the beach. She was jealous.)

3) Who was the woman?

   (No one. She was simply asking the time.)

2. Listen to the passage and answer the following questions.

（小高上個禮拜到東岸談生意，順便去看住在紐約的姑媽。姑媽看到
  他非常高興，給他做了好幾個拿手好菜。小高也把他跟太太和孩子
  照的相片拿出來給姑媽看。因為小高很少來紐約，姑媽想留他多住
  幾天，可是小高來不及改飛機票，只好說下次有機會再來了。）

是非題：
1) _F_ 小高去紐約旅行。
2) _T_ 小高的姑媽請他在家裏吃飯。
3) _F_ 小高的太太、孩子也去了紐約。
4) _F_ 小高不願意在姑媽家多待幾天。

第二部分：口語練習 Speaking Exercises

A: Please practice asking and answering the following questions with a partner before class.

1. 你的父母是從哪兒來的？
2. 你是在什麼地方出生的？
3. 你是在什麼地方長大的？
4. 你去過中國嗎？
5. 快放寒假/暑假了，你打算做什麼？
6. 出國旅行需要辦什麼手續？

B: Please practice speaking on the following topics.

1. 要是你有錢有時間的話，你打算去什麼地方旅行？爲什麼？

2. 請你談一談你最近的一次旅行。

第三部分：閱讀練習 Reading Comprehension

A: Please read the passage and answer the following questions.

(Traditional Characters)

　　王先生和王太太移民來美國已經四年了。他們本來想把孩子小天接到美國來住，但是又怕小天不適應美國的教育和生活。所以只好把他留在老家給小天的姑媽帶。小天今年已經十四歲了，整天閑著沒事做，也越來越不聽姑媽的話，偶爾還威脅姑媽，叫姑媽別管他。姑媽只好給王先生打電話。姑媽跟王先生討論的結果是：放假的時候王太太回老家看看，順便把小天帶回美國。沒想到小天非常反對。他說除非姑媽跟他一起走，否則他是不會來美國的。王先生只好想辦法給他們兩個人辦簽證。

(Simplified Characters)

　　王先生和王太太移民来美国已经四年了。他们本来想把孩子小天接到美国来住，但是又怕小天不适应美国的教育和生活。所以只好把他留在老家给小天的姑妈带。小天今年已经十四岁了，整天闲着没事做，也越来越不听姑妈的话，偶尔还威胁姑妈，叫姑妈别管他。姑妈只好给王先生打电话。姑妈跟王先生讨论的结果是：放假的时候王太太回老家看看，顺便把小天带回美国。没想到小天非常反对。他说除非姑妈跟他一起走，否则他是不会来美国的。王先生只好想办法给他们两个人办签证。

Questions:

1) Why did the Wangs leave their child behind?

(They were afraid that the child would not be able to make the adjustment to American life.)

2) What problems are they having with the child?

   (He does not listen to his aunt.)

3) What was their solution to the problem?

   (Mrs. Want will go back to visit and bring Xiao Tian back with her.)

4) What do you think the chances are for the family to be reunited? Why?

B: 根據閱讀材料，回答下面問題。

Please answer the following questions on the basis of the the itinerary listed below.

去上海你可以坐飞机：

上海虹桥机场是中国最大的机场之一，很多航空公司有班机飞往上海。
（从北美）
中国东方航空公司每星期天从芝加哥经洛杉矶飞往上海。美国西北航空公司每星期四从西雅图飞往上海。中国民航每星期有三个航班飞往上海。
（从欧洲）
东方航空公司每星期五从马德里经布鲁塞尔飞往上海。
（从香港）
东方航空公司每天都有班机飞往上海。香港港龙 (Gǎnglóng: Dragon Air)航空公司每星期有五个航班飞往上海。机票有时非常难买，需要提前订票。
（从日本）
日本航空公司、中国东方航空公司都有航班往返日本与上海。

你也可以坐轮船：

（从香港）
每月有航班往返香港和上海之间，在香港可向中国国际旅行社订船票。

你也可以坐火车：

（从香港）
从香港坐火车去上海，途中需在广州转车。

1) 從香港去上海有哪幾種方法？
2) 從香港坐飛機去上海需要注意什麼？
3) 從巴黎坐東方航空公司去上海應該先去什麼地方？
4) 東方航空公司有那幾條國際航線？
5) 如果你從香港坐船到上海，應該到什麼地方買票？
6) 從香港可不可以坐火車直接到上海？
7) 日本和中國之間有哪兩家航空公司的航班？
8) 如果你想星期四從美國飛往上海應該坐哪家航空公司的飛機？
9) 香港和上海之間有哪兩家航空公司的航班？

C: The following is a newspaper ad for a travel agency.

Questions:

1) In which city is the travel agency located?

   (Boston.)

2) Can they make a domestic reservation for you?

   (Yes.)

3) What other services do they provide?

   (Arranging international trips and taking care of travelers' visa problems.)

4) When can you call them for services?

   (Seven days a week, 9:30AM to 6:30PM.)

D: **Tourist hotels in mainland China, Taiwan and Hong Kong often advertise in newspapers and magazines. The following advertisement is taken from a Taiwanese publication.**

華 堂 煥 彩 桂 冠 增 輝

中 部 最 豪 華 的 國 際 觀 光 旅 館

長 榮 桂 冠 酒 店

於 二 月 十 五 日 隆 重 開 幕

長 榮 桂 冠 酒 店 (台中)

EVERGREEN LAUREL HOTEL

(TAICHUNG)

台中市中港路二段6號 電話：(04)328-9988 傳真：(04)328-8642

訂房專線：台中 (04)328-8766

台北 (02)500-1013，500-1114 傳真 (02)500-9020

豐富您的台中之旅

Questions:

1) Where is the hotel located in Taiwan? Is it in northern Taiwan?

   (Taizhong. No.)

2) If you would like to book a room at the hotel, what number do you need to call?

   ((04)328-8766)

3) If you are in Taipei, what numbers should you call for more information?

   ((02)500-1013,500-1114)

E: 成語故事

Please answer the questions after reading the following story.

1 | 2
3 | 4

(Traditional Characters)

井底之蛙

莊子(1)是中國古代的一個哲學家。有一次，他給別人講了一個故事：

很久很久以前，在一口老井(2)裏住著一只青蛙(3)。一天青蛙在井邊遇見了一隻從東海來的大鱉(4)。青蛙對大鱉說："你看，我住的地方多好啊，世界上沒有比我的井更好的地方了。如果我想玩，就可以跳到井邊玩，玩累了，就回到井裏休息一下。這裏多方便啊！"青蛙問大鱉爲什麼不進來看看呢？

大鱉聽了青蛙的話，就到井裏去看了看。牠覺得井裏並不像青蛙說得那麼好，又小又黑，一點兒意思也沒有，就對青蛙說："你見過大海嗎？鬧水災的時候，海水不會增加很多；鬧旱災的時候，海水也不會減少很多。住在大海裏才真的快樂啊！"

青蛙聽了非常不好意思，它這才明白自己知道的太少了。

(1) 莊子 (Zhuāngzǐ): Zhuangzi   (2) 井 (jǐng): well

(3) 青蛙 (qīngwā): frog   (4) 鱉 (biē): soft-shell turtle

(5) 增加 (zēngjiā): increase   (6) 減少 (jiǎnshǎo): decrease

(Simplified Characters)

井底之蛙

庄子(1)是中国古代的一个哲学家。有一次，他给别人讲了一个故事：

很久很久以前，在一口老井(2)里住着一只青蛙(3)。一天青蛙在井边遇见了一隻从东海来的大鳖(4)。青蛙对大鳖说："你看，我住的地方多好啊，世界上没有比我的井更好的地方了。如果我想玩，就可以跳到井边玩，玩累了，就回到井里休息一下。这里多方便啊！"青蛙问大鳖为什么不进来看看呢？

大鳖听了青蛙的话，就到井里去看了看。牠觉得井里并不像青蛙说得那么好，又小又黑，一点儿意思也没有，就对青蛙说："你见过大海吗？闹水灾的时候，海水不会增加很多；闹旱灾的时候，海水也不会减少很多。住在大海里才真的快乐啊！"

青蛙听了非常不好意思，它这才明白自己知道的太少了。

(1) 庄子 (Zhuāngzǐ): Zhuangzi   (2) 井 (jǐng): well

(3) 青蛙 (qīngwā): frog   (4) 鳖 (biē): soft-shell turtle

(5) 增加 (zēngjiā): increase   (6) 减少 (jiǎnshǎo): decrease

Questions:

1) Where did the frog live?

   (In a well.)

2) Where did the turtle come from?

   (From the East China Sea.)

3) What did the frog brag about to the turtle?

   (That his well was perfact. He could rest in the well when he was tired, and played beside the well.)

4) What did the frog invite the turtle to do?

   (To go in and see the well.)

5) What did the turtle tell the frog?

   (During floods or droughts, there is always enough water in the ocean. Living there is happy.)

6) How did the frog react to what the turtle said about the ocean?

   (He was embarrassed.)

7) What kind of people can be compared to the "frog in the well"?

   (A person with a very limited outlook.)

第四部分：句型與詞語練習　Grammar & Usage

A: 請用 " 除非...不然/否則... " 完成下面對話。

Please complete the following dialogues using "除非 ...不然/否則...".

　　例： A: 去加拿大玩，需要辦簽證嗎？

　　　　 B: 除非你是美國人或是英國人，否則都得辦加拿大簽證。

1. A: 我下個禮拜要到紐約做生意，你買張飛機票跟我一起去，好嗎？

   B: _____ 。

2. A: 給他買飛機票特別麻煩。

   B: 為什麼？

   A: 因為 _____ 。（直飛）

3. A: 這些運動褲看起來都挺不錯的，價錢也不貴。你怎麼不買？
   （純棉的）

   B: _____ 。

B: 請完成下面對話。

Please complete the following dialogues.

   例 ： A: 你想坐哪一家航空公司的飛機去中國？

   B: 哪一家的機票便宜，就坐哪一家的。

1. A: 今天下午體育節目那麼多，你要看哪一個？

   B: _____ 。

2. A: 爸爸，下個學期，我應該選什麼課？

   B: _____ 。

3. A: _____ ？

   B: 你要聽什麼音樂，我就聽什麼音樂。

C: 用「不是...就是...」完成下面對話。

Please complete the following dialogues using "不是...就是...".

   例 ： A: 你週末都做些什麼？（打球/看球賽）

   B: 我週末不是打球就是看球賽。

1. A: 你想學什麼專業？　　　（中國歷史/東亞研究）

   B: _____ 。

2. A: 你找房子找了這麼久，怎麼還沒找到合適的？

   　　　　　　　　　　　　（房租太貴/離學校太遠）

   B: _____ 。

3. A: 你們家平常都吃什麼青菜？　　　（菠菜/小白菜）

   B: _____。

D: 用「難怪」改寫下列句子。

Please rewrite the following sentences using "難怪".

例：最近電視裏的卡通片對兒童的影響越來越不好，所以很多家長不讓他
    們的孩子看卡通片。

   --->最近電視裏的卡通片對兒童的影響越來越不好，<u>難怪很多家長不
       讓他們的孩子看卡通片。</u>

1. 北京一到七月，天氣就很熱，人們連飯都不想吃。所以很多人等到八
   月以後，天氣涼快了才去北京玩兒。

   ---> _____。

2. 他常常喝酒打人，所以他太太跟他鬧離婚。

   ---> _____。

3. 南京夏天熱得叫人受不了，所以叫大火爐。

   ---> _____。

E: 請用「既然...就...」完成下面對話。

例： A: 我們去外邊吃飯，好嗎？

     B: 但是我吃中國飯吃膩了。

     A: <u>既然吃膩了中國飯，咱們今天就吃法國飯吧！</u>

1. A: 我的女朋友跟我吹了。我的心情不太好。

   B: _____。（海邊散步）

   A: 也好，也許散完了步，我的心情會好一些。

2. A: 老李，你有空嗎？我有點兒事想跟你商量。

   B: 我急著到中國領事館去辦簽證，你有什麼事？

   A: _____。（明天）

   B: 好，明天再說。

3. A: 小白這個人什麼都好，就是脾氣有點兒急躁。我母親反對我跟他交
往，你說我應該怎麼辦呢？

   B: _____。

F: 請用 " 然後 " 回答下面問題。

   Please answer the following questions using "然後".

     例： A: 明天是你的生日，打算怎麼過？

        B: <u>我打算先去餐館吃一頓，然後跟幾個朋友一起去跳舞</u>。

  1. A: 出國旅行得辦哪些手續？

     B: _____，_____。

  2. A: 要是有錢，你打算去哪些國家旅行？

     B: _____，_____。

  3. A: 再過幾天就放假了，你有什麼計劃？

     B: _____，_____。

G: 請用 " 多...少... " 完成下面句子。

     例：我父親常說一個人應該<u>多做事，少說話</u>。

  1. 我昨天去看醫生，他讓我_____。

               （清淡的/油的）

  2. 母親對我最近的學習不太滿意，她叫我要_____。

               （復習功課/看卡通片）

  3. 小張覺得自己越來越胖。他決定從今天開始_____。

               （出去散步/在家看電視）

第五部分：翻譯 Translation

A: Please translate the following passage into Chinese.

Lisa doesn't like to watch television. Unless it's something especially good, she won't watch TV. Zhang Tianming is different. He'll watch whatever is on TV.

（麗莎不喜歡看電視，除非有特別好的節目，否則她不看。張天明
跟麗莎不一樣，電視裏有什麼節目他就看什麼節目。）

B: Please translate the following brief exchange into Chinese.

Zhang Tianming: Since you don't like watching TV, let's go and see a movie.

Lisa: Great. Afterwards, we can go to that small restaurant next to the theater and eat.

Zhang Tianming: The food there is not edible. Let's go to Chinatown to have some Chinese food.

（張天明：既然你不喜歡看電視，我們就去看電影吧。

  麗　莎：好極了。然後我們可以去戲院隔壁那家小餐館吃飯。

  張天明：那裏的飯簡直不能吃。我們去中國城吃中國飯吧。）

C: Please translate the following telephone conversation into Chinese.

Xiao Zhang: Eastern Travel Agency? I need to book a plane ticket.

Travel Agent: Where are you going?

Xiao Zhang: I'll fly from Chicago to Korea, and change planes there. Then I'll fly from Korea to Hong Kong.

Travel Agent: How many tickets do you want to purchase?

Xiao Zhang: One.

Travel Agent: We will mail the ticket to you right away.

Xiao Zhang: Thanks.

（小　張：東方旅行社嗎？我想訂一張機票。）

  旅行社：請問您要去哪兒？

  小　張：我想先從芝加哥直飛韓國，在那兒轉機，然後，再從韓國飛
香港。

  旅行社：請問買幾張票？

  小　張：一張。

  旅行社：我們馬上就把機票給您寄去。

  小　張：謝謝。）

D: Please translate the following passage into Chinese.

The airport is far from here. I'm afraid that there is not enough time. We must leave right away.

（機場離這兒很遠，我怕來不及了，我們得趕緊走。）

E: Translate the following sentences into Chinese. Please pay attention to Chinese word order.

1. You have to listen to the tape before you come to class.

（你得先聽錄音再來上課。）

2. My roommate is going to visit his aunt in Nanjing.

（我的同屋去南京看他姑媽。）

3. They plan to go dancing after they finish their homework.

（他們打算做完功課以後去跳舞。）

4. He went to pick up his advisor at the airport in his father's car.

（他開他父親的車去飛機場接他的指導教授。）

5. Xiao Wang gave his boyfriend a ride to the bus stop.　　（送）

（小王送她男朋友去公共汽車站。）

第六部分：寫作練習 Composition

1. 你要去中國旅行，請你把需要做的事情以及需要準備的東西寫出來。

2. 記一次有意思的旅行

第十課　在郵局

第一部分：聽力練習 Listening Comprehension

A: Listen to the tape recording of *Lesson Ten* and answer the following questions.

1. Why were Lisa and Tianming so surprised when they stepped into the post office?

    (They didn't expect the post office to be open on a Saturday afternoon.)

2. What did Lisa and Tianming do at the post office?

    (They bought postcards, stamps, aerograms, called their mothers, wrote some postcards, and sent a telegram to Xi'an.)

3. Did Lisa and Tianming meet with Steve in Hong Kong as planned? Why or why not?

    (No. Steve was on a business trip to Taipei.)

4. Why did Steve go to a post office in Taipei?

    (He went to send a parcel to Lisa.)

B: Listen to the tape for the workbook.

1. Listen to the conversation and answer the following questions.

    （男：小姐，我取包裹。

    　女：好，請你簽個字。⋯這是你的包裹。

    　男：謝謝！包裹這麼大。⋯小姐，我還要買一些郵票，十張六毛的。

    　女：好，一共六塊錢。

    　男：有郵簡嗎？

    　女：有，三毛一張。

    　男：來五張。這是兩塊錢。

    　女：好，找您五毛錢，給您郵簡，您慢走。

    　男：謝謝。）

Questions:

1) Where did the conversation take place?

   (At a post office.)

2) What did he do when he was there?

   (Picked up a package, bought 10 stamps and 5 aerograms)

3) How much money did he spend?

   ($6.25)

2. Please listen to the passage and answer the following questions.

   （王先生前天去香港出差，打算在那兒待兩個星期。沒想到今天卻打回來
   一封電報，說他得改日程，馬上回美國來。大家都覺得很奇怪。他回來
   以後我們才知道，原來他的行李在空運的時候丟了，他在香港不能工
   作，只好趕快回國。）

   1) Why did Mr. Wang go to Hong Kong?

      (He was on a business trip.)

   2) Why did he return so soon?

      (He lost his luggage.)

   3) How did people find out that he was coming back?

      (Through the telegram sent by Mr. Wang.)

3. Dictation: Please write down 海天's letter to his aunt.

   （姑媽：

   　　　　您好。我們移民來美國已經五年多了，一直沒有機會回國看
   您。正好十月我要到南京出差，可以順便看看您老人家和老家的親
   朋好友。我這幾天正在做準備，日程還沒有定。等一切都定了，我
   再寫信告訴您。你們需要什麼，也請寫信告訴我。

   　　　　　　　　祝

   　　　　健康

   　　　　　　　　　　　海天

   　　　　　　　　　　　　　上　　　　）

4. Here is 海天's aunt's reply. Please help transcribe.

（海天：

　　　　收到你的信很高興。我們都希望你趕快回來。大家都對你現在的情況很好奇。趁你這次回來，我們可以好好兒地聊聊。家裏什麼都有，你什麼也不必帶。自己出門旅行要小心，平安最重要。
　　　　　　　　祝
　　　　好
　　　　　　　　　　　　　　　姑媽　　　）

第二部分：口語練習 Speaking Exercises

A: Please practice asking and answering the following questions with a partner before class.

1. 美國的郵局什麼時候辦公？

2. 要是你有一個很重要的包裹要寄回家，你怎麼寄？

3. 你的老家有什麼特產？

4. 中國郵局有哪些服務是美國郵局沒有的？

B: Please practice speaking on the following topics.

1. 請談一談出國旅行的時候應該注意哪些事情，怎樣才能讓家人放心。

2. 請談一談美國郵局的辦公時間，他們有什麼樣的服務，你對他們的服務滿意不滿意。

第三部分：閱讀練習 Reading Comprehension

A: Please answer the question in English after reading the following passage.

(Traditional Characters)

航空郵簡比航空信便宜一些。航空信是寫完信以後，把信紙放進信封裏然後寄出去。航空郵簡只有一張紙，寫完以後，不需要信封就可以寄出去。

(Simplified Characters)

航空邮简比航空信便宜一些。航空信是写完信以后，把信纸放进信封里然后寄出去。航空邮简只有一张纸，写完以后，不需要信封就可以寄出去。

問題：

航空郵簡和航空信有什麼不同？

> *(Aerograms are a little cheaper than regular air mail. No envelopes for aerograms.)*

B: Please answer the questions in English after reading the following passage.

(Traditional Characters)

中國的郵局也叫郵電局。電代表電話，電報，也就是說除了寄信，寄包裹以外，他們也有電話及電報的服務。所以如果要打電話，特別是打國際長途電話，也可以去郵電局。在美國，送信的郵遞員有的步行，有的開車。在中國，大部分的郵遞員送信都是騎自行車。

(Simplified Characters)

中国的邮局也叫邮电局。电代表电话，电报，也就是说除了寄信，寄包裹以外，他们也有电话及电报的服务。所以如果要打电话，特别是打国际长途电话，也可以去邮电局。在美国，送信的邮递员有的步行，有的开车。在中国，大部分的邮递员送信都是骑自行车。

問題：

1) 郵遞員是做什麼的？

> *(They deliver mail.)*

2) 中國的郵電局提供什麼樣的服務？

> *(In addition to mailing letters and parcels, people can make phone calls and send telegrams.)*

C: **Please answer the questions in English after reading the following passage.**

(Traditional Characters)

我昨天收到一張明信片，上面只寫了我家的地址，沒寫是誰寄的。我看著看著笑了起來。原來這是姑媽三年以前去墨西哥旅行的時候寄給我的。姑媽和我都以爲這張明信片早就丟了。沒想到，長途旅行了三年以後卻平平安安地寄到了我家。

(Simplified Characters)

我昨天收到一张明信片，上面只写了我家的地址，没写是谁寄的。我看着看着笑了起来。原来这是姑妈三年以前去墨西哥旅行的时候寄给我的。姑妈和我都以为这张明信片早就丢了。没想到，长途旅行了三年以后却平平安安地寄到了我家。

Questions:

1) Who sent the postcard?

> *(My aunt.)*

2) Why did the person start to smile after she took a look at the postcard?

> *(She realized that it was a postcard that everyone thought was lost in the mail a long time ago.)*

3) When was she supposed to receive the postcard?

> *(About three years ago.)*

D: **Suppose you are mailing a parcel to Zhang Tianming from Taipei. Please fill in your name, his name, his address, and the content of the parcel in the appropriate places.**

Your address:

台北市忠孝東路二段五百號

Zhang's address:
58 Prescott St.
Cambridge, MA 02138
Parcel content:　糖果，餅乾

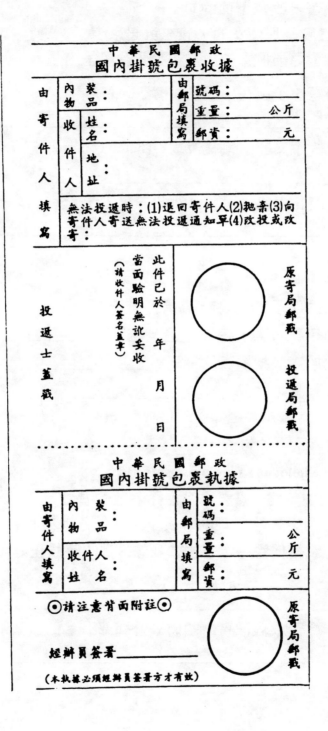

第四部分：句型與詞語練習 Grammar & Usage

A: 請用「V+著+V+著」改寫下面的句子。

例：他一直看著那個女的，後來發起呆來了。

---> 他看著那個女的，看著看著發起呆來了。

1. 他想這個問題想了很久，最後睡著了。

---> _____ 。

2. 他改日程，改了又改，最後改糊塗(hútu: confused) 了。

---> _____ 。

3. 小林聽音樂聽得很高興，後來跳起舞來了。

---> _____ 。

B: 請完成下面的句子。

例：他跟他的女朋友吵架，結果把鏡子打碎了。

1. 他寄了一個包裹回家，結果 _____ 。（丟）

2. 他先生和她吵架，把屋裏的鏡子都_____ 。（破）

3. 他的孩子都是先把功課_____再看電視。（完）

C: 請用「趁」改寫下面的句子。

Please rewrite the following sentences using "趁".

例：你們現在年輕，應該多到世界各地去看看。

--->你們應該趁年輕的時候多到世界各地去看看。

1. 指導教授叫我給他送一本書去，我想送書的時候正好可以問幾個問
   題。

---> _____ 。

2. 平常太忙，今天放假沒事，咱們去看那部有名的法國藝術片吧。

---> _____ 。

3. 飛亞洲的機票一直很貴，可是聽說冬天的機票比較便宜，要去應該
冬天去。

--->_____ 。

D: 請用 " 卻 " 完成下面對話。

Please complete the following sentences using "卻".

例：A: 南京今年的夏天怎麼樣？熱死了吧？

B: 老聽別人說南京的夏天熱得很，<u>沒想到今年卻挺涼快的</u>。

1. A: 學校禮堂演的那個紀錄片，你看了以後覺得怎麼樣？

B: 我一直以為紀錄片沒意思，但是這個片子_____ 。

2. A: 今天小柯怎麼了？是不是有什麼心事？

B: 我也不太清楚。平常看他個性挺開朗的，沒想到今天

_____ 。

3. A: 他今天怎麼說話說個不停，是不是心情特別好？

B: 你說的不錯。他一向挺安靜的，今天_____ 。

E: 請用 " 一直 " 或者 " 一向 " 填空。

Please fill in the blanks with "一直" or "一向".

1. 從上大學以來，他<u>一直</u>住在學校宿舍裏。

2. 他出門旅行<u>一向</u>不買明信片。

3. 小張跟他的女朋友鬧翻了以後，心情<u>一直</u>很受影響。

4. 老李對人<u>一向</u>很熱情，誰的忙，他都幫。

5. 林先生到波士頓上研究所以來，<u>一直</u>適應不了那兒的生活。

6. 我<u>一向</u>不喜歡做菜，只要有人做，我就不做。

F: 請填空。

Please complete the dialogue using the terms provided.

趕快，趁，一向，放心，可靠，正好

A: 快放假了，出國旅行的人越來越多。我打算去英國旅行，但是我的
簽證和護照都還沒辦呢。

B: 你得<u>趕快</u>辦，要不然你一定來不及。

A: 我最近<u>正好</u>特別忙。沒空跑來跑去辦這些事。

B: 那這樣吧，<u>趁</u>這兩天我不太忙，我幫你辦，怎麼樣?

A: 那太好了。你做事情<u>一向 可靠</u>，我最<u>放心</u>不過了。

第五部分：翻譯 Translation

A: Please translate the following passage into Chinese.

Before they knew it, Zhang Tianming and his girlfriend arrived at the post-office. The people at the post-office spoke the Nanjing dialect (南京話) to Zhang Tianming. Zhang Tianming couldn't understand it. It never occurred to him that he wouldn't understand Chinese.

（張天明和他的女朋友走著走著來到了郵局。郵局裏的人跟張天明說
南京話，張天明聽不懂。他沒想到他會聽不懂中國話。）

B: Please translate the following dialogue into Chinese.

Zhang Tianming:	Are you tired from walking?
Lisa:	A little.
Zhang Tianming:	The summer in Nanjing is so hot. No wonder people say Nanjing is like a furnace.
Lisa:	Actually, it's not that horrendous. Where else do you want to go sight-seeing?
Zhang Tianming:	Wherever is not hot.

（張天明：你走了這麼多路，累不累？

麗　莎：有一點兒累。

張天明：南京的夏天真熱，難怪大家都說南京像個大火爐一樣。

麗　莎：其實沒有那麼可怕。你還想去什麼地方玩？

張天明：哪兒不熱，就去哪兒。）

C: Please translate the following passage into Chinese.

On my way to school, I went to the post-office to send parcels to my friends. I had to stand in line for twenty minutes before it was my turn. I waited and waited and fell asleep.

（去學校的路上，我順便去郵局給我的朋友寄一個包裹。人很多，我只好排隊，站著排了二十多分鐘還沒輪到我。沒想到我站著站著睡著了。）

D: Translate the following sentences into Chinese. Please pay attention to the relationship between attributives and "的".

1. Post offices in China do not process passport applications.

（中國的郵局不辦護照。）

2. The house he rented is very close to the track field.

（他租的房子離體育場很近。）

3. The TV program we saw last night was a documentary film.

（我們昨天晚上看的電視節目是一個紀錄片。）

4. The person sitting on the sofa is my roommate Xiao Zhang.

（坐在沙發上的那個人是我的同屋小張。）

5. The person who played with matches and caused the fire burned himself to death.

（那個玩火柴引起火災的人把自己燒死了。）

第六部分：寫作練習 Composition

你剛從美國坐飛機到中國去旅行，請寫一封信給你的父母，告訴他們你一路上都很順利。不要忘了寫信封。

第十一課　一封信

第一部分：聽力練習 Listening Comprehension

A: Listen to the tape recording of Lesson Eleven and answer the following questions.

1. How many places had Tianming and Lisa been to on their sight-seeing trip at the time of the letter?

    (5)

2. What do they like about the Temple of Confucius?

    (The architecture)

3. Why are they most impressed with Sun Yat-sen Mausoleum?

    (The architecture is grand and the view is magnificent.)

4. Which city are they heading to next?

    (Xi'an)

B: Listen to the tape for the workbook.

1. The following is a conversation between Zhang Tianming and his cousin.

（張天明：哎，表哥你到哪兒去了？怎麼一下子你就不見了？

表　哥：唉，別提了。下一次，再也不能星期天出來玩兒了。我在前邊排隊買划船的票，人那麼多，排的隊又不直，我一回頭，就看不見你們了。

張天明：下一次要是排隊買什麼東西，我們一起排。我們還以為你去上廁所了呢！

表　哥：不行，不行，排隊買東西，還得我去。要不然，人家一聽你說話，一看你的女朋友，就知道你們不是本地人，是老外，跟你們多要很多錢。

張天明：真的？沒想到有這種事！那還是你排吧。不過我們一定不能再走丟了！　）

Questions:

1) The dialogue took place

   a. in a restaurant.
   b. outside a movie theater.
   c. in a park.
   d. outside a restroom.

2) Zhang Tianming and his cousin got separated because

   a. his cousin went boating without Zhang Tianming.
   b. there were too many people in the park.
   c. his cousin went shopping without Zhang Tianming.
   d. his cousin didn't want to be seen with foreigners.

3) Zhang Tianming's cousin wouldn't let Zhang Tianming stand in a queue because

   a. Zhang Tianming talked too much and was not very attentive.
   b. Zhang Tianming frequently needed to use the restroom.
   c. Zhang Tianming was too conspicuously foreign.
   d. Zhang Tianming was too lazy, and gave up too easily.

2. Listen to the passage and answer the following questions.

   （ " 親愛的觀眾朋友，這兩天南京的天氣非常炎熱，每天的氣溫都高達三十六、七度，請您注意您和您家裏人的身體健康。要多喝水、儘量少出門。小朋友不要在中午到下午三、四點之間到外邊兒玩。運動後不能馬上用冷水洗澡或者對著冷氣吹。老人要多休息，多吃青菜水果。" ）

Questions:

1) The speaker is very likely

   a. a government official.
   b. the host of a radio program.
   c. the host of a TV program.
   d. a concerned teacher.

2) The weather has been

   a. very seasonable.

b. very hot.

c. very cold.

d. neither too hot nor too cold.

3) The speaker asks the audience to pay attention to

    a. his and his family's health.

    b. his level of activity.

    c. his food intake.

    d. his environment.

4) The audience should

    a. tune in more often.

    b. relax more.

    c. play with children more often.

    d. drink more water and avoid going out frequently.

5) Children

    a. should have three to four hours of play time everyday.

    b. should have at least three to four friends.

    c. shouldn't play between noon and four o'clock.

    d. shouldn't have three to four hours of play time.

6) One shouldn't

    a. eat too much.

    b. exercise in hot weather.

    c. drink cold water immediately after exercising.

    d. take a cold shower immediately after exercising.

7) Old people should

    a. go out more.

    b. eat more fruit and vegetables.

    c. rest more.

    d. b and c.

3. Listen to the passage and answer the following questions.

（ " 遊客們，你們現在看到的就是南京有名的貢院。貢院 是以前科舉
考試的地方。大家可能不知道什麼是科舉考試吧？以前在中國，如

果你想做官的話，你就得考試，這就是科舉考試。那個時候，科舉考試都是在一個特別的地方，叫考場。這個貢院就是中國南方最大的考場。我們左邊兒的那些小屋子，看起來像現在的公共電話亭，可是沒有門。這些小屋子是做什麼用的呢？這就是那些考試的人坐在裏邊考試的地方。那麼為什麼這些小屋子都沒有門呢？對了，因為沒有門，考官才可以看見裏邊的人在做什麼，要是有什麼問題，就會馬上發現。你們想試著考一考嗎？別忘了，考得好，就可以做官兒了啊！"）

Questions:

1) The speaker is a

    a. history teacher

    b. tour guide.

    c. telephone repairman.

    d. government official.

2) A "*gòngyuàn*" is a

    a. park.

    b. public telephone booth.

    c. complex of buildings where examinations were held.

    d. factory.

3) "*kējǔ kǎoshì*" was a(n)

    a. imperial civil service examination.

    b. physical examination.

    c. final examination.

    d. mid-term examination.

4) Examinations were held

    a. everywhere.

    b. at a special place.

    c. at a different place every time.

    d. at a different place every year.

5) The cubicles did not have doors because

  a. it was too hot in Nanjing.
  b. they were in disrepair.
  <u>c</u>. the proctors wanted to see what the candidates were doing.
  d. the proctors wanted to be able to answer the candidates'
    questions.

第二部分：口語練習 Speaking Exercises

A: Please practice asking and answering the following questions with a partner before class.

1. 你去過哪些地方遊覽？

2. 你對美國哪一個城市的印象最深？爲什麼？

3. 你覺得你的老家有什麼吸引人的地方？

4. 請問 " 人老珠黃 " 是什麼意思？

B: Please practice speaking on the following topic.

請你介紹一下美國的一個名勝古蹟。

第三部分：閱讀練習 Reading Comprehension

A: Please answer the questions after reading the following description of Nanjing.

(Traditional Characters)

南京

　　在中國歷史上，南京曾經是好幾個朝代(1)的國都(2)，所以市內和郊區(3) 都有很多歷史古蹟。市區有一條河，叫秦淮河，雖然現在只是一條不太吸引人注意的小河，可是它很有名。兩百年前，秦淮河兩岸曾經是南京最熱鬧的地方之一。一到晚上，河上到處都是遊船，船上的遊客有的喝酒做詩，有的唱歌跳舞，非常熱鬧。在中國文學史上，不少詩人作家曾被秦淮河所吸引，並且寫了一些跟秦淮河有關係的書、詩詞和文章。

(1) 朝代 (cháodài): dynasty   (2) 國都 (guódū): capital of the country

(3) 郊區 (jiāoqū): outskirt

(Simplified Characters)

南京

　　在中国历史上，南京曾经是好几个朝代(1)的国都(2)，所以市内和郊区(3)都有很多历史古迹。市区有一条河，叫秦淮河，虽然现在只是一条不太吸引人注意的小河，可是它很有名。两百年前，秦淮河两岸曾经是南京最热闹的地方之一。一到晚上，河上到处都是游船，船上的游客有的喝酒做诗，有的唱歌跳舞，非常热闹。在中国文学史上，不少诗人作家曾被秦淮河所吸引，并且写了一些跟秦淮河有关系的书、诗词和文章。

(1) 朝代 (cháodài): dynasty   (2) 国都 (guódū): capital of the country

(3) 郊区 (jiāoqū): outskirt

是非題：

1) F 兩百年前秦淮河兩岸有很多學校。

2) F 歷史上不少詩人作家到秦淮河岸邊賣他們寫的書。

3) T 秦淮河在歷史上很有名，是因為不少詩人作家都在作品裏提到它。

4) T 歷史上的秦淮河是很多人喜歡去的地方。

5) T 中國歷史上有不少皇帝(huángdì: emperor)在南京住過。

B: 成語故事

Please answer the questions after reading the following story.

1	2
3	4

(Traditional Characters)

東施效 (1) 顰 (2)

　　中國古代有一個美女叫西施(3)，大家都知道她美麗動人。西施的隔壁住著一個叫東施(4)的女人，長得不怎麼好看。她看見西施那麼好看，聽見別人都說西施漂亮，非常羨慕(5)。有一天，西施病了，皺 (6) 著眉頭(7)，從東施的家門前走過。東施看見了，覺得西施皺著眉頭的樣子非常好看，就模仿西施的樣子，整天皺著眉頭。有錢的人見了她，趕緊關上門不出來了，沒有錢的人見了她，就拉著妻子走開了。

　　東施只知道西施皺眉的樣子好看，可是她不知道為什麼西施皺眉好看。請你們猜猜＂東施效顰＂這句話的意思是什麼？

效 (xiào): to imitate　　　　　　　顰 (pín): to knit one's eyebrows

西施 (Xīshī): a person's name　　　東施 (Dōngshī): a person's name

羨慕 (xiànmù): envious　　　　　　皺 (zhòu): to wrinkle; to knit

眉頭 (méitou): eyebrows

(Simplified Characters)

东施效 (1) 颦 (2)

　　中国古代有一个美女叫西施(3)，大家都知道她美丽动人。西施的隔壁住着一个叫东施(4)的女人，长得不怎么好看。她看见西施那么好看，听见别人都说西施漂亮，非常羡慕(5)。有一天，西施病了，皱 (6) 着眉头(7)，从东施的家门前走过。东施看见了，觉得西施皱着眉头的样子非常好看，就模仿西施的样子，整天皱着眉头。有钱的人见了她，赶紧关上门不出来了，没有钱的人见了她，就拉着妻子走开了。

　　东施只知道西施皱眉的样子好看，可是她不知道为什么西施皱眉好看。请你们猜猜"东施效颦"这句话的意思是什么？

效 (xiào): to imitate　　　　　　顰 (pín): to knit one's eyebrows

西施 (Xīshī): a person's name　　东施 (Dōngshī): a person's name

羡慕 (xiànmù): envious　　　　　皱 (zhòu): to wrinkle; to knit

眉头 (méitou): eyebrows

是非題：

1) _F_ 東施長得也很好看。

2) _T_ 別人都說西施好看。

3) _T_ 東施希望自己和西施一樣地好看。

4) _T_ 西施皺眉頭的樣子很好看。

5) _T_ 東施學西施皺眉的樣兒。

6) _T_ 東施皺眉的樣子一點兒不好看。

7) _T_ 東施不知道西施為什麼好看。

8) _T_ 這個故事是叫人不要隨便地模仿別人。

C: Nanjing is an important metropolis in the lower Yangtze valley. Its long history and rich cultural tradition have left many historic sights, making Nanjing one of the major tourist cities in China. The following passage is taken from a tourist brochure.

中山陵

中山陵，是伟大的革命先行者孙中山先生的陵墓，建于南京市东郊景色秀丽的紫金山南麓。

孙中山先生，原名孙文，号逸仙，1866年11月12日生于广东香山县（今中山县）翠亨村，1925年（民国14年）3月12日逝世于北京。

为了纪念孙中山先生的丰功伟绩，在他逝世以后，为他建造了这座雄伟壮丽的陵墓。

請用中文回答下面的問題：
1) 中山陵在南京的什麼地方？
2) 孫中山原來的名字是什麼？
3) 孫中山的出生地原來的名字是什麼？
4) 那個地方現在叫什麼？

第四部分：句型與詞語練習 Grammar & Usage

A: 選用 " 以來 " 或 " 來 " 填空。

Please fill in the blanks with either "以來"or "來".

1. 柯林上大學<u>以來</u>，一直是白天上課晚上打工。

2. 十年<u>來</u>，他一直在同一家公司工作。

3. 他自從當記者<u>以來</u>，每天都早出晚歸。

4. 兩個星期<u>來</u>，這裏的氣溫每天都是90度以上，非常難受。

5. 柯林自從愛上林雪梅<u>以來</u>，整天吃不下飯，睡不著覺。

B: 選用 "才" 或 "就" 填空。

Please fill in the blanks with either "才"or "就".

1. 一般人大學念四年畢業，我弟弟念了五年<u>才</u>畢業。

2. 小張每次買東西都得買三、四個鐘頭，沒想到今天一個鐘頭<u>就</u>買完了。

3. 郵局的服務員跟我說我寄給我指導教授的掛號信兩天<u>就</u>會到，但是我的老師四天<u>才</u>收到。

4. 別的同學租房子都很容易，一下子<u>就</u>找到合適的房子了。可是我找了三個星期<u>才</u>找到合適的。

5. 小林的表弟說好八點鐘來飛機場接小林，但是他差不多九點<u>才</u>到。

C: 多項定語重組。

Please rearrange the order.

例：好、一種、酒、他喜歡喝 --->他喜歡喝的一種好酒

1. 從圖書館借、昨天、書、舊、一本
   --->昨天從圖書館借的一本舊書

2. 一件、衣服、新、媽媽給我做
   --->媽媽給我做的一件新衣服

3. 秘密、一個、小、他告訴我
   --->他告訴我的一個小秘密

4. 可怕的、電視裏播、那個、故事
   --->電視裏播的那個可怕的故事

D: 請用 " 催 " 完成下面對話。

Please complete the following dialogues using "催".

例：A: 每次跟小林逛街，別人東西都買好了，只有他還沒買完。

B: <u>那你們應該催他快一點兒買。</u>

1. A: 快過新年了，你們卡片寄了沒有？

B: 還沒有。卡片我先生還沒寫完呢。我得＿＿＿＿＿＿＿＿＿＿＿＿。

2. A: 這家餐館的生意真好。

B: 可不是嗎？ 要是你吃得太慢，老板還會＿＿＿＿＿＿＿＿＿＿＿＿。

3. A: 飛機馬上就要起飛了，你能不能開快一點兒。

B: 我開得已經夠快的了。別＿＿＿＿＿＿＿＿＿＿＿＿，來得及。

E: 請用 " 忍不住 " 完成下面對話。

Please complete the following dialogues using "忍不住".

例：A: 小張不是不喜歡喝酒嗎？ 怎麼今天喝了這麼多？

B: 這酒好啊！ <u>誰都會忍不住多喝一點兒</u>。

1. A: 那個女孩長得實在很漂亮。

B: 可不是嗎？ ＿＿＿＿＿＿＿＿＿＿＿＿＿＿＿。（多看兩眼）

2. A: 昨天咱們學校的籃球隊打得真好。

B: 對。我同屋看得大喊大叫，連我也＿＿＿＿＿＿＿＿＿＿＿＿。

3. A: 這個演員演的喜劇都非常有意思。

B: 我也常看他演的戲。每次我都會＿＿＿＿＿＿＿＿＿＿＿＿。

（哈哈大笑）

F: 選擇填空。

1. 他老<u>向</u>別人借錢，可總不還。（ 對、向 ）

2. 他<u>跟</u>我要王老師的電話號碼，可是我沒有。（ 對、跟 ）

3. 他現在的車是<u>跟</u>我買的。（ 跟、對 ）

4. 小張每次買東西都會<u>向</u>售貨員要收據。（ 向、對 ）

第五部分：翻譯 Translation

A: Translate the following passage into Chinese.

New Year will be here soon. This year, it is my turn to do the shopping. My mother has been repeatedly urging me to go shopping. Yesterday I had a free moment, so I took the opportunity to go shopping. There were huge crowds of people in the shopping center, which made me realize what "crowded" really meant. Finally, after two hours I finished shopping. On my way home, I went to the post office to send a package to my friend in China. I hope it won't be lost in the mail.

（新年快要到了，今年輪到我上街買東西。我媽媽再三催我快點去買。昨天我趁中午不忙，就上街去購物中心買東西。購物中心裏頭人山人海，我這才體會到什麼叫 " 擠 "。兩個鐘頭以後，我總算買完了。回家的路上，我順便去郵局給我在中國的一個朋友寄了一個包裹。希望包裹不會寄丟了。）

B: Translate the following passage into Chinese.

Several days ago we went to a park. First, we went boating on the lake. It was a Sunday that day. There were huge crowds of people in the park, which dampened our spirits somewhat. However, we really liked the trees there. There was also a very old, very interesting temple in the park. It had a unique architectural style. Our friend, Anderson, liked the temple very much. He looked at the temple for a long time, and didn't want to leave. We had to urge him again and again. Finally he reluctantly left (that temple) with us.

（幾天前，我們去了一個公園，先在湖上划船。那天是星期天，公園裏人山人海，這讓我們有些掃興。但是我們很喜歡那裏的樹。公園還有一個很老、很有意思的廟，它的建築別具風格。我們的朋友安德森很喜歡那座廟，看了半天也不肯離開，我們再三催他，最後他才戀戀不捨地跟我們走了。）

第六部分：寫作練習 Composition

1. 你最喜歡去什麼地方旅遊？爲什麼？
2. 寫一篇記敘文（遊記、小故事等）

第十二課　中國的節日

第一部分：聽力練習 Listening Comprehension

A: Listen to the tape recording of Lesson Twelve and answer the following questions.

1. What is the pouch for?

   (According to Chinese custom, wearing a pouch will prevent someone from getting sick. But nowadays it is just an ornament.)

2. Why did the poet commit suicide?

   (He was deeply worried about his country, but the king didn't take him seriously.)

3. What are the major holidays in Chinese culture?

   (The Chinese New Year, the Lantern Festival, the Dragon Boat Festival, and the Mid-Autumn Festival.)

B: Listen to the tape for the workbook.

1. Please listen to the story and answer the following questions.

   （ 張天明在南京的時候，姑媽說要帶他到城外的紫金山上去掃墓。一開始他聽不懂什麼叫 “ 掃墓 ”。姑媽跟他解釋說，中國人每年都要在四月五日清明節那天，帶著一家人，準備些鮮花和水果等吃的東西去墓地祭祀祖先。到了墓地，要把墓地前前後後打掃一下，所以叫做 “ 掃墓 ”。姑媽還說今天雖然不是四月五號，可是張天明一家住在美國，沒有機會給祖父、祖母掃墓，趁他這次來南京，正好給祖父、祖母磕頭、掃墓。於是，張天明和麗莎就跟姑媽和表哥一起到紫金山上給祖父、祖母掃墓。那天天氣很好，人不多，他們在山上待了一個多鐘頭。回來的時候，他們順便到有名的紫金山天文台看了看。表哥是學天文的，對天上的星星、月亮、太陽很有研究，他就在紫金山天文台工作。回到姑媽家以後，張天明就為幾天後去西安做準備了。 ）

Questions:

1) Zhang Tianming's aunt took him to

   a. pay respects to his grandfather and grandmother at their tombs.

   b. go mountain climbing.

   c. sell fresh flowers and fruit.

   d. do house cleaning at the family cottage on the mountain.

2) On the fifth day of the fourth month Chinese people

   a. kowtow to their grandparents.

   b. clean their houses thoroughly.

   c. go hiking.

   d. pay respects to their deceased ancestors.

3) Zhang Tiaming's aunt took him to the mountain because

   a. the weather was very good that day.

   b. there were very few people on the mountain.

   c. it was a rare opportunity since Zhang Tianming lived in America.

   d. mountain climbing was Zhang Tianming's passion.

4) Zhang Tianming and his aunt went to the observatory because

   a. Zhang Tianming was interested in astronomy.

   b. Zhang Tianming's cousin was an astronomer and worked at the observatory.

   c. the moon and the sun were in special alignment that day.

   d. they had another hour to kill.

5) Which of the following statements is true?

   a. Zhang Tianming left for Xi'an a few days later.

   b. The observatory was outside of Xi'an.

   c. Zhang Tianming had just been to Xi'an.

   d. Zhang Tianming liked Xi'an better.

2. Please listen to the story and answer the following questions.

（柯林第一次去林雪梅家吃飯的那天正好是春節。林媽媽做了一桌
豐盛的菜，雞鴨魚肉什麼都有。柯林特別喜歡吃魚，他從來沒吃

過這麼好吃的魚，所以一下子把一條魚都吃完了，這時林雪梅一直跟他瞪眼睛，可是他不知道為甚麼。喝茶的時候，他不小心把杯子打破了，覺得非常不好意思，趕緊掃地。林媽媽說：「不用掃，不用掃。」他以為林媽媽是跟他客氣，所以繼續掃，把地掃得非常乾淨。這時候，他又看到林雪梅跟他瞪眼睛。回家的時候，林雪梅送他出來。柯林問林雪梅他做錯了什麼事，為什麼她老跟他瞪眼睛。林雪梅說：「中國人過年吃魚不能把魚都吃完，一定要留一點下來，象徵年年有餘。年年有餘，就是說年年都會有一些花不完的錢。中國人過年的時候也不能掃地，否則就把家裏的錢都掃出去了。」柯林聽了以後非常不好意思。）

Questions:

1) When Ke Lin went to Lin Xuemei's home for the first time, it was

    a. during the Mid-autumn Festival.

    b. during the Spring Festival.

    c. on Christmas.

    d. on New Year's Eve.

2) Ke Lin ate the whole fish because

    a. he didn't like the other dishes.

    b. there was only one main course.

    c. it was very good.

    d. he did not like chicken.

3) Ke Lin kept sweeping the floor because

    a. he felt bad and wanted to pick up the mess.

    b. the floor was very greasy.

    c. Lin Xuemei's mother asked him to.

    d. Lin Xuemei was angry with him.

4) Lin Xuemei kept staring at Ke Lin because

    a. he was being very rude.

    b. he was being too shy.

    c. he had violated Chinese customs.

    d. he was being too greedy.

5) Chinese people always leave some of the fish uneaten on Chinese New Year because

    a. there is too much food.

    b. they don't like fish.

    <u>c</u>. it is a good omen to leave some of the fish uneaten.

    d. they can only eat the rest of the fish next year.

第二部分：口語練習 Speaking Exercises

A: Please practice asking and answering the following questions with a partner before class.

1. 粽子和賽龍舟跟屈原有什麼關係？

2. 你最喜歡過什麼節？為什麼？

3. 對你來說哪個節日最重要？為什麼？

4. 過什麼節你會盡可能回家和家人團圓？

5. 中國人過春節的時候做些什麼？

B: Please practice speaking on the following topics.

1. 請談談美國有哪些風俗習慣。

2. 談談你家過聖誕節或感恩節的情況。如果你的祖籍不是美國，請你談談你家裏過年或過節的情況。

第三部分：閱讀練習 Reading Comprehension

A: Please answer the question aftering reading the following passage.

(Traditional Characters)

    杜甫是中國最偉大的詩人之一。他原來是一個大官，但是皇帝對他說的話不感興趣。他的詩不但寫出當時國家各種各樣的情況，而且也表現出他的愛國精神，以及他生活上和工作上的種種不順利。

(Simplified Characters)

　　杜甫是中国最伟大的诗人之一。他原来是一个大官，但是皇帝对他说的话不感兴趣。他的诗不但写出当时国家各种各样的情况，而且也表现出他的爱国精神，以及他生活上和工作上的种种不顺利。

Questions:

What did Tu Fu write about in his poetry?

(Various social conditions, his own patriotism, and the difficulties he encountered in his life and work.)

B: 成語故事

Read the story and answer the following questions.

$$\begin{array}{c|c} 1 & 2 \\ \hline 3 & 4 \end{array}$$

(Traditional Characters)

嫦娥 (1)奔 (2)月

　　中國有許多關於月亮的故事，嫦娥奔月就是其中之一。據說很久很久以前，天上有十個太陽(3)，大家都熱得受不了，很多人熱死了。嫦娥的丈夫是個有名的獵人，他射下了九個太陽以後，大地才涼快了下來。他有一種仙丹，吃了以後人能飛起來。嫦娥偷偷地把仙丹(4)吃了，飛到了月亮上。每當中秋節的時候，大家常常一邊賞月，一邊吃月餅，有時還說嫦娥奔月的故事。

(1)嫦娥 (Cháng'é)　　　　　(2)奔 (bēn): run ; fly to

(3)太陽 (tàiyang): sun　　　　(4)仙丹 (xiāndān): elixir

(Simplified Characters)

嫦娥 (1)奔 (2)月

　　中国有许多关於月亮的故事，嫦娥奔月就是其中之一。据说很久很久以前，天上有十个太阳(3)，大家都热得受不了，很多人热死了。嫦娥的丈夫是个有名的猎人，他射下了九个太阳以后，大地才凉快了下来。他有一种仙丹，吃了以后人能飞起来。嫦娥偷偷地把仙丹(4)吃了，飞到了月亮上。每当中秋节的时候，大家常常一边赏月，一边吃月饼，有时还说嫦娥奔月的故事。

(1)嫦娥 (Cháng'é)　　　　　(2)奔 (bēn): run ; fly to

(3)太阳 (tàiyang): sun　　　　(4)仙丹 (xiāndān): elixir

問題：

1) 那時候為什麼很多人熱死了？

2) 嫦娥為什麼能飛到月亮上去？

3) 中秋節大家常常做什麼？

C: 成語故事

Please answer the questions after reading the following story.

1	2
3	4

(Traditional Characters)

只許州官放火 (1)，不許百姓點燈

　　很久以前有一個官，他的名字叫田登(2)，可他不許別人叫他的名字。他覺得別人叫他的名字就是對他不尊敬(3)。因為"登"和"燈"念起來一樣，所以大家都不能說"燈"，只能說"火"，也不能說"點燈"，因為"點燈"聽上去好像他的名字"田登"，只能說"放火"。元宵節的時候，大家都要點燈，田登就發告示(4)，說要"放火三日"。因為他是個官，所以老百姓都沒有辦法，只能偷偷生氣地說"只許州官放火，不許百姓點燈。"

放火: set fire	田登(Tián Dēng): a person's name
尊敬(zūnjìng): respect	告示(gàoshi): announcement

(Simplified Characters)

只许州官放火 (1)，不许百姓点灯

很久以前有一个官，他的名字叫田登(2)，可他不许别人叫他的名字。他觉得别人叫他的名字就是对他不尊敬(3)。因为"登"和"灯"念起来一样，所以大家都不能说"灯"，只能说"火"，也不能说"点灯"，因为"点灯"听上去好像他的名字"田登"，只能说"放火"。元宵节的时候，大家都要点灯，田登就发告示(4)，说要"放火三日"。因为他是个官，所以老百姓都没有办法，只能偷偷生气地说"只许州官放火，不许百姓点灯。"

放火: set fire   田登(Tián Dēng): a person's name

尊敬(zūnjìng): respect   告示(gàoshi): announcement

問題：

1) 田登爲什麼不讓別人叫他的名字？

2) 他的名字聽上去像什麼？

3) 他在告示裏爲什麼說"放火三日？"？他的意思是什麼？

4) 老百姓說"只許州官放火，不許百姓點燈"的意思是什麼？

第四部分：句型與詞語練習 Grammar & Usage

A: 用"V+著玩"完成下面的對話。

Please complete the following dialogues using "V+著玩".

1. A: 哎，你唱歌唱得真好！你應該在學校的晚會上唱兩首。

   B: 不行，不行，我只是在家＿＿＿＿＿＿＿，一上台就唱不出來了。

2. A: 你的太極拳打得真好！你能教教我們嗎？

   B: 哪裏，哪裏，我是＿＿＿＿＿＿的。你們真想學，得跟我的老師學。

3. A: 小林，你的故事寫得真好，你應該當作家。

   B: 你別跟我開玩笑了，我只是沒事兒的時候＿＿＿＿＿＿，哪兒能當作家？

B: 用 " 根本 " 完成下面的句子。

Please complete the following sentences using "根本".

1. A: 你覺得小李和他的女朋友合適嗎？

   B: _____。我覺得他們兩個很快就會鬧翻。

2. A: 這個電影你覺得怎麼樣？

   B: 坐在我前邊的人太高了，_____。

3. A: 大家都說這個牌子的衣服質量好，沒想到一洗就變小了。

   B: _____，下次別買這個牌子了。

C: 請用 " . . . 之一 " 完成下面句子。

Please complete the following sentences by using " . . . 之一".

例：中國是<u>世界上人口最多的國家之一</u>。

1. 北京是_____。

2. 張天明是_____。

3. 籃球是_____。

D: 請用 " 儘可能 " 完成下面對話。

Please complete the following dialogues using "儘可能".

例：A: 請你最好在今天晚上八點以前把這個報告翻譯成中文。

   B: <u>我儘可能在八點鐘以前做好。</u>

1. A: 今天下午有重要的客人，你最好不要出去太久。

   B: 好，_____。

2. A: 明天有十幾個人來家裏過端午節，你最好多包一些粽子。

   B: 沒問題，_____。

3. A: 醫生說味精吃多了對身體不好，以後做菜最好不放味精。

   B: 我看到報上也這麼說，_____。

E: 請完成下面對話。

例：A: 我這兩件衣服放到你的櫃子裏去好嗎？　（放/下）

   B: <u>對不起，我的櫃子東西太多，放不下。</u>

1. A: 快過元宵節了，應該買點元宵吃。（買/到）

   B: 我們這兒沒有中國店，＿＿＿＿＿＿＿＿＿＿＿＿＿＿＿＿。

2. A: 老師用中文上課，你覺得怎麼樣？（聽/懂）

   B: ＿＿＿＿＿＿＿＿＿＿＿＿＿＿＿＿＿＿＿。

3. A: 姑媽做了一大盤粽子，大家多吃幾個，儘可能別剩下。　（吃/完）

   B: ＿＿＿＿＿＿＿＿＿＿＿＿＿＿＿＿＿＿＿。

F: 用所給的詞語把下面的這段話連接起來。

Please use the following words and phrases to complete the story.

(Traditional Characters)

" 最後，可是，於是，突然，以後，有一天，從那以後 "

很久很久以前，宋國有一個農人(1)，每天都要到地裏幹活(2)。<u>有一天</u>，他又去地裏幹活，看見一只兔子 (3) 在地裏很快地跑著，<u>突然</u>兔子撞(4) 到一棵樹上。他走到樹下，發現兔子撞斷 (5) 了脖子 (6)，死了，<u>於</u>是他把死兔子拿到市場上去賣了很多錢。回家<u>以後</u>，他想：這比我每天在地裏幹活好多了，又舒服，錢又多。<u>從那以後</u>他就天天坐在樹下，等兔子再來撞死。<u>可是</u>再也沒有兔子撞到樹上，<u>最後</u>這個農人在樹下餓死了。

(1) 農人 (nóngrén): farmer (2) 幹活 (gànhuó): to work

(3) 兔子 (tùzi): rabbit (4) 撞 (zhuàng): run into

(5) 斷 (duàn): break (6) 脖子 (bózi): neck

(Simplified Characters)

" 最后，可是，于是，突然，以后，有一天，从那以后 "

很久很久以前，宋国有一个农人(1)，每天都要到地里干活(2)。<u>有一天</u>，他又去地里干活，看见一只兔子 (3) 在地里很快地跑着，<u>突然</u>兔子撞(4) 到一棵树上。他走到树下，发现兔子撞断 (5) 了脖子 (6)，死了，<u>于是</u>他把死兔子拿到市场上去卖了很多钱。回家<u>以后</u>，他想：这比我每天在地里干活好多了，又舒服，钱又多。<u>从那以后</u>他就天天坐在树下，等兔子再来撞死。<u>可是</u>再也没有兔子撞到树上，<u>最后</u>这个农人在树下饿死了。

(1) 农人 (nóngrén): farmer (2) 干活 (gànhuó): to work

(3) 兔子 (tùzi): rabbit　　(4) 撞 (zhuàng): run into

(5) 斷 (duàn): break　　　(6) 脖子 (bózi): neck

第五部分：翻譯 Translation

A: Please translate the following passage into Chinese.

There are many holidays in America. For many people, the most important holiday is Thanksgiving (感恩節 Gǎn'ēnjié). Thanksgiving is on the fourth Thursday of November. Thanksgiving is a day of family reunion. People who work or study away from home (外地) try their best to go home to celebrate the holiday.

（美國的節日很多，對很多人來說，最重要的是感恩節。感恩節是十一月的第四個星期四。感恩節是一家人團圓的日子。在外地工作和上學的人都儘可能回家過節。）

B: 請用下面詞語和語法點翻譯。

Please translate the following passage into Chinese using the phrases below.

...之一，各種各樣的，好像，跟...有關係，儘可能

...之一，各种各样的，好像，跟...有关系 ，尽可能

There are many parks in Beijing. Zhongshan Park is one of them. In addition to all types of ancient architecture, there are many trees and flowers in the park. One day I went to Zhongshan Park with a friend of mine. My friend seemed uninterested. I asked him, "You don't think the park is interesting?" He said, "It's not that. I'm tired." I asked, "How come you're tired? You just got to the park." He said, "Probably it had to do with the fact that I went to bed really late last night." I said, "Then let's leave early. Try to go to bed as soon as possible tonight."

（北京有很多公園，中山公園是其中之一。公園裏除了有各種各樣的古代建築以外，還有很多樹和花。有一天我跟一個朋友去中山公園玩，我的朋友好像沒有興趣。我問他：「你覺得這個公園沒有意思嗎？」他說：「不是，我累了。」我問：「你怎麼剛到公園就累了？」他說：「可能跟我昨天晚上睡得很晚有關係。」我說：「那咱們早點回去，你今天儘可能早點睡吧。」）

C: 請用下面詞語和語法點翻譯。

Please translate the following passage into Chinese using the phrases below.

吸引，印象，戀戀不捨

吸引，印象，恋恋不舍

This past summer during summer vacation, I traveled to Charleston (查爾斯敦 Chá'ěrsīdūn), South Carolina (南卡). Charleston is a tourist city(旅遊城市) on the southeast coast of America. Every year it attracts many tourists. It has not only beautiful scenery but also a good climate. Charleston's architecture cannot be said to be grand, but it has its own characteristics, especially those buildings along the sea shore. Those European style buildings, and those big trees left a deep impression on me. I went sightseeing there for three days. I left reluctantly on the fourth day.

（ 去年暑假，我去南卡的查爾斯頓旅行。查爾斯頓是美國東南部海邊的一
個旅遊城市，每年都吸引很多遊客。那裏不但風景很美，氣候也很好。
查爾斯頓的建築，雖然說不上壯觀，但很有特點，特別是海邊。那些歐
洲式建築，那些大樹，給我留下了很深的印象。我在那裏遊覽了三天，
第四天才戀戀不捨地離開了。）

D: Translate the following passage into Chinese. Please pay attention to potential complements.

Zhang Tianming wanted to invite his friend Xiao Li to celebrate Chinese New Year with his family. He asked Xiao Li whether he would be able to come. Xiao Li said that if he could finish his paper then he would be able to go. Zhang Tianming's mother prepared an elaborate dinner. Xiao Li really liked the food. He said to Tianming's mom that he wouldn't be able to find such great food elsewhere. Tianming's mom asked him to have some more food. Xiao Li said that he couldn't possibly finish that much food.

（ 張天明想請小李來家裏過年。他問小李來得了來不了。小李說要是他能做完
功課就來。張天明的媽媽準備了一頓豐盛的晚飯。小李覺得菜好吃極了。他對
張媽媽說，在哪兒都吃不到這麼好吃的菜。張媽媽叫他再多吃一點。小李
說他吃得太多了，吃不下了。）

第六部分：寫作練習 (Composition)

作文：《過年》

第十三課　　談體育

第一部分：聽力練習 (Listening Comprehension)

A: **Listen to the tape recording of *Lesson Thirteen* and answer the following questions.**

1. Why did Zhang Tianming call Anderson?

    (He was bored and he missed Anderson.)

2. Who won the ball game last night?

    (Michigan)

3. Who played extremely well for Michigan?

    (No. 5)

4. What is the point of sports according to Zhang Tianming?

    (To be healthy.)

B: **Listen to the tape for the workbook.**

1. Please listen to the passage and answer the following questions.

    （ 李先生雖然已經六十多歲了，但是身體還很強壯，每天早上都要去公園
    跑步，週末還參加老人籃球隊。李太太不打籃球，但是每當李先生比賽
    籃球時，她就跟著去。比賽的時候，李太太總是激動得大喊大叫，讓李
    先生覺得很不好意思。 ）

    Questions:

    1) How old is Mr. Li?

        (Sixty something.)

    2) How is his health?

        (Very good.)

3) What kind of exercise does he do daily?

(Jogging in the park.)

4) What exercise does he do on weekends?

(Playing basketball)

5) What will embarrass Mr. Li?

(His wife cheering him on loudly while he is playing basketball.)

2. Please listen to the passage and answer the following questions.

(張天明學校的足球隊是全美國最好的大學足球隊之一。隊裏有好幾個身體
強壯，速度快的明星球員。這些球員雖然打球打得很好，但是常常喝醉
酒、打架，學習成績也很差，引起老師和其他同學的不滿。但是學校爲了
贏球，爲了賺錢，對這些明星球員的行爲一點辦法也沒有。)

Questions:

1) How good is the Tianming's school's football team?

(One of the best in America.)

2) How are their star players?

(They are strong and fast.)

3) Why are the faculty and other students fed up with the players?

(They get drunk and pick up fights often. They have bad grades.)

4) What does the school plan to do to change the players' behavior?

(Nothing.)

3. Listen to the passage and answer the following questions.

(柯林的父親念大學時是學校籃球隊的隊員。籃球賽季一開始，他就忙著比
賽，沒有時間學習。當時他覺得打球爲學校爭榮譽最重要，學習成績好不
好，他不在乎。可是大學畢業以後，一直找不到好工作，他才後悔上學的
時候沒有好好學習，所以他又回到學校念了一個學位。)

Questions:

1) What was Ke Lin's father's top priority while he was in college?

   (To earn honor for his school.)

2) Why was he too busy to study?

   (He was busy playing basketball.)

3) What did he do later on to better his career opportunities?

   (He returned to school and got another degree.)

第二部分：口語練習　Speaking Exercises

A: Please practice asking and answering the following questions with a partner before class.

1. 學校開學已經多久了？
2. 要是你覺得寂寞，你會做什麼？
3. 奧林匹克運動會多長時間辦一次？
4. 什麼樣的人才可以打籃球？

B: Please practice speaking on the following topics.

1. 你喜歡體育嗎？你為什麼(不)喜歡體育？
2. 你認為體育比賽的目的是什麼？是為了給國家爭榮譽嗎？
3. 談談一個人怎麼可以替他的國家爭榮譽。
4. 談談在什麼情況下你的父母為你感到驕傲。

第三部分：閱讀練習　Reading Comprehension

A: Please answer the questions after reading the following passage.

(Traditional Characters)

喜歡體育的人非常多，有男的，有女的，有老人，也有年輕人。有的人每天都要運動，否則就覺得不舒服，他們一有機會就去打球或者跑步；有的人自己並不怎麼喜歡運動，可是他們喜歡看體育比賽，尤其是球類比賽，如籃球，足球等。每當有重大的比賽時，這些球迷就會想辦法買票去體育場看比賽，有些球迷還會跟他們喜歡的球隊去外地甚至外國看比賽，旅費當然是自己付。有些球迷脾氣比較急躁，如果他們的球隊打得不好，或者輸了，他們就會鬧事。為了看球賽而打架實在沒有必要。

(Simplified Characters)

喜欢体育的人非常多，有男的，有女的，有老人，也有年轻人。有的人每天都要运动，否则就觉得不舒服，他们一有机会就去打球或者跑步；有的人自己并不怎么喜欢运动，可是他们喜欢看体育比赛，尤其是球类比赛，如篮球，足球等。每当有重大的比赛时，这些球迷就会想办法买票去体育场看比赛，有些球迷还会跟他们喜欢的球队去外地甚至外国看比赛，旅费当然是自己付。有些球迷脾气比较急躁，如果他们的球队打得不好，或者输了，他们就会闹事。为了看球赛而打架实在没有必要。

是非題：

1) F 只有年輕人喜歡體育。

2) F 喜歡體育的人都運動。

3) F 喜歡看球賽的人都喜歡打球。

4) T 有時候球票很難買，可是球迷會想辦法買。

5) T 如果球迷想去外地或外國觀看比賽，他們得自己出旅費。

B: **Please answer the questions in English after reading the following passage.**

(Traditional Characters)

足球是可能世界上最受歡迎的體育運動，特別是在歐洲和南美洲。一場精彩的足球比賽能吸引成千上萬的球迷，本地的，外地的，甚至是外國的，都趕到體育場去觀看比賽。再加上電視機前的觀眾，一場足球賽可能有上百萬，上千萬的觀眾。現代足球是英國發明的，可是很少有人知道，中國漢代(206B. C. E220A. D)

有一種跟足球很像的運動，我們現在還可以從古畫中看到當時人們踢球的樣子。只是那時的球場，兩邊各有六個門。另一種在英國非常受歡迎的運動是馬球。馬球和足球不一樣，只有有錢人才能參加。馬球在中國古代也有，這我們可以從出土的俑(1)看出來。後來這些運動在中國都沒有了。和別的國家一樣，中國的現代足球也是從英國來的。

(1) 俑(yǒng): unearthed figurines

(Simplified Characters)

足球是可能世界上最受欢迎的体育运动，特别是在欧洲和南美洲。一场精彩的足球比赛能吸引成千上万的球迷，本地的，外地的，甚至是外国的，都赶到体育场去观看比赛。再加上电视机前的观众，一场足球赛可能有上百万，上千万的观众。现代足球是英国发明的，可是很少有人知道，中国汉代(206B. C. E220A. D)有一种跟足球很像的运动，我们现在还可以从古画中看到当时人们踢球的样子。只是那时的球场，两边各有六个门。另一种在英国非常受欢迎的运动是马球。马球和足球不一样，只有有钱人才能参加。马球在中国古代也有，这我们可以从出土的俑(1)看出来。后来这些运动在中国都没有了。和别的国家一样，中国的现代足球也是从英国来的。

(1) 俑(yǒng): unearthed figurines

問題：

1) 足球在歐洲和南美洲受人歡迎嗎？

2) 一場精彩的球賽最多能吸引多少球迷觀看？

3) 現代足球是在哪個國家最先有人踢的？

4) 我們怎麼知道中國古代也有足球？

5) 馬球和足球有什麼不一樣？

6) 中國古代有馬球嗎？

7) 中國的現代足球為什麼要從外國傳入？

C: Like their counterparts in English-speaking countries, Chinese newspapers, especially those geared towards a large readership, cover sports extensively. There are also newspapers and magazines that are devoted exclusively to the coverage of sports.

中国足球队胜澳门蓝白队

应澳门蓝白体育会的邀请，中国国家足球队今天下午在这里同蓝白队进行了一场友谊赛，以三比零获胜。

中国队在上半时进行到第二十六分钟时攻进第一个球，又分别在下半时第八十四分和第八十九分时又下两城。

Questions:

1) When did the football match take place?

　　(Feb. 27)

2) Where did it take place?

　　(澳門)

3) What are the names of the two teams involved?

　　(中國足球隊和澳門藍白隊)

4) Which team scored a goal in the first half?

　　(中國隊)

5) What's the final score?

　　(3 vs. 0)

6)Which team won?

　　　(中國隊)

第四部分：句型與詞語練習　Grammar & Usage

A: 請用 " 連... 也/ 都... " 完成下面對話。

Please complete the following dialogues using "連... 也/ 都...".

例: A: 你現在住的地方怎麼樣？夏天有沒有空調？ （電扇）

　　B: 空調？<u>我住的地方連電扇都沒有</u>。

1. A: 小張打算什麼時候結婚？ （女朋友）

　　B: 結婚？＿＿＿＿＿＿＿＿＿＿＿＿＿＿＿＿＿＿＿＿。

2. A: 那個人的衣服那麼不乾淨，難道他沒錢買洗衣粉嗎？ （吃飯的錢）

　　B: 洗衣粉？＿＿＿＿＿＿＿＿＿＿＿＿＿＿＿＿＿＿。

3. A: 你的工作真的那麼忙嗎？我覺得你應該休息十分鐘。（喝水的時間）

　　B: 休息？＿＿＿＿＿＿＿＿＿＿＿＿＿＿＿＿＿＿。

B: 請用 " 反正(1) " 完成下面對話。

Please complete the following dialogues using "反正(1)".

例: A: 前面的隊排得那麼長，恐怕得等很長時間，咱們別看了！。

　　　　　　（一定要看）

　　B: 不管等多長時間都沒關係，<u>反正我一定要看</u>。

1. 妹妹：寒假姐姐和弟弟都不回家，哥哥，你還回來嗎？

　　小明：不管他們回不回家，＿＿＿＿＿＿＿＿＿＿＿＿。 （一定回家）

2. A: 大家都說那個電影沒有意思，咱們別去看了。

　　B: ＿＿＿＿＿＿＿＿＿＿＿＿＿＿＿＿＿＿＿＿＿。

3. A: 我累了，今天就在這兒住一個晚上吧，反正明天下午才開會。

　　B: 好吧，我也累了。

A: 誰累了誰就在這兒住吧，＿＿＿＿＿＿＿＿＿＿＿＿＿＿＿＿。

（早一點到開會的地方）

C: 請用 " 反正(2) " 完成下面對話。

Please complete the following dialogues using "反正(2)".

例: A: 這個包裹你要怎麼寄？

B: 寄陸空聯運，寄海運都可以，反正不急。

（陸空聯運、海運，我不急）

1. A: 去他家做客總得帶點東西，你說買糖果還是買餅乾比較合適？

B: ＿＿＿＿＿＿＿＿＿＿＿＿＿＿＿＿＿＿＿＿＿＿＿＿。

（糖果、餅乾，他都喜歡）

2. A: 你想到東岸還是西岸找工作？

B: ＿＿＿＿＿＿＿＿＿＿＿＿＿＿＿＿＿＿＿＿＿＿＿＿。

（東岸、西岸/ 我都有朋友）

3. A: 今天晚上你想看籃球賽還是足球賽？

B: ＿＿＿＿＿＿＿＿＿＿＿＿＿＿＿＿＿＿＿＿＿＿＿＿。

（籃球、足球/ 只要是球賽就行）

4. A: 我聽說昨天的球賽精彩極了。我們學校的球隊打得很不錯。你看了嗎？

B: ＿＿＿＿＿＿＿＿＿＿＿＿＿＿＿＿，打得再好也沒用。（輸了）

5. A: 咱們改了日程以後，就沒有時間去西安了。

B: ＿＿＿＿＿＿＿＿＿＿＿＿＿＿＿＿。（對...沒興趣）

D: 請用 " 所以...是因為... " 完成下面對話。

Please complete the following dialogues using "所以...是因為...".

例: A: 密西根隊為什麼贏球？（速度快,比賽經驗豐富）

B: 他們所以贏球是因為他們球員的速度快,比賽經驗豐富。

1. A: 小張為什麼那麼喜歡中山陵？（那兒的建築很雄偉）

B: ＿＿＿＿＿＿＿＿＿＿＿＿＿＿＿＿＿＿＿＿＿＿＿＿。

2. A: 你為什麼不申請念我們學校的研究所？

                    （我的指導教授建議我申請別的學校）

    B: _____ 。

3. A: 大家為什麼不願意跟他交往？（脾氣很急躁，常常喝醉酒）

    B: _____ 。

第五部分：翻譯 Translation

A: Translate the following telephone conversation into Chinese using the phrases provided.

V＋出來，上＋Number，反正，閑著沒事

A: Oh, Xiao Wang, it's you. Didn't recognize your voice. What's up?

    （哦，小王，是你。沒聽出來你的聲音。什麼事？）

B: I am thinking of getting an old computer for $600.00...

    （我想花六百塊錢買一個舊的電腦...）

A: Why don't you buy a new one?

    （你為什麼不買一個新的呢？）

B: A new one can cost upward of a thousand dollars. I don't have that much money.

    （一個新電腦上千塊錢，我沒有那麼多的錢。）

A: Anyway you don't need a computer right away. Think it over. You don't have much to do this week. You can go to the school computer center, look at some ads there and then make your (a) decision.

    （反正你現在不需要電腦，再想想吧。你這個星期閑著沒事，可以去學校的電腦中心，看看那裏的廣告，然後再做決定。）

B: Please translate the following passage into Chinese.

Whenever there's a holiday, I miss my family even more. I always tell myself since I am abroad I cannot go home anyway. On the surface, it seems that I couldn't care less. Actually, I want to go home to reunite with my family and celebrate the holiday in any way I possibly can.

（ 一到過節，我就更想念我家裏的人。有的朋友問我：「你不想家嗎？」我總是告訴他們：「我在國外，反正回不了家，習慣了。」表面上，我好像不在乎。但是實際上，我希望儘可能早一點回去跟家裏人團圓，一起過節。 ）

C: Please translate the following passage into Chinese.

My brother is one of the players on the school basketball team. He is tall and strong. He can also run very quickly on the court. He practices very hard everyday, and hopes that one day he can earn honor for the school. The coach said that my brother plays well, but he does not have enough experience and needs to sit on the side to watch more games. My brother was very disappointed after he heard that.

（ 我弟弟是學校籃球隊的球員之一。他長得又高又壯，速度也快。他每天都努力練球，希望有一天能為學校爭榮譽。教練說我弟弟球打得是不錯，但是他的經驗還 不夠，得在旁邊多看幾場球。我弟弟聽了以後很失望。 ）

第六部分：寫作練習 Composition

如果你喜歡做或看什麼體育運動，請寫一篇短文，題目是：
　　　　　我最喜歡的體育運動

如果你不喜歡做或看體育運動，請寫一篇短文，題目是：
　　　　　我為什麼不喜歡體育

第十四課　家庭

第一部分：聽力練習 Listening Comprehension

A: Listen to the tape recording of *Lesson Fourteen* and answer the following questions.

1. Why does Zhang Tianming go home for a visit?

    (It is his Thanksgiving break.)

2. What course does Tianming's father want Tianming to take?

    (Computer.)

3. What subjects are Tianming least interested in?

    (Engineering and medicine.)

4. Would Zhang Tianming listen to his father and break up with Lisa? How do you know?

    (No, because he says that he's an adult. He can handle his own business.)

5. Why did Tianming's cousin and his family move out from his aunt's?

    (The tension between Tianming's aunt and her daughter-in-law became unbearable.)

6. Why was Tianming's cousin always fighting with his wife?

    (Because she thought he didn't spend enough time with his daughter.)

B: Listen to the tape for the workbook.

1. Listen to the passage and answer the following questions.

    （安德森的父母去年剛離婚。感恩節快要到了，安德森不知道應該怎麼辦。一方面，他很高興有機會見到他的兄弟姐妹，但是另一方面，他不知道應該去爸爸家過節，還是應該去媽媽家過節。最後，他決定到他女朋友的家去過感恩節。）

True or False:

1) F Anderson's parents moved away last year.

2) T A holiday is coming up.

3) T He's glad that he will be able to see his siblings again.

4) F He decided that it's better that he spent the holiday with his parents.

2. Please listen to the passage and answer the following questions.

（麗莎的表姐結婚以後，發現她的丈夫很懶，家裏的事一點也不管。
下班回家，就坐在沙發上，一邊喝啤酒，一邊看球賽，把屋子搞得
亂七八糟的。表姐工作完回到家，又要做飯，又要洗衣服，實在忙
不過來。偶爾叫她先生幫忙，他要麼找藉口走開，要麼就很不高興
地說做飯、洗衣服本來就是女人應該做的事。夫妻兩個人經常為了
家務事而吵架，關係越來越緊張。）

問題：

1) 麗莎的表姐夫每天下班後都做什麼？

2) 麗莎的表姐為什麼老是那麼忙？

3) 麗莎的表姐叫她表姐夫幫忙時，她表姐夫會怎麼樣？

4) 他們兩個人的關係為什麼越來越緊張？

3. Please listen to the passage and answer the following questions.

（李哲的父母剛從中國移民來美國的時候，由於不懂英文，受的教育
不多，加上適應不了美國文化，只能在中國餐館洗碗。兩個人工作
了十幾年，用省下來的錢，自己開了一家飯館。他們非常希望李哲
能受好一點的教育，將來當個醫生，工程師什麼的，可以賺很多
錢。可是李哲只對哲學有興趣，別的專業都不想學。他的父母不懂
為什麼兒子要學這種將來不能賺錢的專業。李哲說："誰讓你們給
我取，李哲，這個名字呢？"）

Questions:

1) Were Li Zhe's parents born in the United States?

   (No, they were born in China.)

2) Why have his parents always worked in Chinese restaurants?

   (They didn't know too much English, and didn't make immediate adjustment to American life and culture. They washed dishes in Chinese restaurants. Then they opened their own restaurant.)

3) What would they like Li Zhe to become?

   (A well-educated person who can earn a good living.)

4) Why can't they understand Li Zhe's passion?

   (They couldn't understand why Li Zhe is interested in philosophy, a field where there isn't a lot of money.)

5) What does Li Zhe tell them?

   (He cannot help it. His passion comes with his name "zhé" meaning philosophy.)

第二部分：口語練習 Speaking Exercises

A: Please practice asking and answering the following questions with a partner before class.

1. 你的興趣在哪些方面？/你對什麼有興趣？
2. 你覺得什麼樣的工作是鐵飯碗？
3. 你小時候常常跟父母告誰的狀？
4. 什麼叫做獨立？

B: Please practice speaking on the following topics.

1. 要是你的父母要你選你不感興趣的專業，你會跟他們說什麼？
2. 要是你的父母反對你和你的男/女朋友在一起，你會怎麼說？
3. 你認為美國家庭和中國家庭有什麼不同？
4. 請你介紹一下你的家庭。

第三部分：閱讀練習 Reading Comprehension

A: Please answer the questions after reading the following dialogue.

(Traditional Characters)

柯　林：小張，你感恩節過得怎麼樣？

張天明：別提了，本來以為可以好好地跟家人團聚一下，沒想到和我
　　　　父親吵了好幾次。

柯　林：怎麼會呢？你不是和你父親相處得很好嗎？

張天明：我也以為我父親知道我已經長大了，可以為自己的行為負責
　　　　了。現在我才發現，他也跟其他中國父母一樣，實在讓人受
　　　　不了。

柯　林：你別那麼激動，到底發生了什麼事？

張天明：我爸爸不同意我只選那些我有興趣的課，他說這樣畢業以後
　　　　找工作會有問題。

柯　林：為了子女的將來，做父親的有責任提一些建議。那也沒有什
　　　　麼不對的。

張天明：我不是不理解，我是生氣他對我沒有信心，以為我還是不懂
　　　　事的三歲孩子。對了，他還說我不應該再和麗莎來往。他說
　　　　談戀愛是談戀愛，結婚是結婚，要考慮清楚。

柯　林：你應該跟你父親再好好地談談，把話說清楚。不過，說真的，
　　　　現在找工作真不容易，我快畢業了，我有好些同學就有這樣
　　　　的問題。他們都後悔以前沒多選一些有用的課。

張天明：可是他也不能叫我和麗莎分手啊。

柯　林：這個問題比較麻煩。我想你應該讓他了解你和麗莎之間只是
　　　　男女朋友，還沒有談到結婚的事。另外，你也應該找機會把
　　　　麗莎帶回家讓你父母親看看。

(Simplified Characters)

柯　林：小张，你感恩节过得怎么样？

张天明：别提了，本来以为可以好好地跟家人团聚一下，没想到和我
　　　　父亲吵了好几次。

柯　林：怎么会呢？你不是和你父亲相处得很好吗？

张天明：我也以为我父亲知道我已经长大了，可以为自己的行为负责了。现在我才发现，他也跟其他中国父母一样，实在让人受不了。

柯　林：你别那么激动，到底发生了什么事？

张天明：我爸爸不同意我只选那些我有兴趣的课，他说这样毕业以后找工作会有问题。

柯　林：为了子女的将来，做父亲的有责任提一些建议。那也没有什么不对的。

张天明：我不是不理解，我是生气他对我没有信心，以为我还是不懂事的三岁孩子。对了，他还说我不应该再和丽莎来往。他说谈恋爱是谈恋爱，结婚是结婚，要考虑清楚。

柯　林：你应该跟你父亲再好好地谈谈，把话说清楚。不过，说真的，现在找工作真不容易，我快毕业了，我有好些同学就有这样的问题。他们都后悔以前没多选一些有用的课。

张天明：可是他也不能叫我和丽莎分手啊。

柯　林：这个问题比较麻烦。我想你应该让他了解你和丽莎之间只是男女朋友，还没有谈到结婚的事。另外，你也应该找机会把丽莎带回家让你父母亲看看。

問題：

1) 張天明爲什麼跟他父親吵架？

2) 柯林覺得張天明的父親是對的還是錯的？你是怎麼知道的？

3) 張天明能理解他父親的心情嗎？

4) 張天明爲什麼生他父親的氣？

5) 張天明的父親同意他和麗莎交往嗎？

6) 柯林覺得張天明的父親哪些話說得有道理？

7) 他覺得張天明應該怎麼辦？

B: 成語故事

Please answer the questions after reading the following story.

1 | 2
3 | 4

(Traditional Characters)

破鏡重(1)圓

　　陳朝(2)末年有一個駙馬(3)叫徐德言，因為陳朝馬上就要滅亡了，他怕萬一妻子走丟了，找不到他，就把家裏的一面鏡子分成兩半，一半給他的妻子，一半自己留著，並說好元宵節時，他們在街上，一個人買鏡子，一個賣鏡子，用這樣的方法來找對方(4)。陳朝滅亡後，徐德言的妻子真的走丟了。

　　徐德言非常想念妻子，所以元宵節那天就去街上找賣鏡子的人。他看到一位老人正在賣半面鏡子，徐德言拿出自己的半面鏡子，兩面鏡子正好對上(5)。徐德言知道他的妻子就在附近。原來是他的妻子讓老人替她賣鏡子找丈夫的。徐德言就這樣找到了他的妻子。

　　現在中國人常常用＂破鏡重圓＂這句話來說夫妻分開或離婚後又團圓的情況，就是從這個故事來的。

(1) 重(chóng)：again   (2) 陳朝(Chén Cháo)：Chén Dynasty 557-589

(3) 駙馬 (fùmǎ): emperor's son-in-law   (4) 對方 (duìfāng)：each other

(5) 對上 (duì shang)：match

(Simplified Characters)

<h2 align="center">破镜重(1)圆</h2>

陈朝(2)末年有一个驸马(3)叫徐德言，因为陈朝马上就要灭亡了，他怕万一妻子走丢了，找不到他，就把家里的一面镜子分成两半，一半给他的妻子，一半自己留着，并说好元宵节时，他们在街上，一个人买镜子，一个卖镜子，用这样的方法来找对方(4)。陈朝灭亡后，徐德言的妻子真的走丢了。

徐德言非常想念妻子，所以元宵节那天就去街上找卖镜子的人。他看到一位老人正在卖半面镜子，徐德言拿出自己的半面镜子，两面镜子正好对上(5)。徐德言知道他的妻子就在附近。原来是他的妻子让老人替她卖镜子找丈夫的。徐德言就这样找到了他的妻子。

现在中国人常常用"破镜重圆"这句话来说夫妻分开或离婚后又团圆的情况，就是从这个故事来的。

(1) 重(chóng)：again   (2) 陈朝(Chén Cháo)：Chén Dynasty 557-589

(3) 驸马 (fùmǎ): emperor's son-in-law   (4) 对方 (duìfāng)：each other

(5) 对上 (duì shang)：match

Questions:

1) What did Xu Deyan give his wife?

   (He gave her half a mirror.)

2) Why did he take the mirror apart?

   (So they could identify each other in case they got separated.)

3) What did he ask her to do in case they got separated?

   (He asked her to sell the broken mirror on the street.)

4) What time did they decide on to look for each other?

   (On the day of the Lantern Festival.)

5) Did Xu Deyan find his wife on the street?

   (No.)

6) How did Xu Deyan find his wife?

   (A old man was selling the mirror for her. He led him to his wife.)

7) " 破鏡重圓 " is a metaphor for what?

   (For a couple who are reunited with each other after a separation or a divorce.)

C: Please fill in the blanks with the words provided and translate the passage into English.

(Traditional Characters)

念不下，看不出來，看下去，吃不下

小林每次一看籃球賽就會激動得大喊大叫。要是有三，四場球賽，他會一直看下去。他平常很安靜，大家都看不出來他是一個球迷。他自己也覺得奇怪，為什麼一看球賽就念不下書，吃不下飯。

(Simplified Characters)

念不下书，看不出来，看下去，吃不下饭

小林每次一看篮球赛就会激动得大喊大叫。要是有三，四场球赛，他会一直看下去。他平常很安静，大家都看不出来他是一个球迷。他自己也觉得奇怪，为什么一看球赛就念不下书，吃不下饭。

(Every time Xiao Lin watches ball games, he screams and yells with excitement. If there are three or four games, he will keep on watching. Ordinarily, he is very quiet. No one could tell that he is a basketball fan. He wonders himself: why whenever he starts watching a ball game, he is unable to keep on studying or eating.)

D: In recent years, China has witnessed a new phenomenon. There has been a proliferation of talk shows, especially on radios. Advice columns in the print media are equally popular. The following is a fairly typical representation of such articles in Chinese language newspapers. See if you can answer the questions after skimming through it.

(Traditional Characters)

讓孩子吃點苦

城市裏的孩子吃得好，穿得好，玩得好，讀書用功，有的還會彈琴，唱歌，畫畫。做家長的很容易滿足，好像現在的孩子什麼都有，什麼都好。可是也有人說現在的孩子吃不了苦，我認爲說得很有道理。那麼讓孩子學會吃苦呢？

今年寒假，上海一位年輕的爸爸爲了教育女兒，給了她兩個選擇，一是1000元的紅包，二是回老家幫助姑媽做農活。這個小女孩選擇了後者，去經受"吃苦磨練"。對這位有遠見的父親，不妨也獎他一個紅包。

爲了使今天的中國孩子在下個世紀不會輸給美國人，日本人，德國人……做大人的要給我們的孩子上好"吃苦磨練"這一課。

(Simplified Characters)

让孩子吃点苦

城市里的孩子吃得好，穿得好，玩得好，读书用功，有的还会弹琴，唱歌，画画。做家长的很容易满足，好像现在的孩子什麼都好，什麼都有。可是也有人说现在的孩子吃不了苦，我认为说得很有道理。那麼让孩子学会吃苦呢？

今年寒假，上海一位年轻的爸爸为了教育女儿，给了她两个选择，一是1000元的红包，二是回老家帮助姑妈做农活。这个小女孩选择了后者，去经受"吃苦磨练"。对这位有远见的父亲，不妨也奖他一个红包。

为了使今天的中国孩子在下个世纪不会输给美国人，日本人，德国人……做大人的要给我们的孩子上好"吃苦磨练"这一课。

Questions:

1) According to the article, what ability do today's children lack?

    (The ability to endure hardship.)

2) Why does the father deserve an award?

    (He sent his daughter to a winter camp and provided needed challenges.)

第四部分：句型與詞語練習 Grammar & Usage

A: 用「V + 起來」改寫下面的句子。

Please rewrite the following sentences using "V + 起來".

例：她一高興就開始唱歌。--->她一高興就唱起歌來。

1. 小林剛回到家就坐在沙發上開始看電視。

   --->_____。

2. 他們中文課一結束就開始說英文。

   --->_____。

3. 星期六早上起床以後，他就開始洗衣服。

   --->_____。

B: 請用「V + 得 / 不 + 了」完成下面的句子。

Please complete the following sentences using "V + 得 / 不 + 了".

例：她跟她先生鬧翻了，要求離婚，但是她先生不肯簽字，所以
    短時間離不了婚。

1. 一般的退休年齡是六十五歲，老張今年才五十歲，_____。

2. 感恩節大家都回家過節，小李得工作，_____。

3. 排隊買票划船的人很多，可是船很少，我們今天_____。

C: 請用 " 要 " 改寫下面的句子：

Please rewrite the following sentences using "要".

例：這件事情很重要，我應該好好地想想。

---> 這件事情很重要，我要好好地想想。

1. 天太熱，你應該多喝水。

   --->_____ 。

2. 快考試了，你應該多復習一下。

   --->_____ 。

3. 醫生說爲了身體健康應該少吃油的，多吃清淡的。

   --->_____ 。

D: 請用 " 要不是 " 改寫下面的句子：

Please rewrite the following sentences using "要不是".

例：今天晚上的電視節目精彩極了。<u>要不是我功課太多</u>，我一定看下去。

1. 我們學校的籃球隊球員雖然個個速度快，身強體壯，但是比賽經驗不夠。

   昨天_____，我們肯定會輸。

2. 我是一年級的新生，對校園不太熟悉。_____，我的註

   冊手續不會辦得那麼順利。

3. 那個房子又大又漂亮，附近有山有水。_____，我肯定會租

   下來。

E: 請用 " 說不定 " 完成下面的對話。

Please complete the following dialogues using "說不定".

例 ：A: 他什麼時候畢業？

         B: 他平時要是用一點功，<u>說不定早就畢業了</u>。

1. A: 姑媽給我寄的包裹，怎麼還沒寄到？

   B: 別急，_____ 。

2. A: 我給他打電話打了好幾次都打不通。

   B: _____ 。

3. A: 你知道不知道有誰要出租房子？我找房子找了兩個多星期還沒找到

   合適的。

   B: 報紙上有很多出租房子的廣告，_____ 。

第五部分：翻譯 Translation

A: Please translate the following dialogue into Chinese.

Lisa: I can't go to the movies. I don't feel well. （V+不了）

（我看不了電影了。我不舒服。）

Tianming: What's the matter?

（怎麼了？）

Lisa: As soon as I got home this afternoon, I began to have a headache .

（我今天下午一回到家頭就疼起來了。）

Tianming: Have you seen a doctor?

（你看醫生了嗎？）

Lisa: No, I haven't.

（沒有。）

Tianming: Take down my doctor's number and call him. （V+下來）

（你把我的醫生的電話號碼記下來，給他打個電話。）

Lisa: All right.

（好吧。）

B: Please translate the following passage into Chinese using the phrases provided.

聽說，起來，最好，沒想到

听说，起来，最好，没想到

In China, people used to believe that men and women should get married when they have reached a certain age （男大當婚，女大當嫁）, but now I hear that the number of people, especially educated women, who remain single is getting larger and larger numerous. Some women feel that a career （事業） is more important than anything else; others think that it is best not to have a family or children. Only this way can one be free. I left China five or six years ago. Who'd have thought that China could have undergone such big changes （變化：biànhuà）？

（在中國，人們過去都認爲＂男大當婚，女大當嫁＂。可是我聽說現在不結婚的人漸漸多起來了。特別是受教育較多的女性。她們有的覺得事業最重要，有的認爲最好沒有家庭、孩子，一個人才自由。我離開中國已經五、六年了，沒想到中國的變化這麼大。）

第六部分：寫作練習　Composition

你認爲父母應該怎樣教育孩子？

第十五課　男女平等

第一部分：聽力練習 Listening Comprehension

A: Listen to the tape recording of *Lesson Fifteen* and answer the following questions.

1. Why did Lisa's friend quit her job?

   (She is expecting a baby.)

2. On what aspects do Zhang Tianming and Lisa agree with each other?

   (Women get less pay than men do for the same kind of work; there are very few women at the management level.)

3. Who is more optimistic about the issue in question?

   (Zhang Tianming is.)

4. Whom should a Chinese woman obey in the old society?

   (Her father before she was married; her husband after she was married; her son after her husband died.)

5. According to the author, in which period of time did Chinese women start to gain true equality?

   (In the 1950's.)

B: Listen to the tape for the workbook.

1. Please listen to the passage and answer the following questions in English.

（張天明他們學校有男子籃球隊，也有女子籃球隊。男子籃球隊的表現每年都讓球迷很失望。但是女籃年年都進入決賽，為學校爭得了許多榮譽。由於一般的球迷對女籃比賽沒有什麼興趣，電視幾乎從來不播女子籃球比賽，所以女籃雖然表現好，但是不能給學校賺什麼錢。男籃雖然老輸，可是每次比賽，電視都播，給學校賺了一大筆錢，所以女籃教練的薪水比男籃教練低得多。有的人認為這是歧視婦女的現象，但也有人覺得這是做生意，沒有什麼歧視不歧視的問題。）

Questions:

1) Who has a better record?

(The women's basketball team)

2) Why do men's basketball teams in general get much more TV coverage?

(Fans are not interested in women's basketball games as much.)

3) Why is the salary of the coach of the women's basketball team get much lower than the coach of the men's basketball team?

(Because the school claims that the women's basketball team does not bring in as much revenue as the men's basketball team does.)

4) On the basis of the incident, do you think the school discriminates against women? Why or why not?

2. Please listen to the passage and answer the following questions in Chinese.

（以前在中國大陸，婦女被叫做＂半邊天＂，意思是說男女是平等的。改革開放以後，歧視婦女的現象越來越多。公司在報上登廣告找人的時候，經常是只要男的，偶爾要女的，但不是要年輕的，就是要漂亮的，而且常常是一些薪水很低的職位。）

問題：

1) 中國婦女找工作是改革開放以前容易還是以後容易？

2) 要是一個女的想在公司裏找一個做主管的工作，她找到工作的機會大不大？為什麼？

3) 從報紙的廣告裏，怎麼能看出來社會上有男女不平等的現象？

3. Please listen to the passage and answer the following questions.

（婦女去體育場看球賽時，常常覺得排隊上廁所是一件很痛苦的事。因為隊排得那麼長，可是休息時間卻那麼短。有的女的實在憋不住了，只好跑到男廁所去，這是一件很丟人的事。體育場女廁所所以不夠，是因為一般人認為，體育迷大部分是男的，不需要那麼多女廁所。但是現在看球的婦女越來越多，人們的想法也應該變一變，以後蓋體育場時應該多替婦女想想。）

Questions:

1) What do women find so painful when they go to a ball game in a sports stadium?

> *(They have to wait in long lines to go to the bathroom.)*

2) What do women have to do when they cannot wait any longer?

> *(They will go into men restrooms.)*

3) What preconception do people have about women and sports?

> *(They assume that the majority of the people who go to see ball games are men. Therefore, they don't need that many restrooms for women.)*

4) Why should people change their preconceptions?

> *(Female fans are increasing.)*

第二部分：口語練習 Speaking Exercises

A: Please practice asking and answering the following questions with a partner before class.

1. 在你的家裏，誰負責帶孩子？誰負責教育孩子？

2. 你幫不幫父母分擔家務？

3. "老鼠見了貓"是什麼意思？

4. 社會上有哪些男女不平等的現象？

B: Please practice speaking on the following topics.

1. 你認爲怎樣才算男女平等？你認爲男女能平等嗎？

2. 談談從五十年代以來中國婦女的社會地位有什麼樣的變化。

第三部分：閱讀練習 Reading Comprehension

A: Please fill in the blanks with the words provided.

(Traditional Characters)

> 要不是，沒想到，甚至，實際上，說不定

　　自從小李辭掉工作以來，她的婆婆常跟她吵架。<u>要不是</u>小李的先生在旁邊，她的婆婆<u>說不定</u>還會打她呢。小李所以辭職是因爲想待在家裏帶孩子。<u>沒想到</u>婆婆不讓小李帶，有時候<u>甚至</u>不讓小李跟孩子一起吃飯。婆婆說小李不是個好妻子，好母親。<u>實際上</u>，大家都知道小李是個模範母親。不但體貼先生，而且非常愛孩子。

(Simplified Characters)

> 要不是，没想到，甚至，实际上，说不定

　　自从小李辞掉工作以来，她的婆婆常跟她吵架。<u>要不是</u>小李的先生在旁边，她的婆婆<u>说不定</u>还会打她呢。小李所以辞职是因为想待在家里带孩子。<u>没想到</u>婆婆不让小李带，有时候<u>甚至</u>不让小李跟孩子一起吃饭。婆婆说小李不是个好妻子，好母亲。<u>实际上</u>，大家都知道小李是个模范母亲。不但体贴先生，而且非常爱孩子。

B: Please answer the questions after reading the following passage.

(Traditional Characters)

　　林雪梅的父母親非常重男輕女。他們生第一個孩子的時候，一看是個女的，就給她起名 " 林招弟 "，希望她能帶來一個弟弟。生老二的時候，沒想到又是個女的，就把老二的名字取做 " 林來弟 "，希望老二下面能生個弟弟。林雪梅是老三，出生的時候，父母看她還是個女的，但是不願意再生了，就給她起一個名字叫 " 林若男 "，希望她能像個男孩一樣。父母從小就把她當男孩一樣養：不給她裙子穿，只讓她穿牛仔褲，也不讓她留長頭髮。林雪梅從小就認爲男的能做的，自己也能做，特別反對重男輕女。她認爲女孩子沒有什麼不好，所以上大學以後，就把自己的名字從 " 林若男 " 改成了 " 林雪梅 "。

(Simplified Characters)

　　林雪梅的父母亲非常重男轻女。他们生第一个孩子的时候,一看是个女的,就给她起名"林招弟",希望她能带来一个弟弟。生老二的时候,没想到又是个女的,就把老二的名字取做"林来弟",希望老二下面能生个弟弟。林雪梅是老三,出生的时候,父母看她还是个女的,但是不愿意再生了,就给她起一个名字叫"林若男",希望她能像个男孩一样。父母从小就把她当男孩一样养:不给她裙子穿,只让她穿牛仔裤,也不让她留长头发。林雪梅从小就认为男的能做的,自己也能做,特别反对重男轻女。她认为女孩子没有什么不好,所以上大学以后,就把自己的名字从"林若男"改成了"林雪梅"。

Questions:

1) How many brothers and sisters does Lin Xuemei have?

   (Two sisters.)

2) Why is her eldest sister named 招弟?

   (Her parents hoped that she could bring a brother along.)

3) What is her second sister's name?

   (來弟)

4) What is the meaning of the name given to Lin Xuemei originally?

   (Be like a boy.)

5) How did Lin Xuemei get her current name?

   (She saw nothing wrong to be a female, and changed her name to a more feminine one.)

C: Please answer the questions after reading the story.

<u>1 | 2</u>
3 | 4

(Traditional Characters)

花木蘭的故事

　　中國古時候有一個叫花木蘭的女性。有一天，她在家裏一邊幹活，一邊想著父親前一天說的話。父親昨天很著急地告訴她，他們家必須有一個人去當兵(1)。雖然父親已經很老了，身體又不好，可是因為木蘭沒有哥哥，木蘭的弟弟又太小了，看來只能父親自己去當兵了。木蘭想來想去決定自己替父親去當兵。木蘭當了兵以後，和男兵一樣，男兵能做的，她也能做，而且做得非常好，大家都以為她是男的。幾年以後，木蘭回到了家裏，換上女人穿的衣服，化了妝，男兵們看了都非常驚訝(2)。木蘭說，"兩隻兔子(3)在地上一起跑，誰能看得出哪個是雌(4)的，哪個是雄(5)的呢？"

(1) 當兵 (dāng bīng): serve in the army   (2) 驚訝 (jīngyà): surprised

(3) 兔子 (tùzi): rabbit   (4) 雌 (cí): (of animal) female

(5) 雄 (xióng): (of animal) male

(Simplified Characters)

<h1 style="text-align:center">花木兰的故事</h1>

　　中国古时候有一个叫花木兰的女性。有一天，她在家里一边干活，一边想着父亲前一天说的话。父亲昨天很着急地告诉她，他们家必须有一个人去当兵(1)。虽然父亲已经很老了，身体又不好，可是因为木兰没有哥哥，木兰的弟弟又太小了，看来只能父亲自己去当兵了。木兰想来想去决定自己替父亲去当兵。木兰当了兵以后，和男兵一样，男兵能做的，她也能做，而且做得非常好，大家都以为她是男的。几年以后，木兰回到了家里，换上女人穿的衣服，化了妆，男兵们看了都非常惊讶(2)。木兰说，"两只兔子(3)在地上一起跑，谁能看得出哪个是雌(4)的，哪个是雄(5)的呢？"

(1) 当兵 (dāng bīng): serve in the army   (2) 惊讶 (jīngyà): surprised

(3) 兔子 (tùzi): rabbit   (4) 雌 (cí): (of animal) female

(5) 雄 (xióng): (of animal) male

問題：

1) 父親告訴木蘭什麼了？

2) 父親爲什麼很著急？

3) 木蘭的父親有幾個兒子？

4) 木蘭是個好兵嗎？爲什麼？

5) 木蘭回家後, 大家看見她爲什麼很驚訝？

6) 木蘭怎麼回答他們？

7) 她說的話是什麼意思？

第四部分：句型與詞語練習 Grammar & Usage

A: 請用 " 就拿...來說 " 完成下面句子。

Please complete the following sentences using "就拿...來說".

例：他對他太太非常體貼，就拿昨天來說，他不但送花給太
太，還親自下廚做了幾道拿手好菜給太太吃。

1. 在社會上，有許多男女不平等的現象，＿＿＿＿＿＿＿＿＿＿，
＿＿＿＿＿＿＿＿＿＿＿＿＿＿。

2. 小張在學校各方面都表現得非常好，＿＿＿＿＿＿＿＿＿＿，
＿＿＿＿＿＿＿＿＿＿＿＿＿＿。

3. 中國人過不同的節，吃不同的東西，＿＿＿＿＿＿＿＿，＿＿＿＿＿＿，
＿＿＿＿＿＿＿＿＿，＿＿＿＿＿＿。 （端午節，中秋節）

B: 請用 " 甚至 " 完成下面對話。

Please complete the following sentences using "甚至".

例： A: 你平常看什麼電視？ （看/廣告）

B: 看甚麼電視？我什麼都看，甚至連廣告都看 。

1. A: 你什麼時候結婚啊？

B: 結婚？！我＿＿＿＿＿＿＿＿＿＿＿＿＿＿。（沒有/女朋友）

2. A: 你先生在家幫不幫你做家務事？

B: 幫忙做家務事！他＿＿＿＿＿＿＿＿＿＿＿。（不洗 / 碗）

3. A: 聽說他在國際比賽中得到了很好的成績。（打破了世界記錄）

B: 他不但拿了好幾面金牌，銀牌，＿＿＿＿＿＿＿＿＿＿＿。

C: 請用 " ...以來 " 改寫下面句子。

例：從結婚到現在，老張從來沒有跟太太吵過架。

---> 結婚以來，老張從來沒有跟太太吵過架。

1. 退休到現在，王老師一直沒閒著，不是寫文章，就是出國旅行。

--->＿＿＿＿＿＿＿＿＿＿＿＿＿＿＿＿＿＿＿＿＿。

2. 那部電影從上演到現在，已經打破美國商業片的票房記錄。

   --->_____ 。

3. 那個公園從開門到今天，已經吸引了成千上萬的遊客。

   --->_____ 。

第五部分：翻譯 Translation

A: **Translate the following passage into Chinese. Please pay attention to Chinese word order.**

It's been three years since Mr. and Mrs. Wang got divorced. They fought fiercely before they parted company. Things have been much better since the divorce. Now they even joke when they speak to each other. Every year their kids spend six months with dad, and six months with mom, but every New Year they go back together to Washington, D. C. by plane to see grandma. Now they get along with one another much better. People all say that Mr. and Mrs. Wang were right to get divorced.

（ 王先生和王太太離婚已經三年了。他們分手以前，吵架吵得非常厲害。離婚
　以後反而好多了，在一起說話時還會開玩笑。他們的孩子每年跟爸爸住六個
　月，跟媽媽住六個月。但是每個新年他們都一起坐飛機回華盛頓去看奶奶。
　現在一家人的關係好多了。很多人都說他們離婚離對了。 ）

B: **Please translate the following passage into Chinese using the phrases provided.**

以後，雖然，甚至

以后，虽然，甚至

After Zhang Tianming came back from China, he felt that even though he had spent a lot of money, it was worth it (很值得). Who knows when he would be able to go to China again? Ever since he came back, he had been thinking about writing to his aunt, but he had been very busy. He didn't even have the time to call his friends.

（張天明從中國回來以後，覺得雖然花了很多錢，但是很值得。誰知道
　什麼時候他能再去中國呢？從中國回來後他一直想給他的姑媽寫信，
　可是他很忙，甚至連給他的朋友打電話的時間都沒有。 ）

C: Please translate the following passage into Chinese using the phrases provided.

就拿...來說，明顯，實際上

就拿...来说，明显，实际上

Equality between men and women is not an issue that could be easily settled. Take me for an example, I think women's status is already very high. Men sometimes do not fare as well as women. Isn't it true that it's easier for women to find jobs? My wife does not agree with me. She says in terms of position and salary society as a whole flagrantly favors men over women. She believes that so long as people are discussing equality between men and women, it must be because inequality exists in reality. Furthermore she says that equality between men and women may never be achieved.

（男女平等問題是一個很難說清楚的問題。就拿我來說，我覺得婦女的地
位已經很高了，男人有時候還不如女人，女的不是常常比男的更容易找
到工作嗎？可是我太太不同意我的看法。她說從職位和薪水的高低來
看，整個社會明顯地重男輕女。她認為只要還有人在討論男女平等的問
題，就是因為實際上還有男女不平等的現象。她還說，男女平等恐怕永
遠也實現不了。）

D: Please translate the following passage into Chinese.

Many people believe that women's social status has been elevated and that gender equality is slowly manifesting itself in families and in society. However, feminists are not that optimistic. They feel that there is still plenty of discrimination against women.

（很多人認為婦女的社會地位已經有了很大的提高，男女平等在家庭裏和工作上
慢慢地得到體現。但是女權主義者沒有那麼樂觀。他們覺得社會上還有許多歧
視婦女的現象。）

第六部分：寫作練習 Composition

請寫一篇短文，題目是：

1. 我生活中的一位女性。（可以寫你的母親，姐姐或妹妹）
2. 我對男女平等問題的看法

第十六課 健康與保險

A: Listen to the tape recording of *Lesson Sixteen* and answer the following questions.

1. Why couldn't Tianming go to the movie?

   (He had to go to pick up his aunt at the airport.)

2. Why didn't the aunt have the operation in Canada?

   (She would have to wait for a long time if she wanted to have an operation in Canada.)

3. What is the drawback of having the operation in America?

   (Her insurance company won't cover the bill.)

4. Why does Lisa think the Canadians have a better health care system?

   (Because everyone can have medical treatment no matter if you are rich or poor.)

5. Why does Lisa want to meet with Tianming's aunt?

   (Because she hears his aunt used to be a movie star.)

B: Listen to the tape for the workbook.

1. Listen to the passage and answer the following questions.

   （張天明的姑媽年輕的時候在台灣拍了許多武打片，是有名的電影明
   星。那個時候拍武打片不像現在可以買保險，要是不小心受了傷，
   只能自己花錢看醫生。後來，她不敢再拍武打片了。幾年後，她移
   民到多倫多，在一家保險公司做事。公司讓她在中國移民中做生
   意。因為她會說北京話、台灣話和廣東話，加上她以前在台灣、香
   港非常有名，她的客戶越來越多，生意越做越好。現在她自己開
   了一家保險公司。）

選擇題：

1)   a. 張天明的媽媽年輕時是一個電影明星。

         b. 張天明的姑媽年輕時在電影院工作。

         c. 張天明的姑媽年輕時是一個電影演員，可是沒有名。

         d. 張天明的姑媽年輕時是一個有名的電影演員。

2) 那個時候

         a. 拍武打片可以買保險。

         b. 電影公司會替明星買保險。

         c. 張天明的姑媽很有錢，她自己買保險。

         d. 拍武打片不能買保險。

3) 張天明的姑媽

         a. 買了保險才敢拍武打片。

         b. 不敢再拍武打片了，因爲拍武打片不能買保險。

         c. 不再拍武打片了，因爲武打片沒有意思。

         d. 不再拍武打片了，因爲她想移民到加拿大去。

4) 保險公司讓張天明的姑媽在中國移民中做生意，因爲

         a. 她只會說中文，不懂英文。

         b. 她會說廣東話，多倫多有很多香港人。

         c. 她會說很多方言(fāngyán： dialect)，而且在中國移民中非常
            有名。

         d. 她經常去台灣、香港和東南亞。

5) " 客戶 " 的英文意思是

         a. guest.

         b. client.

         c. polite.

         d. guest room.

6) 張天明的姑媽現在

         a. 自己開保險公司。

         b. 還在別人的保險公司做事。

         c. 有保險。

         d. 她的一家人都有保險。

2. Listen to the passage and answer the following questions.

（很多中國人剛到美國的時候，看到美國人買各種各樣的保險，覺得很不理解。比如說，平時要買健康保險；買了車，得為車子買保險；買了房子，還要買火險 …，各種各樣的保險費加起來，對很多家庭來說是一個很大的負擔。許多來美國不久的中國人都覺得花那麼多錢買保險很不值得。但是他們在美國生活久了以後，就發現，非買保險不可，要不然萬一生了病，出了事，沒有保險的話，就真的一點辦法都沒有了。）

Questions:

1) What is the one thing that many Chinese people don't understand when they first come to this country?

   (Various kinds of insurance)

2) According to the passage, what kinds of insurance do Americans purchase?

   (Health, auto, home liability)

3) Why do many Chinese people start buying insurance after they've been in the United States for awhile?

   (Because they realize that they need to purchase insurance to protect themselves in cases of accidents.)

3. Listen to the passage and answer the following questions.

（約翰的弟弟大衛前兩天突然肚子疼得不得了，家裏人開車把他送到醫院去看急診。開始醫生以為他只是吃壞了肚子，但是經過檢查，發現問題相當嚴重，需要馬上做手術。約翰的父親在同意書上簽了字，護士就把大衛推進手術室。大衛看到那麼多的護士醫生，心裏有些緊張。這個時候，大衛聽到一個護士說："你別緊張。"大衛回答說："好，我不緊張。"護士說："哦，對不起，我不是說你，我是叫醫生不要緊張。"）

Questions:

1) Why was David sent to the hospital?

   (Because he was having pain in the stomach.)

2) What was the doctor's evaluation?

   (That the illness was rather serious.)

3) What did the doctor decide to do?

   (To operate on David.)

4) Why was David nervous?

   (Because there were many nurses and doctors.)

5) Did he have a reason to feel nervous? Why?

   (Yes, because the surgeon was very nervous himself.)

第二部分：口語練習 Speaking Exercises

A: Please practice asking and answering the following questions with a partner before class.

1. 你/你家買了什麼保險？
2. 你覺得美國的醫療保險制度有什麼缺點？
3. 你會怎麼改革美國的醫療保險制度？
4. "羊毛出在羊身上" 是什麼意思？

B: Please practice speaking on the following topics.

1. 請談談美國政府應該怎麼照顧窮人。
2. 請談談怎麼樣才能有健康的身體。
3. 你認為政府是不是應該給所有的人買保險？(可以分成兩組進行辯論)

第三部分：閱讀練習 Reading Comprehension

A: Please answer the questions after reading the passage .

(Traditional Characters)

　　在中國的城市裏，大部分人都是公費醫療，生了病就到醫院去掛號看病，醫藥費大多由政府負擔，自己幾乎不花錢。這方面與美國非常不同。在美國，子女不滿十八歲，多是父母替子女買健康保險。成年人從學校畢業或找到工作以後，就應該由公司和個人分擔保險費用。要是沒有工作或是失業了，就得自己花錢買保險。不過，美國一般的保險只保某些項目，像眼睛和牙齒還得另外保。所以一家人的保險費加起來是一個很大的負擔。難怪有人說在美國生不起病。

(Simplified Characters)

　　在中国的城市里，大部分人都是公费医疗，生了病就到医院去挂号看病，医药费大多由政府负担，自己几乎不花钱。这方面与美国非常不同。在美国，子女不满十八岁，多是父母替子女买健康保险。成年人从学校毕业或找到工作以后，就应该由公司和个人分担保险费用。要是没有工作或是失业了，就得自己花钱买保险。不过，美国一般的保险只保某些项目，像眼睛和牙齿还得另外保。所以一家人的保险费加起来是一个很大的负担。难怪有人说在美国生不起病。

　　問題：
　　1) 請問，＂公費＂是什麼意思？
　　2) 中國的保險和美國有什麼不同？
　　3) 爲什麼在美國生不起病？

B: Please answer the questions after reading the following passage.

(Traditional Characters)

　　中醫，中藥有幾千年的歷史，出了許多有名的醫學家，如華陀(1)，張仲景(2)，李時珍(3)等。華陀生活在公元(4)二世紀到三世紀，他能夠用一種藥來麻醉(5)病人，然後在病人身上做手術。張仲景(公元二--三世紀)也是漢代的醫學家；他的《傷寒論》(6)對中醫的發展產生了很大的影響，在書中他提出了防病(7)比治病更重要的觀點。李時珍是中國明代(1368-1644)的醫學家和藥物學家。他寫了《本草綱目》(8)，對中國藥物學的發展作出了極大的貢獻(9)。

　　(1) 華陀 (Huà Tuó): a person's name 　　(2) 張仲景 (Zhāng Zhòngjǐng): a person's name

　　(3) 李時珍 (Lǐ Shízhēn): a person's name　(4) 公元 (gōngyuán): common era

　　(5) 麻醉 (mázuì): anaesthetize

　　(6) 《傷寒論》(Shānghán Lùn): *On Febrile Diseases*

　　(7) 防病 (fángbìng): prevent

　　(8) 《本草綱目》(Běncǎo Gāngmù): *Materia Medica*

　　(9) 貢獻 (gòngxiàn): contribution

(Simplified Characters)

　　中医，中药有几千年的历史，出了许多有名的医学家，如华陀(1)，张仲景(2)，李时珍(3)等。华陀生活在公元(4)二世纪到三世纪，他能够用一种药来麻醉(5)病人，然后在病人身上做手术。张仲景(公元二--三世纪)也是汉代的医学家，他的《伤寒论》(6)对中医的发展产生了很大的影响，在书中他提出了防病(7)比治病更重要的观点。李时珍是中国明代(1368-1644)的医学家和药物学家。他写了《本草纲目》(8)，对中国药物学的发展作出了极大的贡献(9)。

(1) 华陀(Huà Tuó): a person's name　　(2) 张仲景(Zhāng Zhòngjǐng): a person's name

(3) 李时珍(Lǐ shízhēn): a person's name　　(4) 公元(gōngyuán): common era

(5) 麻醉(mázuì): anaesthetize

(6)《伤寒论》(Shānghán Lùn): *On Febrile Diseases*

(7) 防病(fángbìng): prevent

(8)《本草纲目》(Běncǎo Gāngmù): *Materia Medica*

(9) 贡献(gòngxiàn): contribution

是非题：

1) T　華陀和張仲景都是漢代的醫學家。

2) T　華陀也很懂藥。

3) T　張仲景認爲醫生應該想辦法使人儘量不生病。

4) F　《本草綱目》和《傷寒論》一樣，都是藥物學方面的書。

C: Up till a few years ago insurance in any form was all but unknown in China. There is now a fledgling insurance industry in China. Foreign insurance companies are also trying to cash in on the potentially huge insurance market in China. One of them, the American International Group, has returned to Shanghai, where it was first founded before 1949. The following is an insurance card.

中國平安保險公司

西湖游船游客人身安全保险证

贰　　　角

Questions:

1) Who issued it?

   (中國平安保險公司 *an insurance company*)

2) Who is it for?

   (For tourists)

3) What is it for?

   (Personal safety)

4) How much does it cost?

   (Twenty cents)

第四部分：句型與詞語練習 Grammar & Usage

A: 請用 " V+得 / 不+起 " 完成下面的句子。

  Please complete the following sentences using "V +得 / 不 +起".

  例： 這件衣服太貴了，<u>我買不起</u>。

1. 沒有醫療保險的人 _____醫生。

2. 現在大學的學費越來越貴，很多人 _____。

3. 那家餐館的菜好吃是好吃，但是每道菜的價錢都那麼貴，

   _____。

B: 請用 " 不如 " 改寫下面的句子。

Please rewrite the following sentences using "不如".

　　例：這家醫院的心臟科醫生沒有那家醫院有名。

　　　　--->這家醫院的心臟科醫生不如那家醫院有名。

1. 很多人覺得美國的醫療保險制度沒有加拿大好。

   ---> _____。

2. 今年申請這所大學的人沒有去年多。

   ---> _____。

3. 我的房租沒有小王的房租貴。

   ---> _____。

C: 請用 " 毫無 " 改寫下面的句子。

Please rewrite the following sentences using "毫無".

　　例：這個情況很糟糕，我一點辦法也沒有。

　　　　--->這個情況很糟糕，我毫無辦法。

1. 他這個人做事一點計劃都沒有。

   ---> _____。

2. 他對哲學一點興趣都沒有。

   ---> _____。

3. 小張大學剛畢業，一點工作經驗都沒有，找工作肯定不容易。

   ---> _____，找工作肯定不容易。

D: 請用 " 至少 " 完成下面對話。

Please complete the following dialogues using "至少".

　　例：A: 你怎麼申請這個學校？

　　　　B: 這個學校雖然不太有名，但至少學費便宜。

1. A: 他好像不是一個模範丈夫嗎。

   B: 雖然他不是一個模範丈夫，但＿＿＿＿＿＿＿＿＿＿＿＿＿＿＿。(體貼)

2. A: 小王感恩節居然沒回家跟家裏人一起過節，真奇怪。

   B: 他雖然沒回家過節，但＿＿＿＿＿＿＿＿＿＿＿＿＿，不像小李，連
      電話都沒打。

3. A: 這個工作真沒意思，真想辭職不幹了。

   B: 你千萬別辭職。這個工作是個鐵飯碗，雖然沒意思，但＿＿＿＿＿＿＿。

E: 請用 " 畢竟 " 完成下面對話。

   例： A: 你覺得這個餐館的菜怎麼樣?

        B: 這個餐館的菜不錯，但是畢竟沒有你太太做的菜好吃。

1. A: 媽，我已經是二十多歲的大人了。你別像管孩子那樣管我，好不好？

   B: 我知道你長大了，但是＿＿＿＿＿＿＿＿＿＿＿＿＿＿＿＿＿＿＿。

2. A: 你現在租的房子怎麼樣？安靜不安靜？

   B: 偶爾有人從窗戶外邊經過，但是＿＿＿＿＿＿＿＿＿＿＿＿＿＿＿。

3. A: 這套運動服跟那套運動服看起來一樣，爲什麼價錢差那麼多？

   B: 這套是阿迪達斯的，＿＿＿＿＿＿＿＿＿＿＿＿＿＿＿＿＿。(名牌)

第五部分：翻譯 Translation

A: Please translate the following passage into Chinese using the words provided.

V+不起，不如，V+得起，至少

Many people cannot afford to see a doctor when they are ill. No wonder some people think that America's health insurance system is not as good as Canada's. At least everybody can afford to see a doctor in Canada. However, the Canadian health care system has problems, too. Sometimes patients have to wait a long time before they can see a doctor. Besides some people feel that medical facilities in Canada are not as good as those in America.

（很多人生了病看不起醫生，怪不得有些人覺得美國的健康保險制度不如
  加拿大好。因爲在加拿大至少每個人都看得起醫生。但是，加拿大的醫

療制度也有問題。有時候病人看醫生得等很長時間。另外，有的人覺得加拿大的醫療設備不如美國好。）

B: Please translate the following passage into Chinese.

My teacher takes good care of his health. Not only does he exercise every day, he is also very careful about what he eats. He doesn't eat greasy or salty food, and does not take even the tinniest amount of sugar. He eats a lot of fruit. Although he is not a vegetarian, he seldom eats meat. His health is very good. But it seems to me while health is very important, what meaning would life have if one could not eat good food?

（我的老師很注意身體健康。他不但每天運動，而且吃飯也特別注意。他不吃很油的，也不吃很鹹的，甚至一點糖都不吃，他吃很多青菜和水果。他雖然不吃素，但很少吃肉。他的身體不錯。可是我覺得身體好雖然很重要，可是如果不能吃好吃的，生活還有什麼意思呢？）

C: Translate the following passage into Chinese. Please pay attention to the use of multiple attributives.

The little narrow river outside the town is very appealing to the town's residents. It's a great place to take a walk by. There is often a pleasure boat on the river. The tourists on board all like to greet the people selling flowers and newspapers by the river. It's a sight that looks like a painting.

（城外的那條窄窄的小河非常吸引人，是大家散步的好地方。河上有一條小遊船。船上的遊客很喜歡跟河邊賣花賣報紙的人打招呼。看起來好像是一張畫。）

第六部分：寫作練習 Composition

You are having a dispute with your insurance company, which does not think the drug that your doctor prescribed (醫生開的藥) for you was necessary. Write a letter in which you explain that you owed your recovery to the drug, and that you have asked your doctor to write a supporting letter. Tell the insurance company that you have tried several times to call its representatives, but nobody was there to take your calls, and that you are very unhappy with this service.

第十七課　　教　育

第一部分：聽力練習　Listening Comprehension

A: Listen to the tape recording of *Lesson Seventeen* and answer the following questions.

1. Which education system does Tianming's father prefer?

   (The Chinese one.)

2. Which part of the sister's comment indicates American education system has its flaws?

   (She said that without her parents' supervision she wouldn't be doing well solely relying on what she had learned from school.)

3. What is the most important thing in teaching?

   (Teachers should teach according to the talent, the level and the need of each individual.)

4. What do the parents who immigrated from China think of education?

   (They thought they are providing their children with a stress-free childhood in America. But, they also worry their kids might not be competitive in the future.)

B: Listen to the tape for the workbook.

1. Listen to the phone conversation and answer the following questions.

   （---喂？

   ---媽，是我。

   ---哦，是小龍。好久沒給家裏打電話了，怎麼今天想起給家
   　　裏打電話了？是不是又沒錢花了？

   ---不是。我只是想跟您說說話。我們這幾天天天考試，忙得我連睡
   　　覺的時間都沒有。

   ---你考得怎麼樣？

   ---不太好。

   ---爲什麼沒考好？是不是玩得太多了？是不是整天打球和朋友去

酒吧喝酒？

---沒有。媽，您不知道這幾門課多沒意思……

--- 既然你已經選了這些課，沒有意思也得想辦法學好。你多用點功，大考要考得好一些。要不你下學期拿不到獎學金怎麼辦？

--- 那就只能借錢或者暑假裏打工了。您怎麼樣？

--- 我也很忙。我們學校很多學生都是移民，在家不說英文，學習有困難。我們想開中文和英文雙語班，用中文來上課，等他們英文學好了，再全部用英文上課。另外，我們想多開些數學、物理、化學方面的課，所以我們要申請錢。我正在替學校找錢。有個銀行答應給我們十萬塊錢。我們的壓力也很大，如果這些班辦得不好，兩年後我們就拿不到薪水了。

--- 說到錢，媽，您能不能借給我兩百塊？

--- 不是兩個星期前才給你寄去兩百塊錢嗎？怎麼都花完了？

---下個週末我要去女朋友家，要買些禮物。

---好吧，我明天寄給你。）

Questions:

1. Xiao Long had not called his parents for a long time because

      a. he had forgotten.

      b. he did not need money.

      c. he had been too busy.

      d. he had been away on a basketball tournament.

2. Xiao Long did not do well on the examinations because

      a. he had been bar hopping every night.

      b. he was not interested in his classes.

      c. he had had to work.

      d. he had been hanging out with his girlfriend.

3. Xiao Long's mother was a(n)

      a. immigration lawyer.

      b. school teacher.

      c. banker.

      d. pensioner.

4. She had been looking for money to

    a. fund bilingual classes and more science classes.

    b. open a private school.

    c. enable her to go back to school.

    d. supplement her income.

5. Xiao Long needed money to

    a. pay his debt.

    b. visit his girlfriend.

    c. buy new shoes.

    d. see a friend in another state.

2. Please listen to the description and answer the following questions.

（我們學校已經有一百二十多年的歷史了，有大學生兩萬五千個，另外還有五千多個研究生。學生是從全國五十個州和世界八十多個國家來的。這個城市在中西部，很小，人口只有三萬多，可是我們學校的文化活動很豐富。我們學校的音樂學院是美國最大的，幾乎每天晚上都有免費的音樂會，週末還有歌劇演出。學校的美術館經常放外國電影。如果你花十二塊錢買一張季票的話，每次看電影再付一塊錢就可以了，一個學期差不多放二十多部電影。我們學校的籃球隊也很有名，曾經三次獲得全美大學籃球比賽第一。我們學校附近很美，有一個國家公園，公園裏有一個湖，可以划船、游泳。如果你們選這所大學，一定不會後悔。）

Questions:

1) The audience of this speech is very likely

    a. a group of tourists from abroad.

    b. a group of championship rowers.

    c. a group of high school students and their parents.

    d. a group of education experts.

2) The school is

    a. less than a hundred years old.

    b. more than a hundred years old.

    c. a hundred years old.

    d. just twenty years old.

3) The students come from

    a. the midwest.

    b. fifteen states and thirty foreign countries.

    c. small towns with populations of thirty-thousand.

    d. all fifty states and eighty foreign countries.

4) The school can boast of having

    a. the largest national park nearby.

    b. the cheapest film tickets on the college campus.

    c. the best rowing team in the country.

    d. the largest conservatory of music in the country.

第二部分：口語練習 Speaking Exercises

A: Please practice asking and answering the following questions with a partner before class.

1. 你每天一放學回家就做什麼？
2. 你覺得你自己的學習態度夠不夠認真？
3. 你覺得美國的中小學教育有什麼優點，有什麼缺點？
4. 你覺得美國的大學教育有什麼優點，有什麼缺點？
5. "望子成龍，望女成鳳" 是什麼意思？
6. 你的童年過得怎麼樣？

B: Please practice speaking on the following topics.

1. 請談談對你影響最大的老師。

2. 請談談什麼樣的老師才是個好老師。

第三部分：閱讀練習 Reading Comprehension

A: Please read the passage and answer the following questions.

(Traditional Characters)

　　現在在中國的城市裏，尤其是大城市，很多家庭只有一個孩子。這些孩子從小就吃好的，穿好的。很多家長還花錢請老師教他們的孩子鋼琴、英語等等，他們把大部分的時間和金錢都花在孩子身上。爸爸媽媽把這些獨生子女當成太陽(1)一樣，圍著(2)他們轉(3)。這些孩子要什麼，大人就給他們買什麼。有些孩子因此變得非常自私(4)，什麼事都以自己為中心。現在的孩子不太聽父母的話，也不尊敬(5)老人。這跟中國文化強調的完全不同。這種現象已經引起某些社會學家的重視。

     (1)太陽（tàiyang）: sun   (2)圍著（wéi zhe）: around

     (3)轉（zhuàn）: turn; revolve   (4)自私（zìsī）: selfish

     (5)尊敬（zūnjìng）: respect

(Simplified Characters)

　　现在在中国的城市里，尤其是大城市，很多家庭只有一个孩子。这些孩子从小就吃好的，穿好的。很多家长还花钱请老师教他们的孩子钢琴、英语等等，他们把大部分的时间和金钱都花在孩子身上。爸爸妈妈把这些独生子女当成太阳(1)一样，围着(2)他们转(3)。这些孩子要什么，大人就给他们买什么。有些孩子因此变得非常自私(4)，什么事都以自己为中心。现在的孩子不太听父母的话，也不尊敬(5)老人。这跟中国文化强调的完全不同。这种现象已经引起某些社会学家的重视。

     (1)太阳（tàiyang）: sun   (2)围着（wéi zhe）: around

     (3)转（zhuàn）: turn; revolve   (4)自私（zìsī）: selfish

     (5)尊敬（zūnjìng）: respect

是非題：

1) F 在中國的每個地方，只有一個孩子的家庭很多。

2) T 除了鋼琴、英文外，很多家長還出錢請老師教他們的孩子別的東西。

3) T 這些家長把很少的時間和金錢留給自己。

4) T 這些獨生子女像太陽一樣因爲他們是家庭的中心。

5) T 有些孩子以爲自己最重要。

6) T 中國文化要求孩子關心、照顧父母。

B: Read the passage and answer the following questions.

(Traditional Characters)

　　最近十幾年來，去中國學習的外國學生越來越多，其中不少是去學習漢語的，也有些學生是學中國歷史或醫學的。當然，外國人去中國學習不是最近才有的現象。早在唐朝(1)就有日本和韓國的學生去唐朝的首都(2)長安，也就是現在的西安，學習中國文化。現在，外國留學生主要是去北京、上海、南京等大城市。一般來說，如果外國學生想在中國上大學，需要先學一到兩年的漢語，或者參加漢語水平考試，然後才能進入專業學習。很多外國留學生，除了學習以外，還經常參加各種社會活動。如參加中國有些電視台舉辦的外國人唱中國歌的比賽，這些活動很受歡迎(3)。今後，去中國學習的外國學生將會更多，因爲中國的經濟發展得很快，中國將會變得越來越吸引人。

> (1)唐朝(Táng Cháo): the Tang dynasty 618-907   (2)首都 (shǒudū): capital
>
> (3)歡迎(huānyíng): welcome

(Simplified Characters)

　　最近十几年来，去中国学习的外国学生越来越多，其中不少是去学习汉语的，也有些学生是学中国历史或医学的。当然，外国人去中国学习不是最近才有的现象。早在唐朝(1)就有日本和韩国的学生去唐朝的首都(2)长安，也就是现在的西安，学习中国文化。现在，外国留学生主要是去北京、上海、南京等大城市。一般来说，如果外国学生想在中国上大学，需要先学一到两年的汉语，或者参加汉语水平考试，然后才能进入专业学习。很多外国留学生，除了学习以外，还经常参加各种社会活动。如参加中国有些电视台举办的外国人唱中国歌的比赛，这些活动很受欢迎(3)。今后，去中国学习的外国学生将会更多，因为中国的经济发展得很快，中国将会变得越来越吸引人。

(1)唐朝(Táng Cháo): the Tang dynasty 618-907   (2)首都(shǒudū): capital

(3)欢迎(huānyíng): welcome

問題：

1)外國學生去中國主要學習什麼？

2)今天的外國學生和唐朝的外國學生有什麼不同？

3)外國學生怎樣才能在中國上大學？

4)除了學習以外，外國學生還做些什麼？

C: It is estimated that there are as many as two hundred thousand Chinese studying abroad. These students represent some tremendous human resources that the Chinese government wants to tap into. To that end, it has been trying to attract more students to go back to China by offering different incentives and advertising in magazines that are targeted towards overseas Chinese students. The following is what such an advertisement could look like. See if you can answer the following questions.

西江大学现急需引进以下专业具有硕士以上学位的骨干教师，欢迎有志于教育事业的海外留学人员应聘来江大施展才华。

1. 国际工商管理	1 人
2. 国际金融	1—2 人
3. 英　语	1—2 人
4. 计算机硬件、软件	1—2 人

凡应聘到西江大学工作的教师，学校负责解决住房和液化气，其中获国外硕士学位者，一对夫妇可安排2室1厅70米²住房一套；获国外博士学位者，一对夫妇可安排3室1厅78米²住房一套。

就聘人员可将本人履历及有关证件的复印件寄中国××省西江市梁溪路100号西江大学人事处。联系人：陈××. 联系电话：中国0××—668761—401。

Questions:

1) What is the name of this institution?

    （西江大學）

2) How many positions is it trying to fill? Give the maximum number.

    （7）

3) How many of these positions can you decipher?

4) What is the most important incentive that this institution is offering?

    (housing)

5) Where is this institution?

    （中國西江市）

D: 成語故事

Please answer the questions after reading the story.

(Traditional Characters)

畫　蛇(1) 添(2) 足(3)

　　古時候有一個人，有一天他請朋友們喝酒，可是他的酒不夠多，所以他對朋友們說：「我的酒你們幾個人喝，不夠，一個人又喝不了。請你們在地上畫條蛇，誰先畫完，誰就先喝酒。」有一個人先畫好了，他拿起酒杯喝了一口，然後看了看，他看別人都沒畫完，就說：「我還能給蛇畫上幾隻腳呢！」他還沒把腳畫好，另一個人就把一條蛇畫完了，他把酒杯拿過去說：「蛇本來沒有腳，你怎麼能給蛇加上腳呢？這杯酒應該是我的。」說完他就把酒都喝了。

(1)蛇(shé): snake　　　　　(2)添 (tiān): add

(3)足 (zú): foot

(Simplified Characters)

画　蛇(1) 添(2) 足(3)

　　古时候有一个人，有一天他请朋友们喝酒，可是他的酒不够多，所以他对朋友们说：「我的酒你们几个人喝，不够，一个人又喝不了。请你们在地上画条蛇，谁先画完，谁就先喝酒。」有一个人先画好了，他拿起酒杯喝了一口，然后看了看，他看别人都没画完，就说：「我还能给蛇画上几隻脚呢！」他还没把脚画好，另一个人就把一条蛇画完了，他把酒杯拿过去说：「蛇本来没有脚，你怎么能给蛇加上脚呢？这杯酒应该是我的。」说完他就把酒都喝了。

(1)蛇(shé): snake　　　　　(2)添 (tiān): add

(3)足 (zú): foot

Questions:

1) Why did the host ask his guests to draw a snake on the ground?

　　(To decide who can drink the wine.)

2) Why did the first person to finish decide to add a few feet to the snake?

　　(He finished before others did and had some time to kill.)

3) Why did the second person end up winning the contest?

  (Because snakes don't have legs.)

4) What do you think is the moral of this parable?

  (Don't spoil a perfectly good thing by adding something unnecessary.)

第四部分：句型與詞語練習 Grammar & Usage

A: 請用 " 自然 " 完成下面句子。

 Please complete the following sentences using "自然".

  例：A: 聽說中國菜很難做。

    B: 中國菜一點也不難做，<u>多做幾次自然就會了</u>。

1. A: 我剛到，對校園還不太熟悉。連圖書館在哪兒都不知道。

 B: 別急，_____。

2. A: 這麼多漢字，我記不住。

 B: 慢慢來，_____。

3. A: 我太久沒運動了。才跑了五分鐘就累得喘不過氣來。

 B: 沒關係，_____。

B: 請用 " 害得 " 完成下面句子。

 Please complete the following sentences using "害得".

  例：我的同屋昨天聽音樂聽到半夜，<u>害得我沒睡好覺</u>。

1. 最近報上有文章說中國菜太油，卡路里太多，_____。

2. 我跟他說好七點在電影院門口見，他差不多八點才來，_____。

3. 張先生和張太太常常吵架吵得很厲害。偶爾還當著孩子的面說些很難聽的話，_____。

C: 選用下列詞語填空。

Please fill in the blanks with the words provided.

餓壞了，氣壞了，急壞了，累壞了，樂壞了

饿坏了，气坏了，急坏了，累坏了，乐坏了

1. 你去哪兒了？你媽媽給你打了三天電話都沒找到你，她<u>急壞了</u>，你趕快給她打個電話吧。

2. A: 你有吃的東西嗎？今天我從早上一直忙到現在,沒有時間吃飯。

   B: 那你一定<u>餓壞了</u>。

3. 爲了準備考試，柯林三天沒睡覺，<u>累壞了</u>，他決定考完試以後，多睡一會兒。

4. A: 柯林，這次考試你考了第一，高興麼？

   B: 總算沒有白準備。我跟我爸爸說下學期我能拿到獎學金(jiǎngxuéjīn: scholarship)，他不用替我付學費，他聽了以後 <u>樂壞了</u>.。

5. A: 哎，柯林，張天明想選《中國歷史》，選上了嗎？我聽說很多人想選這門課。

   B: 沒有。爲了選這門課，他早上八點就去排隊了，結果還是沒選上，他<u>氣壞了</u>。

D: 完成句子。

Please complete the following dialogues using potential complements.

例： 學生：老師，明天我把課文都背下來，能考好嗎？(考不好)
　　老師： <u>明天的考試，只會背課文考不好</u>。

1. A: 你今天能做完功課嗎？

   B: ＿＿＿＿＿＿＿＿＿＿＿＿＿ , ＿＿＿＿＿＿＿＿＿＿＿。（做不完）

2. A: 如果我都考A，能得到獎學金嗎？

   B: ＿＿＿＿＿＿＿＿＿＿＿＿＿ , ＿＿＿＿＿＿＿＿＿＿＿。（得不到）

3. A: 要是沒有醫療保險，能看病嗎？

   B: ＿＿＿＿＿＿＿＿＿＿＿＿＿ , ＿＿＿＿＿＿＿＿＿＿＿。（看不起）

E: 請用 " 即使 ... 也 " 完成下面句子。

Please complete the following sentences using "即使 ... 也".

例：我弟弟對人特別好，<u>即使不認識的人他也願意幫助</u>。

1. 這道數學習題難極了，_____。

2. 王叔叔的病非常嚴重，_____。

3. 那個航空公司的飛機常常出問題，很不安全。_____。

第五部分：翻譯 Translation

A: Please translate the passage into English.

(Traditional Characters)

　　在一些第三世界國家，重男輕女的現象十分嚴重。有時候婦女在社會上有沒有地位，完全要看她能不能生男孩，或者是她能生幾個男孩。男孩生得越多，她的地位就越高。

(Simplified Characters)

　　在一些第三世界国家，重男轻女的现象十分严重。有时候妇女在社会上有没有地位，完全要看她能不能生男孩，或者是她能生几个男孩。男孩生得越多，她的地位就越高。

B: 把下面的句子譯成中文，注意中文被動意義的表達方法

Translate the following sentences into Chinese. Pay special attention to how one expresses passivity in Chinese.

1) We can eat now. Dinner is ready (cooked).

（可以吃飯了，飯做好了。）

2) The report is done. We can relax now.

（報告寫完了，我們可以輕鬆一下了。）

3) His car was stolen. He has to walk to school now.

（他的車被偷了，他只能走路去學校了。）

4) Last year she was elected "best student" by her classmates.

（去年她被同學選爲 " 最佳(最好的)學生 "。）

5) I finished reading the book. I can lend it to you if you want to read it.

(書我看完了。如果你想看的話，我可以借給你。)

C: Please translate the following passage into Chinese.

In many Asian countries the pressure on students is very great. Everyday they have a lot of homework. They cannot even take a break on weekends: they have to attend cram schools. Teachers emphasize rote-learning. In America teachers encourage students to think independently, emphasize free-wheeling development, but many people criticize the American educational system. They think that American teachers are not strict enough with the students so that the students do not have a solid foundation.

（在亞洲國家，學生的壓力很大，他們每天都有很多功課，甚至連週末也
不能休息，得上補習班。老師強調死記硬背。在美國，老師鼓勵學生獨
立思考，強調學生自由發展。可是很多人批評美國的教育制度，認為美
國的老師對學生太不嚴了，結果學生的基礎不紮實。）

D: Please translate the following passage into Chinese.

My elder brother went to high school in China. His teachers were very strict. That's why he has a very good foundation in Chinese, English and mathematics. Naturally he feels that the Chinese pedagogy is better. My younger sister did not go to elementary school till after she came to America. She never had to memorize anything through mechanic repetition. Her teachers emphasized free-wheeling development. However, when she graduated, her math was rather shaky. Her English and history were very good. Apparently although the American education method is good, there indeed are some problems.

（我哥哥是在中國上的中學。他的老師很嚴，所以他的中文英文和數學基
礎都很好。他自然覺得中國的教育方法好。我小妹是來美國以後上的小
學，從來不必死記硬背。她的老師強調讓學生自由發展。但是小妹中學
畢業以後，英文，歷史很好，可是數學的基礎不太好。看來，美國的教
育方法雖然不錯，但的確有一點問題。）

第六部分：寫作練習 Composition

談談你的中小學教育對你的學習態度和學習方法有什麼樣的影響。
要是你有孩子，你希望他在什麼樣的教育制度下長大。

第十八課　槍枝與犯罪

第一部分：聽力練習 Listening Comprehension

A: **Listen to the tape recording of *Lesson Eighteen* and answer the following questions.**

1. Why does Tianming have a gun in his room?

   (It's a birthday present for his brother.)

2. What do John and his family think of guns?

   (His father is a member of the National Rifle Association. His mother hates guns. John thinks the country is crazy when it comes to guns.)

3. What is Zhang Tianming's view on owning a gun?

   (He thinks everyone should have a gun to protect him/herself.)

4. What is John's opinion on gun control?

   (He thinks the government is not tough enough on legislation. The implementation of gun control legislation is also too lax. He also thinks all gun commercials should be banned.)

B: **Listen to the tape for the workbook.**

1. Listen to the passage and answer the following questions.

   （麗莎去中國前，她的父母很擔心，他們怕麗莎和張天明兩個人在中國旅行不安全，所以一定要麗莎和張天明參加一個旅行團，這樣每到一個地方都有導遊陪著，加上很多遊客一起活動，所以會比較安全。可是麗莎和張天明覺得參加旅行團不自由，再說，他們要在南京張天明姑媽家待好幾天，沒有辦法參加旅行團。但是不管麗莎和張天明怎麼說，麗莎的父母還是不放心，於是他們就打電話給張天明的父母，了解中國社會犯罪的情況。張天明的爸爸說，他前年去過一次中國，去了很多地方，雖然他聽說有的遊客的東西被偷了，但覺得總的來說中國還是比較安全的。他還說，在南京，麗莎和張天明去什麼地方，表哥都會陪著，所以不會有問題。如果實在不放心，他可以讓張天明的表哥跟麗莎和張天明一塊兒去西安。他這樣說了以後，麗莎的父母才放心，同意讓麗莎和張天明兩個人去中國。）

Questions:

1) What were Lisa's parents worried about?

    a. That it was not safe to travel to China.

    b. That Lisa would not get along with other tourists.

    c. That Lisa would not get along with Zhang Tianming.

    d. That Lisa and Zhang Tianming would exhaust themselves going to so many places.

2) Lisa and Zhang Tianming did not want to join a tour group because

    a. it would be more expensive.

    b.none of the itineraries included Nanjing.

    c. they wanted to stay put in Nanjing for several days.

    d. they could not find a tour group.

3) Lisa's parents called Zhang Tianming's father because

    a. They wanted to invite him to have dinner before Lisa and Zhang Tianming left for China.

    b. They were worried and wanted to know if it's safe to travel in China.

    c. Lisa wanted them to call Zhang Tianming's father.

    d. They wanted to say 'hello' to him.

4) Zhang Tianming's father told Lisa's parents it'd be safe for Lisa and Zhang Tianming because

    a. wherever Lisa and Zhang Tianming went in China, they would be accompanied by Zhang Tianming's cousin.

    b. there's virtually no crime in China.

    c. he had seen no serious crime on his last trip.

    d. he was going with them.

2. Listen to the passage and answer the following questions.

（　從前有一個小偷，在一對年輕夫婦結婚的那天，趁著房間裏沒人，
　　藏在床底下，想等到晚上他們睡著了以後出來偷東西。誰知道那對
　　年輕夫婦三天三夜不睡覺，最後那個小偷餓壞了，實在受不了了，
　　就偷偷地從床底下爬出來，可是被人看見了。小偷很害怕，他說他
　　是那位太太的醫生，太太有一種奇怪的病，她家裏人怕她晚上發
　　病，所以讓他藏在床下，如果小姐病了，他就出來給小姐看病。聽
　　了他的話，大家都不相信，可是不知道怎麼辦。有一個人出了這樣
　　一個主意：因為小偷從來沒見過那位太太，所以他讓另外一個小姐
　　出來，問小偷這是不是他家的太太，小偷說 " 是 "。大家馬上把他
　　抓起來了。）

Questions:

1) The thief hid himself

> **a**. under the bed.
>
> b. by the window.
>
> c. behind the door.
>
> d. under the table.

2) The two young people

> a. were insomniacs.
>
> **b**. were newlyweds.
>
> c. were starving.
>
> d. could not take it any more.

3) The thief came out of hiding because he

> a. repented.
>
> **b**. was starving.
>
> c. became afraid.
>
> d. got sick.

4) The thief claimed to be the bride's

    a. doctor.

    b. tutor.

    c. student.

    d. cousin.

5) The thief was exposed when

    a. people discovered things that he had stolen on him.

    b. he failed to identify the bride.

    c. the bride denied that he was her doctor.

    d. he confessed.

第二部分：口語練習 Speaking Exercises

A: Please practice asking and answering the following questions with a partner before class.

1. 過生日的時候，你希望你的好朋友送給你什麼生日禮物？

2. 什麼情況會讓你很緊張？

3. 美國哪些城市的犯罪率比較高？

4. 美國憲法保障哪些權利？

B: Please practice speaking on the following topics.

1. 美國政府應該通過什麼樣的手段來減少犯罪？

2. 你怎麼跟別人解釋一個人應該擁有槍枝？

3. 辯論：應該／不應該允許私人擁有槍枝

第三部分：閱讀練習 Reading Comprehension

A: Please read the passage and answer the following questions.

(Traditional Characters)

　　這是美國南部的一個小城。一個秋天的夜晚，約翰和他的太太從朋友家回來。約翰推開門，在黑暗中看見一個人向他跑來，約翰拿出手槍開了三槍，那個人一下子倒在了地上。約翰把燈打開，發現躺在地上的不是別人，正是他的女兒。原來，他的女兒想跟他開個玩笑，故意藏在衣櫃裏，想嚇嚇(1)他們。那天晚上，約翰的女兒在醫院裏死去。這件事情發生後，大家都沒有怪約翰開槍。當地的人多半都有槍，很多人說要是他們遇到這個情況，他們也會開槍，錯不在槍。他們認爲約翰的女兒不該開那樣的玩笑。

　　　(1)嚇嚇(xiàxia): frighten

(Simplified Characters)

　　这是美国南部的一个小城。一个秋天的夜晚，约翰和他的太太从朋友家回来。约翰推开门，在黑暗中看见一个人向他跑来，约翰拿出手枪开了三枪，那个人一下子倒在了地上。约翰把灯打开，发现躺在地上的不是别人，正是他的女儿。原来，他的女儿想跟他开个玩笑，故意藏在衣柜里，想吓吓(1)他们。那天晚上，约翰的女儿在医院里死去。这件事情发生后，大家都没有怪约翰开枪。当地的人多半都有枪，很多人说要是他们遇到这个情况，他们也会开枪，错不在枪。他们认为约翰的女儿不该开那样的玩笑。

　　　(1)吓吓(xiàxia): frighten

Questions:

1. When and where did the tragedy take place?

    (In an Autumn night, in a southern town.)

2. Where had John and his wife been?

    (Went to a friend's house.)

3. Why did John fire three shots?

   (He saw someone running towards him in the dark.)

4. Whom had he shot?

   (His own daughter.)

5. How did his neighbors react to the tragedy?

   (They didn't blame him for firing the shots. They might have done the same thing if they were John.)

6. Who did they think was at fault?

   (John's daughter.)

B: 成語故事

Please answer the questions after reading the following story.

(Traditional Characters)

樑(1)上君子(2)

你知道爲什麼中國人把小偷叫做 " 樑上君子 " 嗎？原來，中國漢朝(3)有一個叫陳是的人很會教育人。有一天晚上，陳是看見一個小偷爬到他家的屋樑上，準備等沒有人時偷東西。陳是沒有馬上叫人來抓小偷。他把他的孩子叫來，很認真地對他們說：" 一個人一定要經常提醒自己不能作壞人。壞人不是生下來就是壞人，而是因爲經常作壞事，慢慢變成壞人的，就像樑上的那位君子一樣。" 小偷聽了後嚇得從屋樑上掉(4)了下來。

(1)樑(liáng)：beam   (2)君子(jūnzi)：gentleman

(3)漢朝(Hàn Cháo)：the Han dynasty (206 B.C.E-220)

(4)掉(diào)：fall

(Simplified Characters)

梁(1)上君子(2)

你知道为什么中国人把小偷叫做 " 梁上君子 " 吗？原来，中国汉朝(3)有一个叫陈是的人很会教育人。有一天晚上，陈是看见一个小偷爬到他家的屋梁上，准备等没有人时偷东西。陈是没有马上叫人来抓小偷。他把他的孩子叫来，很认真地对他们说：" 一个人一定要经常提醒自己不能作坏人。坏人不是生下来就是坏人，而是因为经常作坏事，慢慢变成坏人的，就像梁上的那位君子一样。" 小偷听了后吓得从屋梁上掉(4)了下来。

(1)梁 (liáng)：beam   (2)君子(jūnzi)：gentleman

(3)汉朝(Hàn Cháo)：the Han dynasty (206 B.C.E-220)

(4)掉(diào)：fall

Questions:

1. What was Chen Shi good at?

   (Educating people.)

2. What was the thief doing on the beam?

   (Waiting to steal things when where was no one around.)

3. What did Chen Shi do when he spotted the thief?

  (He called in his children.)

4. What did he say to his children?

  (Bad people were not born bad. They became bad because they got used to doing bad things.)

5. What was the thief's reaction?

  (He fell down from the beam.)

6. What is "a gentleman on the beam"?

  (A thief.)

第四部分：句型與詞語練習　Grammar & Usage

A: 請用 "萬一" 完成下面對話。

Please complete the following dialogues using "萬一".

  例：A: 現在交朋友真難！我覺得由父母介紹也不錯。

    B: 我反對，<u>萬一碰上一個不好的，那怎麼辦</u>？

 1. A: 現在醫療保險那麼貴，加上我的身體一向很健康，等過兩年
   再保吧！

   B: 那不行，＿＿＿＿＿＿＿＿＿＿，到時候後悔就來不及了。

 2. A: 我想把我現在這份工作辭了。

   B: 你的工作是鐵飯碗，辭了多可惜。再說，現在沒有工作的人那
   麼多，＿＿＿＿＿＿＿＿＿＿＿＿＿，那你怎麼辦？

 3. A: 他們兩個吵得那麼厲害，好像還打架呢。你覺得我們應該不應該
   打電話給警察？

   B: 趕快找警察。＿＿＿＿＿＿＿＿＿＿＿，那就來不及了。

B: 請用 "簡直" 完成下面對話。

Please complete the following dialogues using "簡直".

  例：A: 他說話那麼衝，<u>我簡直不能跟他討論事情</u>。

    B: 可不是嗎？難怪没有人願意跟他交往。

1. A: 我隔壁同學放音樂，聲音大，＿＿＿＿＿＿＿＿＿＿＿＿＿＿＿＿。

   B: 我看你要麼到圖書館去念書，要麼趕緊搬家吧。

2. A: 那個紀錄片又長又沒意思，＿＿＿＿＿＿＿＿＿＿＿＿＿＿＿。

   B: 這個紀錄片是沒有什麼意思，但是沒辦法，為了寫報告你最好看下去。

3. A: 昨天放假，我帶朋友去夫子廟遊覽。那兒到處人山人海，

   ＿＿＿＿＿＿＿＿＿＿＿＿＿＿＿＿＿＿＿＿＿＿＿＿。

   B: 你怎麼選放假的時候去呢？人擠人肯定沒意思。

C: 請用 " 只要 " 完成對話。

Please complete the following dialogues using "只要".

例：A: 家裏有槍太危險了！要是走了火，那可不是開玩笑的。

B: 只要你把槍放在安全的地方，不要讓小孩碰，是不會有問題的。

1. A: 升學的壓力太大了，我受不了了。

   B: 別緊張，＿＿＿＿＿＿＿＿＿＿＿＿＿＿＿＿＿，一定會考上好大學。

2. A: 他這一次病得這麼厲害，真讓人擔心。

   B: 不要擔心，＿＿＿＿＿＿＿＿＿＿＿＿＿，他的病一定會好起來的。

3. A: 漢字這麼多，怎樣才能記住呢？

   B: ＿＿＿＿＿＿＿＿＿＿＿＿＿＿＿＿＿＿＿＿，就能把漢字記住。

D: 請用 " 基本上 " 完成對話。

Please complete the following dialogues using "基本上".

例： A: 這個法案只有兩三個地方解釋得不太清楚。(清楚)

B: 這個法案除了那兩三點以外，基本上還是很清楚的。

1. A: 她的未婚夫不太喜歡分擔家務。(不錯)

   B: 她的未婚夫＿＿＿＿＿＿＿＿＿＿，＿＿＿＿＿＿＿＿＿＿。

2. A: 今天老師講的語法，只有 " 了 " 的用法不太清楚。(聽懂)

   B: ＿＿＿＿＿＿＿＿＿＿，＿＿＿＿＿＿＿＿＿＿＿＿。

3. A: 這個孩子愛看卡通片，但是還是挺用功的。(用功)

   B: 這個孩子＿＿＿＿＿＿＿＿＿＿＿，＿＿＿＿＿＿＿＿＿＿。

E: 請用 " 通過 " 改寫句子。

Please rewrite the following sentences using "通過".

例：警察調查了以後，發現那些東西不是他偷的。

--->警察通過調查，發現那些東西不是他偷的。

1. 醫生檢查了以後，老張才知道自己有心臟病。

--->_____，老張才知道自己有心臟病。

2. 大家討論了以後，決定選王先生為公司的新主管。

--->_____，決定選王先生為公司的新主管。

3. 李先生介紹了以後，大家才知道今天的客人是美國有名的詩人之一。

--->_____，大家才知道今天的客人是美國有名的詩人之一。

第五部分：翻譯 Translation

A: 把下面的句子翻譯成中文，注意 " 和 " 和 " 並 " 的用法。

Translate the following sentences into Chinese. Take care to distinguish between "和" and "並".

1. Freedom of speech and assembly are rights that are guaranteed by the American Constitution.

（言論和聚會自由是美國憲法保障的權力。）

2. At the meeting we discussed Ke Lin and Zhang Tianming's suggestion, and decided to adopt it. （採納）.

（在會上我們討論並決定採納柯林和張天明的建議。）

3. The government has passed the legistration and decided to implement it immediately.

（政府通過了那項法規並決定馬上執行。）

4. His cousin studied very hard. He passed (the examinations), got into a good college, and got a scholarship.

（他的表弟(哥、姐、妹)學習非常努力，結果考進了一所好大學，並得到了獎學金。）

B: Fill in the blanks with the words provided and translate the passages into English.

並，只要，即使，正，害得，通過，看來，萬一

并，只要，即使，正，害得，通过，看来，万一

1. (Traditional Characters)

很多人認為美國的社會講究男女平等，<u>只要</u>有能力，願意做事，<u>即使</u>是女的也有機會做高職位主管。但有許多人有不同的觀點。他們指出政府<u>通過</u>各種不同手段來鼓勵婦女受教育，就業，<u>害得</u>有些男的喪失公平競爭的機會。<u>看來</u>男女平等的問題還沒有<u>真</u>正地解決。

(Simplified Characters)

很多人认为美国的社会讲究男女平等，<u>只要</u>有能力，愿意做事，<u>即使</u>是女的也有机会做高职位主管。但有许多人有不同的观点。他们指出政府<u>通过</u>各种不同手段来鼓励妇女受教育，就业，<u>害得</u>有些男的丧失公平竞争的机会。<u>看来</u>男女平等的问题还没有真正地解决。

2. (Traditional Characters)

非法移民在社會上不但沒有什麼地位，<u>並</u>常受各方的批評。<u>正</u>因為是非法進的美國，所以<u>萬一</u>出了什麼事,還不能指望警察的幫助。

(Characters)

非法移民在社会上不但没有什么地位，<u>并</u>常受各方的批评。<u>正</u>因为是非法进的美国，所以<u>万一</u>出了什么事,还不能指望警察的帮助。

C: Please translate the following passage into Chinese.

America is a free country. The Constitution ensures people have freedom of speech, freedom of assembly, freedom to bear arms. In school, teachers encourage students to give free rein to imagination and seldom require students to do mechanical memorizing. Many students do not respect their teachers. Some even verbally abuse their teachers, and bring drugs and guns into classrooms. The crime rate has gone up. The government tries to fight crime by hiring more cops and building more jail cells. However some policemen don't treat their jobs seriously and some even become criminals. Perhaps there is too much freedom in the society.

（美國是個自由的國家。憲法保障人民有言論自由，聚會自由，以及買賣槍枝的自由。在學校裏，老師鼓勵學生發揮想象力，很少要求學生死記硬背。但是很多學生不尊師重道，有的還罵老師，還有學生甚至帶毒品和槍來上課。犯罪率越來越高。爲了打擊犯罪，政府多雇了一些警察，多蓋了一些監獄。但是有些警察不認真工作，有的甚至變成了犯罪份子。也許這個社會太自由了。）

D: Translate the following passage into Chinese:

Many Americans think that having a gun to protect oneself is an important right guaranteed by the Constitution. In their view, this right is as important as freedom of speech. These Americans want the government to hire more policemen to deter crime. Others disagree. They believe too many Americans have guns, and that it is too easy to buy guns; the government should ban gun commercials on TV.

（很多美國人認爲有槍保衛自己是憲法保障的權力。在他們看來，這個權利和言論自由一樣重要。他們要求政府多僱警察。 但是有些人不同意他們的看法，他們認爲美國有槍的人太多，買槍太容易，他們還認爲政府應該禁止電視播賣槍的廣告。 ）

第六部分：寫作練習 Composition

你認爲每個人都應該有權利買槍嗎？爲什麼？

第十九課　　動物與人

A: Listen to the tape recording of *Lesson Nineteen* and answer the following questions.

1. How many protests has Ke Lin participated in the past few days?

   (Two: one in front of the biology department; the other in New York.)

2. Why is Zhang Tianming looking for Ke Lin?

   (He has two tickets for a basketball game. He wants Ke Lin to go with him.)

3. Is Ke Lin going to see the game with Zhang Tianming? Why or why not?

   (No, he is going to take part in another protest.)

4. What's Zhang Tianming's view on animal experiments?

   (If it is for finding a cure for human diseases, then he is for it.)

5. Does Ke Lin think it is right to sacrifice animals to save people's lives?

   (No, he doesn't think people are more important than animals.)

B: Listen to the tape for the workbook.

1. Listen to the passage and answer the following questions.

   （大熊貓長得十分可愛，是世界上大家最喜歡的動物之一。孩子們更喜歡它們了。說起來可能有人會不相信，西方國家大概是在二十世紀初才知道有熊貓的。開始大家都不知道熊貓到底是熊還是貓，所以中國人把這種動物叫做熊貓。熊貓每次只生一兩隻小熊貓，而且存活率很低，很多小熊貓生下來就死了，加上熊貓的主食竹子有時會大量死亡，所以熊貓的數量越來越少。現在世界上的熊貓不到一千隻。七十年代，中國政府送給了美國、日本、英國等國家一些熊貓。現在外國的動物園可以向中國借大熊貓，但是中國不再送了。）

Questions:

1) Why do the Chinese call the panda "*xióngmāo?*"

   (Because no one knew whether it was a bear or a cat.)

2) What did the Chinese government do in the seventies?

   (They gave some pandas to other countries as gifts.)

3) What could foreign zoos do to exhibit pandas?

   (They could borrow them from China.)

4) What other facts can you recall from this passage?

2. Please listen to the passage and answer the following questions.

   New Vocabulary:

   代表 (dàibiǎo): represent   羊 (yáng): lamb

   兔 (tù): rabbit   尾巴 (wěiba): tail

（ 中國人用十二種動物來代表十二年。這十二種動物叫十二生肖。比
如說，1974年是虎年，如果你是1974年出生的，你就是屬虎的，虎
就是你的生肖。1976年是龍年，如果你是1976年出生的，那你就是
屬龍的，龍就是你的生肖。1978年是馬年，如果你是1978年出生
的，你就屬馬，你的生肖就是馬。以前，很多中國人不願意在羊年
生女孩子，因爲他們認爲羊年出生的女孩子將來生活不好，命會很
苦。還有的中國人不願意在兔年結婚，因爲他們怕他們的婚姻會像
兔子的尾巴那樣短，所以很多人會趕在兔年以前，也就是在虎年結
婚，或者等到下一年，也就是龍年結婚。雖然現在已經是二十世紀
了，還是有些人相信這些。）

Questions:

1) 1974 was the year of the

   a. rabbit.

   b. lamb.

   c. horse

   d. tiger.

2) 1976 was the year of the

    a. dragon.

    b. lamb.

    c. rabbit.

    d. horse.

3) 1978 was the year of the

    a. lamb.

    b. horse.

    c. tiger.

    d. rabbit.

4) People were reluctant to have children in the year of the lamb because they believed that

    a. their children would have unhappy lives.

    b. it was usually a time of famine.

    c. their children would die young.

    d. their children would be less intelligent.

5) People were reluctant to get married in the year of the rabbit because they feared that

    a. their marriage would not last.

    b. their marriage would be an unhappy one.

    c. they would have too many children.

    d. their spouse would commit adultery.

6) The year of the rabbit comes after the year of the

    a. lamb.

    b. horse.

    c. tiger.

    d. dragon.

7) The year of the rabbit comes before the year of the

    a. lamb.

    b. horse.

    c. tiger.

    d. dragon.

8) What is "*shēngxiào?*"

第二部分：口語練習 Speaking Exercises

A: Please practice asking and answering the following questions with a partner before class.

1. 你會為了什麼事情上街抗議？
2. 你覺得什麼樣的抗議行為有點兒太過分？
3. 要是你發現有人虐待孩子，你會怎麼辦？
4. 美國政府現在面臨的最大難題是什麼？

B: Please practice speaking on the following topics.

1. 如果通過動物實驗來研究藥物，結果會怎麼樣？
2. 請談談生態不平衡會帶來什麼樣的問題。

第三部分：閱讀練習 Reading Comprehension

A: Please fill in the blanks with the words provided.

(Traditional Characters)

禁止，手段，採取，通過，犯罪，降低，保障，提高

最近十幾年來，中國政府為了降低人口出生率，採取了各種手段。但是社會學家指出，解決人口問題最根本的方法是提高婦女的社會地位，從法律上保障婦女的權利。為此，中國人大通過了婦女和兒童權利保護法，禁止販賣婦女等各種犯罪行為。

(Simplified Characters)

禁止，手段，採取，通过，犯罪，降低，保障，提高

　　最近十几年来，中国政府为了<u>降低</u>人口出生率，<u>採取</u>了各种<u>手段</u>。但是社会学家指出，解决人口问题最根本的方法是<u>提高</u>妇女的社会地位，从法律上<u>保障</u>妇女的权利。为此，中国人大<u>通过</u>了妇女和儿童权利保护法，<u>禁止</u>贩卖妇女等各种<u>犯罪</u>行为。

B: Please answer the questions after reading the following passage.

(Traditional Characters)

　　　　動物在世界各國文化中都佔有很重要的地位，中國也一樣。比如，在中國的農村男孩子常常戴虎頭帽(1)，穿虎頭鞋。端午節的時候，中國人要賽龍舟。過新年的時候，中國人要舞獅(2)。在國外，每當中國新年的時候，中國城的舞獅表演往往吸引很多人去觀看。在中國，不僅漢族舞獅，有的少數民族也有舞獅的習慣，例如中國南方的僮族(3)。僮族的舞獅很有特色，他們把很多凳子(4)擺(5)起來，前邊的一個人拿著球引獅子爬(6)到凳子頂上。獅子是由兩個人扮演的，所以要爬到最上邊的凳子上，非常困難。大家敲鑼打鼓(7)，又喊又叫，十分熱鬧。雖然快二十一世紀了，大家對這些民間風俗習慣還是很喜歡。

(1)帽 (mào: hat)	(2)獅 (shī: lion)
(3)僮族 (Zhuàng: the Zhuang nationality)	(4)凳子 (dèngzi: bench)
(5)擺 (luò: pile up)	(6)爬 (pá: climb)
(7)敲鑼打鼓 (qiāo luó dǎ gǔ: beat gongs and drums)	

(Simplified Characters)

　　　　动物在世界各国文化中都占有很重要的地位，中国也一样。比如，在中国的农村男孩子常常戴虎头帽(1)，穿虎头鞋。端午节的时候，中国人要赛龙舟。过新年的时候，中国人要舞狮(2)。在国外，每当中国新年的时候，中国城的舞狮表演往往吸引很多人去观看。在中国，不仅汉族舞狮，有的少数民族也有舞狮的习惯，例如中国南方的壮族(3)。壮族的舞狮很有特色，他们把很多凳子(4)擺(5)起来，前边的一个人拿着球引狮子爬(6)到凳子顶上。狮子是由两个人扮演的，所以要爬到最上边的凳子上，非常困

难。大家敲锣打鼓(7)，又喊又叫，十分热闹。虽然快二十一世纪了，大家对这些民间风俗习惯还是很喜欢。

(1)帽 (mào: hat)

(2)狮 (shī: lion)

(3)壮族 (Zhuàng: the Zhuang nationality)

(4)凳子 (dèngzi: bench)

(5)摞 (luò: pile up)

(6)爬 (pá: climb)

(7)敲锣打鼓 (qiāo luó dǎ gǔ: beat gongs and drums)

Questions:

1) Can you give an example of the popularity of the tiger in Chinese folk costumes?

   (Boys wear tiger hats and tiger shoes.)

2) Is the lion dance confined to the Han people?

   (No, some minorities also have lion dance.)

3) Can you describe the Zhuang lion dance?

   (The lion, played by two people, follows a ball and climbs up to the top of a pile of benches.)

4) In Chinese communities the dragon boat race is often associated with a particular festival. What is that festival?

   (the Dragon Boat Festival or Duanwu Jie)

5) Where is the custom of wearing "tiger-head" hats most prevalent in China?

   (In rural areas)

C: 成語故事

Please answer the questions after reading the following story.

(Traditional Characters)

朝(1)三 暮(2)四

　　從前有個養(3)猴子的人，大家都叫他狙公(4)，意思是猴子先生。狙公養了很多猴子，他很了解猴子。他說的話猴子們也能聽懂。

　　狙公的猴子都很喜歡吃一種果子，每天都要吃很多，狙公沒有錢給猴子買那麼多的果子了，他想少給猴子吃點果子，可是他怕猴子不高興，於是就想了個辦法。

　　一天早上，狙公對猴子們說：〝從現在起，我每天早上給你們三個果子、晚上四個，你們說好不好？〞猴子們聽了都說不好，覺得給得太少。狙公於是笑著說：〝那麼，早上四個，晚上三個，好不好？〞猴子們聽了，個個都很高興，都不吵了。

　　" 朝三暮四 " 這句話就是從這個故事來的。但是這個成語有特別的意思：一個人一會兒這樣，一會兒那樣，不可相信。

(1)朝(zhāo)：morning	(2)暮(mù)：dusk
(3)養(yǎng)：raise	(4)狙公(jūgōng)：a person's name

(Simplified Characters)

朝(1) 三 暮(2) 四

　　从前有个养(3)猴子的人，大家都叫他狙公(4)，意思是猴子先生。狙公养了很多猴子，他很了解猴子。他说的话猴子们也能听懂。

　　狙公的猴子都很喜欢吃一种果子，每天都要吃很多，狙公没有钱给猴子买那么多的果子了，他想少给猴子吃点果子，可是他怕猴子不高兴，于是就想了个办法。

　　一天早上，狙公对猴子们说：" 从现在起，我每天早上给你们三个果子、晚上四个，你们说好不好？" 猴子们听了都说不好，觉得给得太少。狙公於是笑着说：" 那么，早上四个，晚上三个，好不好？" 猴子们听了，个个都很高兴，都不吵了。

　　" 朝三暮四 " 这句话就是从这个故事来的。但是这个成语有特别的意思：一个人一会儿这样，一会儿那样，不可相信。

(1)朝(zhāo)：morning	(2)暮(mù)：dusk
(3)养(yǎng)：raise	(4)狙公(jūgōng)：a person's name

Questions:

1) Why was the man called Jugong?

   (He raised many monkeys.)

2) Why did Jugong want to stop feeding so many nuts to the monkeys?

   (He couldn't afford it.)

3) Why did the monkeys prefer the second plan?

   (They thought they were getting more nuts out of the second plan.)

4) How did the second feeding plan differ from the first one?

*(The first one would give 3 nuts in the morning and 4 in the evening. The
second plan was just the opposite.)*

   5) What does the idiom "朝三暮四" mean?

     *(It refers to someone who cannot make up his/her mind or someone is not
trustworthy.)*

第四部分：句型與詞語練習 Grammar & Usage

A: 請用 " 憑什麼 " 完成下面對話。

Please complete the following dialogues using "憑什麼".

  例 ： A: 小李又加薪了。

      B: 我們工作得那麼努力都沒有人給我們加薪，<u>小李憑什麼加
薪</u>？

  1. A: 請你不要吸煙，我受不了煙味。

     B: 這又不是你家，＿＿＿＿＿＿＿＿＿＿＿＿＿＿＿＿？

  2. A: 我不懂老師為什麼只給我一個B，沒給我A。

     B: 你做實驗常常做不出結果，＿＿＿＿＿＿＿＿＿＿＿＿？

  3. A: 請你不要說這些難聽的話。

     B: 憲法保障我有言論自由，＿＿＿＿＿＿＿＿＿＿＿＿＿？

B: 請用 " 儘量 " 完成下面對話。

Please complete the following dialogues using "儘量".

  例：A: 醫生, 我父親出院以後，應該注意些什麼？

     B: 他應該按時吃藥，<u>儘量多休息</u>。

  1. A: 她懷孕以後，先生對她特別體貼。

     B: 可不是嗎？家務事都是他做，＿＿＿＿＿＿＿＿＿＿＿。

  2. A: 這兩天放假，你為什麼不出去走走？

     B: 過年過節到哪兒都是人，我＿＿＿＿＿＿＿＿＿＿＿＿。

  3. A: 最近的電視節目越做越糟糕。孩子看了很容易學壞。

B: 可不是嗎?因為我怕我的孩子受不好的影響，＿＿＿＿＿＿＿＿＿＿。

C: 用「因為」或「為了」填空。

Please fill in the blanks using "因為" or "為了".

1. 為了節省錢，我決定畢業後搬回家裏住。
2. 因為我沒有工作、沒有錢，畢業後我只能搬回家裏住。
3. 爸爸說：「我這樣做是為了你好。」
4. 許多人認為為了減少犯罪，政府應該立法禁止槍枝買賣。
5. 因為很多中國人重男輕女，很多女孩生下來沒人要，真可憐。
6. 為了保護動物，很多人設立了私人的動物保護區。

D: 請用「而」完成下面的句子。

Please complete the following sentences using "而".

例：她為了學習美國文化而到美國留學。

1. 他為了提高中文水平＿＿＿＿＿＿＿＿＿＿＿＿＿＿＿＿。
2. 為了＿＿＿＿＿＿＿＿＿＿＿＿＿＿＿＿是非常沒有必要的。
3. 因為輸了場球＿＿＿＿＿＿＿＿＿＿＿＿＿是很不應該的。

E: 請用「其中」完成下面的對話。

Please complete the following dialogues using "其中".

例： A: 那個人為什麼被警察帶走了？

B: 他犯了很多罪，其中有非法賭博，吸毒，偷竊，和搶劫等等。

1. A: 你昨天去動物園看到什麼動物了？
   B: 那個動物園的動物很多，＿＿＿＿＿＿＿＿＿＿＿＿。

2. A: 昨天報上有一篇關於中國的報導，談到中國現在面臨的難題。
   B: 對，我也看到了。文章中提到了好幾個方面的問題，
      ＿＿＿＿＿＿＿＿＿＿＿＿＿＿＿＿。

3. A: 你去年暑假去什麼地方旅行了？
   B: 我遊覽了中國的許多城市。＿＿＿＿＿＿＿＿＿＿＿＿。

F: 請用 " 由於 " 改寫下面句子。

Please rewrite the following sentences using "由於".

例：中國南方地少人多，許多人移民他處，往外發展。

--->由於中國南方地少人多，許多人移民他處，往外發展。

1. 中西部在鬧水災，我們不能坐火車，得改坐飛機。

   --->＿＿＿＿＿＿＿＿＿＿＿＿＿＿＿＿＿＿＿＿＿＿＿＿。

2. 前幾年美國經濟情況不好，很多人找不到工作。

   --->＿＿＿＿＿＿＿＿＿＿＿＿＿＿＿＿＿＿＿＿＿＿＿＿。

3. 我們學校的教練很努力，學校的運動員在比賽中拿到了好幾面金牌和
   銀牌。

   --->＿＿＿＿＿＿＿＿＿＿＿＿＿＿＿＿＿＿＿＿＿＿＿＿。

第五部分：翻譯 Translation

A: Translate the following passage into Chinese.

There is an elementary school near our home. Yesterday I saw many parents arrive at the school. I heard that a teacher had hit a boy. The principal said that the reason that the teacher had hit the student was that he made fun of the teacher. The parents thought even if the student had done something wrong, the teacher should only have educated him. In order to avoid causing parents' protesting, the principal fired the teacher. Some teachers thought that the principal was being unfair. However, the parents thought the teacher had brought the consequence on himself.

（我們家附近有一所小學。昨天，我看見很多學生家長到學校來。據說，因爲有一個老師打了一個男學生。可是，校長說那個老師所以打學生，是因爲學生開老師的玩笑。家長們認爲，即使學生有錯，也只能教育。校長爲了避免引起家長的抗議，就把那個老師辭了。有的老師認爲校長這麼做不公平，但是家長們認爲那個老師是自食其果。）

2. Please translate the following passage into Chinese.

I think animal abuse is barbaric behavior. Neither do I approve animal dissection for the sake of curing humans of diseases. We should protect animals and maintain the ecological balance as much as we can, and make our habitat (生存的地方) better and better.

（我認爲虐待動物是很野蠻的行爲。我也不同意爲了給人治病，就去解剖動物。我們應該儘量保護動物，保持生態平衡，使我們生存的地方越來越好。）

第六部分：寫作練習 Composition

請你談談對某些動物保護組織如PETA的看法。

What do you think of some animal protection groups such as PETA? Do you think some of the people involved are overly sentimental and go overboard sometimes?

第二十課　　環境保護

A: Listen to the tape recording of *Lesson Twenty* and answer the following questions.

1. Why couldn't Zhang Tianming find Li Zhe?

    (He was in the lab doing research and writing reports.)

2. Who was the culprit for the pollution?

    (A chemical plant in town.)

3. Why did the government sponsor the research rather than the chemical plant?

    (The chemical plant claimed that it couldn't afford to clean up the mess.)

4. Why did the chemical plant claim that it couldn't afford to clean up the mess?

    (Because it would increase the production cost too much and make the plant less competitive on the world market.)

5. What kind of environmental damage had the chemical plant caused? Give two examples.

    (The pine grove had died. Because of acid rains, the reservoir was heavily polluted.)

B: Listen to the tape for the workbook.

1. Please listen to the passage and answer the following questions.

（安娜住在加州，是一位有三個孩子的中年婦女。安娜已經有一年半沒有看報、看電視了。別人覺得很奇怪，因為安娜在大學學的是新聞專業，雖然她畢業後沒有當記者，可是她一直很愛看報、看電視，特別是愛看電視新聞。她的先生解釋說，現在報紙、電視經常報導有關環境污染的消息，安娜看了後覺得很緊張。比如說，前一陣子，報紙、電視說超級市場上賣的蘋果對健康有害，不能吃，一個有名的電影女明星也跟著人說美國的蘋果不安全。本來安娜天天讓她的孩子吃蘋果，這樣一來，她再也不敢買蘋果了。可是過了幾個月，報紙又說蘋果很安全，大家可以放心地吃。安娜不知道應該相信誰。又比如，兩年前，很多電視節目和報紙文章說住在高壓電線旁對身體不好，安娜看了以後就非要搬家不可。她要把她原來的房子賣了，搬到另外一個地方去，可是沒有人願意賣她的房子。最後她只能大減價，才把房子賣了，安娜很生氣，從此以後，安娜再也不看報、不看電視了。）

Questions:

1) Anna has not read a newspaper or watched TV for a year and a half because

    a. she is too busy raising her three children.

    b. she can no longer afford newspapers or cable TV.

    c. the media coverage makes her nervous.

    d. she has never been interested in any form of journalism.

2) According to the media, apples

    a. are a good source of nutrition.

    b. are unsafe.

    c. have been endorsed by a well-known film star as a health food.

    d. are in short supply.

3) Anna insisted on moving from her old house because

    a. it was too small for her family.

    b. the mortgage was getting too high.

    c. it sat near a high-voltage power line.

    d. she wanted to be near her children.

4) Anna had to lower the price of the house because

    a. no one wanted to buy it.

    b. she wanted to sell it immediately.

    c. others advised her to do so.

    d. the house was crumbling.

2. Listen to the passage and answer the following questions.

New Vocabulary: 泡沫 pàomò: foam

（這是中國南方的一個小鎮，1994年夏天的一天。那一天小鎮的居民醒來後突然發現鎮裏的小河的河水變白了，河面上出現一些白色的泡沫和大片的死魚。大家都不知道出了什麼事。經過當地環保局的調查，原來是鎮上的一家工廠偷偷地向河裏排放了大量的工業廢水。廠長說他的壓力很大，現在競爭很厲害，他們的工廠無法自己解決廠裏的廢水問題。可是，他不承認是他叫工人向河裏排放廢水的。政府環保局問工人，工人說是廠領導讓他們在深夜向河裏倒污水的。事情發生後一個多星期，鎮上的居民不能喝河裏的水，日常生活出現了很大的困難，很多人身體不舒服。雖然這幾年鎮上的居民生活改善了，但是附近的環境卻一天不如一天。鎮上有很多人在那家工廠工作，工廠給他們帶來了很多好處。廠裏向河裏排放廢水後，大家都開始考慮是經濟發展重要還是環境保護重要。）

Questions:

1) When did the incident described in the passage happen?

   (In the summer of 1994)

2) Where did it happen?

   (In a town in southern China)

3) How did the inhabitants of the town find the river when they woke up?

   (They found a lot of white foam and dead fish)

4) What had happened to the river?

   (A factory had discharged waste water directly into the river.)

5) What was the factory director's excuse?

   (They couldn't afford to treat the waste water.)

6) What were the consequences of the calamity for the town's inhabitants?

   (Many people felt sick. The water of the river was not drinkable.)

7) What changes had the factory brought to the town?

   (Living situation had improved but the environment had suffered.)

8) What question did the town's inhabitants begin to ponder?

(They had to ask themselves which was more important: economic development or environmental protection?)

第二部分：口語練習　Speaking Exercises

A: Please practice asking and answering the following questions with a partner before class.

1. 這幾天你都在忙些什麼？
2. 什麼樣的地方是大學城？
3. 怎麼樣可以減少對空氣的污染？
4. 什麼樣的污染會對人體健康造成很大的危害？

B: Please practice speaking on the following topics.

1. 請談談政府應採取什麼措施來鼓勵私人工廠治理三廢問題。
2. 請談談核能發電的優缺點。

第三部分：閱讀練習　Reading Comprehension

A: Please answer the questions after reading the following passage.

(Traditional Characters)

對許多發展中國家來說，在發展經濟的同時如何保護環境是一個大難題。很多第三世界國家認為，對他們來說發展經濟比環境保護更重要，等經濟發達了再來考慮環境保護也不晚，他們對西方國家對第三世界國家提出的要求也表示不滿。在他們看來，保護熱帶雨林雖然重要，但是他們首先要解決的是老百姓的吃飯問題。西方國家不能不考慮第三世界國家的生存問題。他們也認為西方發達國家對環境造成的污染遠遠超過發展中國家，所以西方國家應該負更大的責任。

(Simplified Characters)

对许多发展中国家来说，在发展经济的同时如何保护环境是一个大难题。很多第三世界国家认为，对他们来说发展经济比环境保护更重要，等经济发达了再来考虑环境保护也不晚，他们对西方国家对第三世界国家提出的要求也表示不满。在他们看来，保护热带雨林虽然重要，但是他们首先要解决的是老百姓的吃饭问题。西方国家不能不考虑第三世界国家的生存问题。他们也认为西方发达国家对环境造成的污染远远超过发展中国家，所以西方国家应该负更大的责任。

True or false:

1) T 很多第三世界國家認爲環境保護不是最重要的事情。

2) T 很多發展中國家認爲對她們來說發展經濟更重要。

3) T 發展中國家人民吃飯和穿衣的問題很重要。

4) T 第三世界國家認爲發達國家應該對世界環境保護多負責任。

B: As China's economy develops at a break neck speed, its environment is taking a heavy toll. News of environmental degradation now appears regularly in the Chinese media. Answer the questions after you skim through the following paragraph. (New words：噸 dūn：ton，逾 yú：surpass)

長江沿岸排污嚴重
每年逾百四十億噸

(本報綜合報道)據長江流域水資源保護局提供的資料，近年來長江沿岸五十多個城市和十五萬多家企業每年排放到長江的工業和生活廢水不下一百四十億噸。而地處長江與大運河交匯處的江蘇錫江諫壁發電廠，近年每年有近八十萬噸煤灰渣排入長江。成爲全國聞名的污染大戶。

1) What is the gist of the title?

   (The pollution problem is very serious along the Yangtze River.)

2) How much industrial and residential waste water is discharged into the Yangtze River each year?

   (14 billion tons)

3) Where does the waste water come from?

   (From the fifty cities and 150 thousand industries along the Yangtze River.)

4) Who is the largest culprit?

   (The power plant along the river.)

5) How many tons of coal cinders does it discharge each year?

   (800 thousand tons)

6) Where is it located?

   (At the confluence of the Yangtze River and the Grand Cannel.)

C: 成語故事

Please answer the questions after reading the following passage.

(Traditional Characters)

竭澤而漁 (1)

　　春秋時期(770-476 B.C.E.)楚國攻打晉國(2)。當時楚國強，晉國弱。晉文公(3)問他的大官狐偃(4)怎樣才能打敗(5)楚國。狐偃說："如果是送禮物，越精美(6)越好，如果是打仗，越奸詐(7)越好。所以打楚國您得用計策(8)。"
晉文公把狐偃的主意說給他的另一個大官雍季(9)聽。雍季不同意狐偃的主
意，他說："把池塘(10)裏的水都抽乾了(11)，當然能捉到魚，可是第二年
就沒有魚了。把樹林裏的草都燒光了，當然能打得到動物，但是第二年就
沒有動物了。奸詐也一樣，可能偶爾用一次會成功，但是下一次就不能再
用了，所以這不是長遠的辦法。"可是雍季沒有更好的建議，晉文公只能採
用狐偃的辦法。晉文公用狐偃的建議打敗了楚國，可是他卻重賞(12)雍季，
大家都覺得很奇怪。晉文公解釋說："雍季的話對我一輩子都有用，而狐
偃的話只是暫時有用。我當然得重賞雍季。"

現在大家用"竭澤而漁"來比喻(13)人沒有限度的不顧後果的索取(14)。

(1)竭澤而漁(jié zé ér yú)	(2)晉(Jìn)國: State of Jin
(3)晉文公: Duke Wen of Jin	(4)狐偃(Húyàn): a person's name
(5)打敗(bài): defeat	(6)精美(jīngměi): exquisite
(7)奸詐(jiānzhà): deception; treachery	(8)計策(jìcè): scheme
(9)雍季(Yōngjì): a person's name	(10)池塘(chítáng): pond
(11)抽乾(chōu gān): drain completely	(12)重賞(zhòng shǎng): reward lavishly
(13)比喻(bǐyù): describe	(14)索取(suǒqǔ): take; exhaust

(Simplified Characters)

竭泽而渔 (1)

春秋时期(770-476 B.C.E.)楚国攻打晋国(2)。当时楚国强，晋国弱。晋
文公(3)问他的大官狐偃(4)怎样才能打败(5)楚国。狐偃说："如果是送礼物，
越精美(6)越好，如果是打仗，越奸诈(7)越好。所以打楚国您得用计策(8)。"
晋文公把狐偃的主意说给他的另一个大官雍季(9)听。雍季不同意狐偃的主
意，他说："把池塘(10)里的水都抽乾了(11)，当然能捉到鱼，可是第二年
就没有鱼了。把树林里的草都烧光了，当然能打得到动物，但是第二年就
没有动物了。奸诈也一样，可能偶尔用一次会成功，但是下一次就不能再
用了，所以这不是长远的办法。"可是雍季没有更好的建议，晋文公只能採
用狐偃的办法。晋文公用狐偃的建议打败了楚国，可是他却重赏(12)雍季，
大家都觉得很奇怪。晋文公解释说："雍季的话对我一辈子都有用，而狐
偃的话只是暂时有用。我当然得重赏雍季。"

现在大家用"竭泽而渔"来比喻(13)人没有限度的不顾后果的索取(14)。

(1)竭泽而渔 (jié zé ér yú)

(2)晋 (Jìn)国: State of Jin

(3)晋文公: Duke Wen of Jin

(4)狐偃 (Húyàn): a person's name

(5)打敗 (bài): defeat

(6)精美 (jīngměi): exquisite

(7)奸诈 (jiānzhà): deception; treachery

(8)计策 (jìcè): scheme

(9)雍季 (Yōngjì): a person's name

(10)池塘 (chítáng): pond

(11)抽乾 (chōu gān): drain completely

(12)重賞 (zhòng shǎng): reward lavishly

(13)比喻 (bǐyù): describe

(14)索取 (suǒqǔ): take; exhaust

Questions:

1) Why couldn't Jin have defeated Chu without resorting to some sort of a scheme?

   (Because Jin was much more powerful than Chu.)

2) What was Huyan's suggestion to Duke Wen?

   (His suggestion was to defeat Jin through a clever scheme.)

3) Why did Yongji disapprove of Huyan's suggestion?

   (He said that any scheme could only work onc; it wouldn't help the country in the long run.)

4) Why did Duke Wen reward Yongji lavishly instead of Huyan?

   (He felt Yongji's advice would benefit him for the rest of his life.)

第四部分：句型與詞語練習 Grammar & Usage

A: 請用 " 爲什麼 " 或 " 怎麼 " 填空。

Please fill in the blanks using "爲什麼" or "怎麼".

1. <u>怎麼</u>他還沒有來？平時他八點就到學校了，現在都十點半了。

2. 你<u>爲什麼</u>上這所大學？這所大學很有名吧？

3. 平平，你已經十歲了，<u>怎麼</u>還要媽媽給你穿衣服？

B: 請用 " 往往 " 或 " " 填空。

Please fill in the blanks using "往往" or "常常".

1. 你有十年沒來看我了，以後你要<u>常常</u>來看我。

2. 我<u>常常</u>想去歐洲，可是一直沒有時間去。

3. 研究新藥治病<u>往往／常常</u>得用動物做實驗。

C: 填空。

Fill in the blanks.

1. 改革開放以後的犯罪率比改革開放以前的犯罪率<u>高多了</u>。(很高／高多了)

2. 你母親現在的身體怎麼樣？<u>好多了</u>。(好多了／好得多)

3. 發展中國家的環保意識比發達國家<u>薄弱得多</u>。(薄弱得多／有一點薄弱)

D: 完成下面句子。

Please complete the following sentences.

1. 下個月我的女朋友結婚，她請我參加他的婚禮，我實在不知道應該怎麼辦。去吧，_____，不去吧，_____。

2. 她找男朋友很挑剔，男朋友長得怎麼樣她特別在乎。_____吧，她不喜歡，_____吧，她也不喜歡。

3. 這件事情很重要，我要不要現在給張教授打個電話告訴他？可現在已經是晚上十一點了。打吧，_____，不打吧，_____。

4. 這套運動服顏色樣子都不錯，就是價錢有點貴。買吧，_____，不買吧，_____。

E: 請用 " 以為 " 完成下面的對話。

Please complete the following dialogues using "以為".

例： A: 你怎麼現在才來？我等你已經等了一個多鐘頭了。

B: 我以為現在才八點。我的錶慢了，非常對不起。

1. A: 那門課你怎麼上了一半就不上了？

B: 我_____，沒想到難得很，所以就不上了。(容易)

2. A: 你條件那麼好，為什麼不申請那個工作？

   B: 我＿＿＿＿＿＿＿＿＿＿，所以沒申請。（工作經驗不夠）

3. A: 哎，你怎麼病了？你身體不是挺好的嗎？

   B: 我太胖了，最近在減肥。我＿＿＿＿＿＿，沒想到反而病了。

   （對身體好）

F: 請用"造成"完成下面的對話。

   Please complete the following dialogues using "造成".

   例：最近這場大雪，給交通造成很大的困難。

1. A: 在附近建化學工廠，增加就業機會，有什麼不好？（污染）

   B: 當然不好，＿＿＿＿＿＿＿＿＿＿＿＿＿＿＿。

2. A: 他們整天不是吵架就是打架，是不是要離婚了？　　　（影響）

   B: 他們想過要分手，但是怕對孩子＿＿＿＿＿＿＿，所以不離了。

3. A: 現在的電腦真厲害，什麼事都能做。（造成）

   B: 就是因為電腦什麼都能做，＿＿＿＿＿＿＿＿＿。

第五部分：翻譯　Translation

A: Please translate the following passage into Chinese.

America is one of the world's big energy [producing and consuming] nations. But America is unlike China. In America most power plants use oil to generate electricity. Besides there are many nuclear power stations in America. Although nuclear energy causes little pollution to the environment, many people oppose nuclear energy because they are concerned that nuclear stations are not safe enough.

（美國是世界上的能源大國之一。可是美國和中國不一樣，在美國，大多數的發電廠用石油來發電。另外，美國有很多核電站。雖然核能對環境造成的污染很小，但很多人反對核能，因為他們擔心核電站不夠安全。）

B: Please translate the following passage into Chinese.

My family lives in a small town in the southern part of America. The natural environment there is very good. The sky is blue, the mountains green; the water is very clean. Because there are no factories there, there is no pollution. Recently the state government proposed to build an incinerator (焚化爐) near our home, which attracted the opposition of the all the residents of the town. They all went to the local government to protest. They believed that if this kind of incinerator were built, it would cause environmental pollution, and that the consequences would be unthinkable. Eventually, the municipal government decided to build the incinerator elsewhere.

（我家住在美國南部的一個小城市。那裏的自然環境很好。天空是藍色的，山是綠色的，水很清。因爲那兒沒有工廠，所以沒有污染。最近州政府想在我家附近建一個焚化爐，引起全市居民的反對。他們都到當地政府去抗議。他們認爲如果建這個焚化爐，會造成環境污染，後果將不堪設想。最後市政府決定把焚化爐建到別的地方去了。）

C: Translate the following passage into Chinese.

Because of the need to develop the economy, many countries underestimate the importance of protecting the environment. As a result, the decrease of rain forests has led to ecological imbalance. Many animals are on the verge of extinction. In addition, the global weather has become abnormal. More and more people have incurable diseases. In order to find the medicine for these diseases, researchers have to use animals for medical experiments. However, there are organizations protesting this and claiming that animal experiments are barbaric. On the other hand, is it humane to see people die from diseases?

（爲了發展經濟，很多國家忽略了環境保護的重要。結果，熱帶雨林減少了，造成生態不平衡。許多動物瀕臨滅絕。此外，世界各地的天氣也不正常。越來越多人得一些治不了的病。爲了研究治病的藥，科學家得用動物做實驗。但是有些組織抗議說用動物做實驗太野蠻。反過來，難道讓人死於疾病就人道嗎？）

第六部分：寫作練習 Composition

請你談談對發展中國家經濟和環境哪個更重要。

APPENDIX

TEACHER'S GRAMMAR NOTES

第一課　開學

1. "了"：

　　動態助詞"了"的意思是"實現、完成"，有兩種位置，一是在動詞後，一是在句末。用"了"時，通常表示在某一個時間出現了某事，完成了某種動作或發生了某種變化，句中往往有一個表示時間的詞語。

　　"了"位於動詞後時，表示動作的實現或完成：

　　(1)昨天上午我看了一個電影。

　　(2)去年我媽媽去了一次北京，在那兒住了很長時間。

　　(3) A：這本書你看了嗎？

　　　　B：看了。

　　如果動詞和"了"後有賓語，後面又沒有另外一個"了"或後續句時，賓語前應該有定語，最常用的是數量詞，如例(1)、(2)的第一個分句，也可以是形容詞、名詞等等，如例(2)的第二個分句。

　　"了"用在句尾時，常常表示出現了一種新情況、一種新的變化，或一件事情、一種狀態發生、完成了。例如：

　　(4)四月了，天氣慢慢暖和了。

　　(5)我原來打算今天晚上看電影，可是明天要考試，所以不看了。

　　(6)A：你昨天做什麼了？

　　　　B：看電影了。

　　有時句子中沒有出現時間詞語，表示的時間就是"現在"或"到現在為止"如例(3)。再如：

　　(7)A：你吃飯了嗎？

　　　　B：吃了。

　　　　A：花了多少錢？

　　　　B：十塊錢。

有時用"了"的句子，沒有時間詞語，這種句子一般包括有兩個動詞短

語，動作發生的時間是一個相對的時間，即前一個動詞短語所表示的動作
完成的時間就是後一個動詞短語所表示的動作發生的時間。如：

(8) 他下了課就來了。

(9) 我吃了飯就去。

在例(8)中，＂來＂的時間是＂下了課＂以後，例(9)中，＂吃了飯＂
是＂去＂的時間。

2. ＂是...的＂結構：

當聽話、說話雙方知道一個動作或一件事情已經發生，而要說明事情
發生的時間、地點、方式、目的以及動作者等等情況時，就應該用
＂是...的＂結構，＂是＂可以用，也可以不用。

(1) A：王老師來了嗎？

B：來了。

A：(是)什麼時候來的？

B：昨天晚上來的。

A：(是)跟誰一起來的？

B：是跟他姐姐一起來的。

A：是坐飛機來的還是開車來的？

B：開車來的。

(2) 張天明是在波士頓出生的。

(張天明已經出生，聽話人當然已經知道了。)

(3) A：你是大學生嗎？

B：不，我是研究生。

A：你是在哪兒上的大學？

B：在波士頓大學。

因此，如果已經知道動作發生了，而要問或要說明動作發生的時間、
地點等等時，就應該用＂是...的＂結構，而不要用＂了＂。

3. ＂除了...以外，還...＂：

"除了...以外，還..."是一個包括式，"除了"和"還"後的詞語所表示的人或事都包括在所談論的人或事中。

(1)他除了學中文以外，還學法文。

（＝他學中文，也學法文。）

(2)我們班除了小王以外，還有小林去過中國。

（＝小王和小林都去過中國。）

(3)我晚上除了看書以外，還願意看電視。

（＝我晚上願意看書，也願意看電影。）

相反，"除了...以外，都..."是排除式，後面的句子所表示的情況不包括"了"後的詞語所表示的人或事物。例如：

(4)除了小柯以外，我們班都去過中國。

（＝小柯沒去過中國。）

(5)除了看書以外，晚上什麼事我都願意做。

（＝我晚上不願意看書。）

4. "再說"：

"再說"用於進一步說明原因：

(1)你別走了，天太晚了，再說我們要說的事還沒說完呢。

(2) 我不打算學日文，日文太難，再說對我的專業也沒有幫助。

(3) 她不應該跟那個人結婚，那個人不太聰明，再說對她也不是特別好。

注意，"而且"也表示"進一步"的意思，但是不是只說明原因。

(4)我去年不但選了英文課，而且選了中文課。

(5)他姐姐不但聰明，而且漂亮。

例(1)、(2)、(3)的"再說"可以用"而且"替換，但是例(4)、(5)的"而且"不能用"再說"替換。

第二課 宿舍

1. 漢語的詞序（一）：

當謂語為動詞時，句子的結構有時會很復雜，這就有一個怎樣組織安排句子的問題。在一般情況下，漢語的詞序是：

主語--動詞--賓語

如：

我　　打　　球了。

作為主語和賓語的詞如果有修飾語（表示領有、數量、修飾關系等等）--定語，定語都要放在被修飾語的前面，我們把定語放在（）裏面：

(1)（我的）（小）妹妹買了（一本）（很有意思的）書。

(2)我很喜歡（媽媽給我寄來的）衣服。

(3)這就是（我以前住的）地方。

如果有表示動作（或事情）發生的時間、處所、協同者、方式等等狀語，都要放在動詞前。時間、處所等有時可以放在主語前。我們把狀語放在< >中。如：

(4) 我們<昨天>去了（一個）（很遠的）地方。

(5) 他<在房間裏><慢慢地>走著。

(6) <明天>我要<跟一個朋友><從學校>開車去南方旅行。

應該注意，漢語的定語和狀語總是在它所修飾、限制的詞的前面。但漢語的動詞後常常出現表示結果狀態的補語。我們把補語放在[ ]裏面。

(7) 我<剛才>寫[錯]了(一個)字。

(8) 請你坐[下]。

上面講的是漢語的基本詞序。很多因素可以影響漢語的詞序。關於漢語中某些改變基本詞序的情況，我們在後面將會說明。

2. 存在句 ：

存在句的詞序與一般詞序不同。存在句的結構是 ：

處所詞＋動詞＋（了／著＋）數量詞＋名詞

存在句表示某一處所存在（有）某一事物。比如 " 桌子上放著一本書 "、" 門前有一棵樹 "、" 房後是一片綠地 "。存在句的動詞有三類，一是 " 有 "；一是 " 是 "，一類是表示人體、肢體動作的動詞：

(1) 黑板上有一些字。

(2) 桌子上是一本書。

(3) 書架上放著三本書。

(4) 床上坐著一個人。

表示存在時，" 有、是 " 的不同在於，" 是 " 後的名詞一般是該處所存在的唯一事物，" 有 " 則不然。比較：

(5) 桌子上有一本書，一個本子，一張報和一些紙。

(6) A: 你看，桌子上放著什麼？

B: 桌子上是書。

(7) 我們學校的前面是一條馬路，後面是一個公園。

存在句的作用是描寫一個地方或描寫一個人的穿著打扮。例(1)--(7)是描寫處所的。下面是描寫人物的：

(8) 這時從前面走來一個人，他頭上戴著一頂紅帽子，身上穿著一件運動衫，腳上穿著一雙運動鞋。

(9) 那個女孩手裏拿著一封信。

3. " 比較 " ：

在中文裏，" 比較 " 的意思與英文的比較級不同。它並不是用來比較的，是表示程度不夠高。

(1) 這本書比較貴，你別買了吧。

(2) 我比較矮，才五尺四，不能打籃球。

(3) 今天比較冷，你多穿點衣服吧。

(4) A: 你喜歡看什麼電影？

　　B: 我比較喜歡看中國電影。

注意下面的句子：

(1) A: 你的病怎麼樣了？

　　B: 好一點兒了。(*比較好。)

(2) 我很高，我哥哥更高。

　　(*我很高，我哥哥比較高。)

4. "(方便)得很"：

"得很"可以用在形容詞和表示心理活動的動詞後表示較高的程度：

(1) 外面冷得很，別出去了。

(2) 那所學校學費貴得很。

(3) 我們的學校大得很。

(4) 張天明想家得很。

"冷得很"比"很冷"程度要高。

5. "那(麼)"：

"那(麼)"可以承接上文，即把後面的句子跟前邊的句子連接起來，後面的句子表示由前邊的句子引出的結果或判斷。"那麼"也可以說"那"。例如：

(1) A: 晚上去看電影好嗎？

　　B: 可是今天晚上我沒有空兒。

　　A: 那(麼)就明天吧。

　　B: 好吧。(OK.)

(2) A: 媽媽，我不喜歡當醫生。

B: 那（麼）學電腦怎麼樣？

A: 我也沒有興趣。

B: 那就什麼都不學，在家裏當家庭主婦吧。

A: 看您說的！

6. " 恐怕 " (I'm afraid)：

副詞 " 恐怕 " 表示說話人的一種估計，例如：

(1) 住這兒恐怕很不方便吧？

(2) 下雨了，恐怕我們不能打球了。

(3) 十一點了，現在給他打電話恐怕太晚了。

(4) 窗戶外有一條路，這兒恐怕很吵吧？

　　注意：" 恐怕 " 前通常不用主語 " 我 "。例如一般不說 " 我恐怕他不能去了 "，" 我恐怕你會不高興 "。如果說 " 我恐怕不能去了 "，意思是 " （我）恐怕我不能去了 "，" 他恐怕不能去了 "，意思是 " （我）恐怕他不能去了 "。

第三課　飯館

1. 關於 " 話題 " :

　　如果一個人、一個東西或一件事情是前面提到過，也就是說對說話人和聽話人已經不是新的信息，而是已知信息，這時就要把表示已知信息的詞語放在句子的開頭作為話題。話題在句首是漢語的重要特徵。例如：

　　(1) 其實，<u>那個記者的看法</u>我也不同意.。（第三課）

　　(2) <u>他剛才告訴我的那件事</u>我早就聽說了。

　　(3) 你<u>手續</u>都辦完了嗎？

　　(4) 這兒<u>魚</u>做得很好。

　　話題在句首與我們在第二課中講的漢語句子的一般詞序不同。在例 (1)中，如果 "<u>那個記者的看法</u>" 不是已知信息，例（1）的詞序應該是 " 我給你們介紹一下一個記者對中國菜的看法，好嗎？" 這是一個典型的 " 主--動--賓 " 詞序的句子。例(2)做話題的部分如果不是已知信息，例 (2)的句子將是 " 我聽說了一件事，……那件事他早就告訴我了 "

　　所謂已知信息是指前面剛剛說過的，或像人每天都吃飯、睡覺，學生一般總要上課、做功課之類。例如：

　　(5) <u>功課</u>你做完了嗎？

　　(6) <u>飯</u>要慢慢吃，吃得太快對身體不好。

當我們說漢語的詞序是 " 主--動--賓 " 的時候，那是指一個孤立的句子或不受上下文影響的句子。但是在實際語言中，句子中詞的順序會受很多因素影響。話題就是在一定的上下文、語境中出現的現象。

2. 狀語和 " 地 " :

　　有些<u>狀語</u>表示動作的方式或者人做某種動作時的情態，這時通常後面要用 " 地(de) " :

　　(1) 他慢慢地走進了教室。

　　(2) 我用力地把桌子搬起來。

(3) 看見了我，妹妹很高興地問："姐姐，你跟我玩球，好嗎？"

3. "一+V"：

"一"後加上一個動詞（常用單音節動詞），表示實現了一個短暫的動作：

(1) 外面有人叫我，我開門一看，是送信的。

(2) 他把書往桌子上一扔，跑了出去。

"一"這樣用時，有時後面接著出現表示動作的結果的句子，用"就"來連接：

(2) 這個句子很容易，他一看就懂。

(3) 你的聲音我很熟，一聽就知道是你。

(4) 他病了，一看書就頭疼。

4. "原來"：

"原來"有兩個意思：

A. "以前、沒有改變的"：

(1) 他原來學中文，後來改學電腦了。

(2) 我原來不認識他，上大學以後在一起上課，才認識了。

(3) 我的中學老師還是原來的樣子，一點都沒變。

(4) 你還住在原來的宿舍嗎？

B. 發現了以前不知道的情況，有恍然大悟的意思：

(1) 我早就聽說有一個重要人物要來，原來就是你呀。

(2) 房間裏冷得很，原來暖氣壞了。

(3) 我覺得好像在哪兒見過你，原來你是我的同學的姐姐。

5. "極了"：

"極了"用在形容詞和表示心理活動的動詞後表示很高的程度：

(1) 我聽媽媽說暑假帶我去中國旅行，高興極了。

(2) 妹妹說她離開家以後，想家想極了。

(3) 這本書好極了，你應該看看。

(4) 那個地方遠極了，你別去了。

6. “又...又...” :

“又...又...” 中間可以用兩個形容詞或兩個動詞，表示同時出現的兩種情況或兩個動作：

(1) 他的女朋友又聰明又漂亮。

(2) 今年夏天天氣真不好，又熱又悶。

(3) 孩子們又跑又跳，玩得十分高興。

(4) 那個小孩又哭又鬧，我們一點辦法也沒有。

注意，用形容詞時，如果用褒義的，兩個都必須是褒義的，同樣，如果用貶義的，兩個都得是貶義的，而且在這一特定場合，這兩個形容詞的意義應該是有聯繫的。比如，描寫一個人，常常說 “聰明、漂亮，高、矮，胖、瘦”；寫天氣時用 “熱、悶，冷、濕” 等等。用動詞時，兩個動作也應該是常常一起發生的，如 “說、笑，喊、叫，打、罵” 等等。

我們也可以發現 “也...，也...” 這樣的結構，這個用法要求有一定的上文，即要求上文提到了 “也” 後用的形容詞所表示的意思。例如：

A：你幫我找一個工作好嗎？

B：好啊，你要找什麼樣的工作？

A：我要找一個又不累錢又多的工作。

B：我知道有一個醫院有工作，也不累，錢也多，可是對

       身體不太好。你願意去嗎？

7. “多/少” + V (+ NU+M+N)

在祈使句中，應該說： “多買一點東西、多吃一點、多寫兩遍，少看幾本、少看電視、上課少說英文。而不應該說 “買多一點東西...，看少幾本書...”。

第四課 買東西

1.時間詞語在句子中的位置：

　　時間詞語有兩類，一類是像 " 今天、星期一、1996年、三天前、...
的時候 " 這樣的表示一個具體的時間的詞語，我們稱為時點。一類是像 "
一個小時、三天、兩年 " 這樣的表示一段時間的詞語，我們稱為時段。表
示時點的詞通常在句子中做狀語，位於句首或動詞之前，我們在前幾課已
有說明。本課主要介紹表示時段的時間詞的用法。表示時段的詞語常常表
示動作或狀態持續的時間。例如：

　　(1) 我來了兩天了，覺得很方便。（第二課）

　　(2) 開學已經兩個多星期了。（第三課）

　　(3) 我昨天做功課做了兩個小時。

　　(4) 你學中文學了多長時間？

表示時段的詞語通常都位於動詞之後。在這種句子中，如果動詞表示的動
作是可以持續的，如 " 學、做、寫、走 " 等等，後面有賓語時，要重復動
詞，如例(2)、(3)。如果動詞表示的動作是不能持續的，如 " 來、結婚、
畢業、死 " 等，則不能重復動詞，如例(1)。

　　如果通常表示時段的詞語，並不表示動作持續的時間，比如動詞前有
否定詞，或 " 一天吃三次、三天來一次 " 等，這些詞語就位於動詞前：

　　(5) 我一個星期沒有看見他了。

　　(6)很長時間沒吃中國飯了，他很想去中國飯館吃一頓。

　　　　（第三課）

　　(7) 這種藥一天吃三次。

2. " 無論... ，都... " ：

　　" 無論 " 表示在任何條件或情況下結果都不變，" 無論 " 後必須用：

A.表示任指的疑問代詞；B.表示選擇關係的並列成分。例如：

(1) 明天無論誰請客我都不去。（"誰"表示任指）

(2) 今天無論什麼地方我都去過了，太累了。

　　（"什麼地方"表示任指.）

(3) 我們已經決定明天去逛街，你無論同意不同意都得跟我
　　們去。（"同意不同意"是表示選擇關係的並列成分）

(4) 他無論在家裏還是在學校，總是看書，很少看見他玩。

　　（"在家裏還是在學校"是表示選擇關係的並列成分.）

3. "於是"：

連詞"於是"表示由於前面的某種情況，引起的一個自然結果。例
如：

(1) 我給他打了很多次電話都沒有人接，於是就寫了一封
　　信。

(2) 晚飯後，他去一家購物中心買運動鞋，那裏沒有他喜
　　歡的，於是又開車去了另一個購物中心。

(3) 本來週末孩子們要去爬山，沒想到星期六早上下雨了，
　　於是他們就不去了。

(4) 小明在書店看見一本新書，他很喜歡，於是就買下來
　　了。

注意，"於是"雖然也表示結果，但與"所以"不同。"於是"前
面一定有一種情況，雖然這種情況也可能是一種原因，但兩個句子的因果
關係沒有用"因為...，所以..."的句子那麼強，所以上述句子中的"於
是"不宜換成"所以"；此外"於是"所引出的結果往往是一個動作或一
種變化，"所以"所引出的結果要廣得多。例如：

(1) 這次考試，因為我沒有準備，所以考得很不好。

(2) 上海人多車多，所以開車很容易緊張。

(3) 天要下雨，所以非常悶。

這幾個句子都不能用 " 於是 " 。在例 (1) 中，雖然前面一個分句表示的是一種情況，但後一個分句不是一個動作或變化，例 (2) 、例 (3) 與例 (1) 同。

4. " 真 " :

" 真 " 可以表示確定、感嘆的語氣，用在形容詞和表示心理活動的動詞前：

(1) 今天真冷，穿三件毛衣都不行。

(2) 你們老師給的功課真多，你做了三個鐘頭了還沒做完。

(3) 你真聰明，這麼難的字也會寫。

應該注意的是， " 真 " 的主要作用並不是表示程度高，跟 " 很、十分、特別 " 不一樣，它的作用是為了表示一個肯定的或感嘆的語氣，不是為了告訴別人什麼新的情況或信息。因此在一般敘述的句子中，不要隨意用 " 真 " 。比如：

(4) A：喂，小張，你聽天氣預報了嗎？明天的天氣怎麼樣？

  B：天氣預報說明天的天氣會到二十度，很冷。

這裏不能說：*天氣預報說明天的天氣會到二十度，真冷。
" 真 " 有時表示 " 真正 " 的意思，這時後面可以加上 " 的 " 。如：

(5) 我真的不想去看電影。

(6) A：畢業以後我想去賣東西。

  B：你真這麼想嗎？

5. " adj. / V+是+adj. / V，可是 / 但是... " :

這種結構的意思是 " 雖然...，可是 / 但是... " ：

(1) A：我決定學文學了。

  B：學文學好是好，可是找工作不太容易吧？

(2) A：這件衣服太貴了，別買！

  B：這件衣服貴是貴，可是牌子好。

(3) A：明天的晚會你去不去？

　　B：我去是去，不過可能晚一點。

(4) A：你不吃肉嗎？

　　B：我吃是吃，可是吃得很少。

6. "難道"：

　　"難道"用於反問句.可以加強反問的語氣。例如：

(1)這麼容易的題，難道你還不會做嗎？

(2)他來美國十年了，難道他連一句英文都不會說嗎？

(3)這件事不是他做的，難道是你做的？

　　注意，"難道"可以用在主語前，也可以用在主語後，用"難道"的句子，因為是反問句，所以只能是用"嗎"的是非問句，不能是其他幾種疑問句。例如不能說：*"這件事情不是你，難道是誰？"*"你難道去不去？"等等。

　　另外要注意，用反問句時，前面應該有上下文，所以通常不能在句子的一開頭就用"難道"。

7. 動詞重疊(Reduplication of verbs)：

　　動詞可以重疊，當動詞重疊形式 表示尚未發生的動作時，可以使語氣更加緩和、客氣，常用於祈使句。例如：

(1) 我陪你去化妝品那邊看看。（第四課）

(2) 你看看我寫得對不對？

(3) 你好好跟他說說，叫他不要不高興了。

"一下"也有同樣的作用：

(1) 你們不認識，我來介紹一下。

(2)你看一下我寫得對不對？

(3) 等一下，晚飯還沒好。

第五課 選 專 業

1. " 只 是 / 就 是 " (it's just that)：

" 只是/ 就是 " 可以表示轉折，與 " 不過 " 用法接近，比 " 但是、可是 " 所表示的轉折語氣要輕。" 就是 " 比 " 只是 " 更加口語化。

(1) 你要跟他結婚，我不是不同意，只是我覺得太早了一點。

(2) 他這個人好是好，就是身體差一些。

(3) 那兒冬天的天氣暖和是暖和，只是常常颱風。

應該注意的是，用 " 只是/ 就是 " 的句子，第一個分句的意思往往是正面的、好的，第二個句子則常常對第一個句子的意思進行修正，指出美中不足之處，這一點與 " 但是、可是、不過 " 不同。

2. " 對他來說 " (to him)：

" 對他來說 " 的意思是 " 從他的角度來談問題 " 例如：

(1) 對妹妹來說，今年最重要的事情是選一個好大學。

注意，" 對他來說 " 和 " 他認為 " 意思不同，" 對...來說 " 實際上是說話人的一種看法。又如：

(2) (我認為)對他來說，有工作總比沒工作好，可是他認為工作不好還不如沒有工作。

(3) 對她媽媽來說，她是最重要的。

(4) 對我來說，找一個好工作是第一位的事情。

3. " 至 於 "：

" 至於 " 的作用是引出一個與上文不同、但是有關係的句子。例如：

(1) A：我們明天去旅行還是後天去？

　　B：我們先討論去不去，至於明天去還是後天去，我想
　　　都可以。.

(2) A：你認識那兩個人嗎？

　　B：我認識那個男的，至於那個女的，我從來沒見過。

(3) 我喜歡吃中國飯，至於我太太，她喜歡吃日本飯。

(4) 買日用品，這個商店不錯，比較便宜，至於買衣服，還
　　是去大一點的購物中心吧。

4. " 要麼..., 要麼... " (either...or)：

" 要麼..., (要麼)... " 是選擇連詞，表示在幾種(往往是兩種可能
中)，選擇一種，常常用於選擇意願，所以一般用於尚未發生的事。比如：

(1) 你要麼學醫，要麼學工程，反正不能學文科。

(2) A：你說明天做什麼？

　　B：要麼聽音樂，要麼看電影。

　　A：去公園看紅葉怎麼樣？

　　B：不行。

(3) A：明天誰去送你爸爸去飛機場？

　　B：要麼你去，要麼我哥哥去。

5. " 另外 " (another; other)：

" 另外 " 有兩個用法，一個在名詞前：

(1) 另外兩門課選什麼，還不知道。

(2) 這裏有兩個大學，一個男校，另外一個是女校，都很
　　不錯。

(3) 他有三個妹妹，一個上大學，另外兩個已經工作了。

(4) 我的四個中文老師，三個是從中國大陸來的，另外一個
　　是從台灣來的。

"另外"還可以用在動詞或句子前，這是我們在第四課的詞語練習中
練習過的。再如：

(5) 再選一門物理課，另外再選兩門電腦系的課，學分就
　　夠了。

(6) 我明年想去日本旅行，另外還想去中國看看。

(7) 上個週末我看了一個電影，另外還聽了一個音樂會。

6. 結果補語 Resultative Complements：

漢語的動詞後邊可以用一個形容詞或另一個動詞，表示前一個動詞
的結果，我們把後一個動詞或形容詞稱爲結果補語。結果補語主要有以下
幾類：

A: 結果補語說明前面的動詞所表示的動作：

(1) 我做完了功課再看電視。（完）

(2) 一個字得反復練習才能記住。（住）（第五課）

(3) 下學期的課你選好了嗎？（好）（第五課）

B: 表示通過第一個動詞所表示的動作，引起主語（動作者）出現新的狀態
或變化：

(4) 老師講的我聽懂了。（懂）

(5) 你吃飽了嗎？（飽）

C: 表示通過動作，引起賓語（動作接受者）出現新的狀態或變化：

(6) 你怎麼把妹妹打哭了？（哭）

(7) 他把椅子搬走了。（走）

(8) 我洗乾淨了衣服就睡覺。（乾淨）

應該注意的是，一個動詞可以用什麼動詞和形容詞做結果補語不都是隨意的，所以最好把動詞和結果補語當作一個詞來記。

7. "再"、"又"、"還"比較：

"又"和"再"都可以表示動作狀態得重復，"又"一般用於已經發生的情況，"再"用於尚未發生的情況。例如：

(1) 我上星期看了一個中國電影，昨天又看了一個。

(2) 您剛才說的我沒聽清楚，請您再說一次。

但"想、能、可以、要"以及"是"等前邊要用"又"：

(3) 她今天下午又要去見指導教授了。

(4) 明天又是星期天了。

"還"可以表示數量增加範圍擴大等，一般也用於尚未發生的情況：

(5) 這本書我買了一本了，還得買一本。

(6) 這個電影我看了一次了，還想再看一次。

第六課 租房子

1. 帶 " 得 " 的補語句 :

帶 " 得 " 的補語,叫情態補語(也有人叫程度補語),從結構和作用上可以分成三類:

A: 補語對前面的動詞進行判斷,例如:

    (1) 我每天起得很早。

    (2) 他跑得很快。

    (3) 妹妹寫字寫得很好。

動詞後有賓語時,要重復動詞(如例(3))。

B: 補語描寫主語或賓語等的情態,這種情態是由於補語前的動詞和形容詞所表示的動作或狀態產生的結果。例如:

    (1) 他聽到老師說明天不考試了,高興得跳了起來。

    " 跳了起來 " 是 " 高興 " 的結果,也是對 " 他 " 的描述。

    (2) 同學開他玩笑,說得他很不高興。

    " 很不高興 " 是 " 說 " 的結果,是對 " 他 " 的描述。

    (3)她把房子打掃得乾乾淨淨的。

    " 乾乾淨淨 " 是 " 打掃 " 的結果,是對 " 房子 " 的描述。

此類補語是描寫性的,用於已然(已經發生)的情況,此種補語不用否定形式。

C: 補語表示程度,例如:

    快過年了,飛機場裏人多得很。

此類表示程度的補語,也用於已然的情況,不用否定形式。

2. " ...以後 " 與 " ...的時候 " 比較 :

    " ...以後 " 的意思是 " 在...以後 " , " ...的時候 " 的意思是 " 在...的同時 " 。比較:

    (1) a. 我看見他的時候,他正在打電話。

　　b. 我看見他以後，跟他打了聲招呼。

(2) a. 他出去的時候忘了帶錢。

　　b. 他出去以後想起來沒有帶錢。

(3) a. 沒有事情的時候，他常常打電話。

　　b. 下了課以後，他給小王打了一個電話。

3. "...的話"：

　"...的話"是助詞，用在表示假設的分句後，後面一定有另一個分句。例如：

(1) 你要是去的話，一定給我打電話。

(2) 媽媽要是非讓我學醫不可的話，我就不上大學了。

(3) 電影，有意思的話，我就看完，沒有意思的話，我看一點就不看了。

4. "最...不過了"：

　"最...不過了"意思是"沒有比...更...的了"，語氣很強。例如：

(1) 她過生日，買花送她最好不過了。

(2) 這本書對東亞史的介紹最清楚不過了。

(3) 小王的妹妹最聰明不過了。

5. 趨向補語（一）：表示方向

　　趨向動詞可以用在動詞之後做補語。趨向動詞有"來、去、上、下、進、出、回、過、起、開、到"；"來、去"還可以與其他趨向動詞構成"上來、上去，下來、下去，進來、進去，出來、出去，回來、回去，過來、過去，起來，開來、開去，到......來、到......去"等，我們統統稱為趨向補語。趨向補語表示的意義可以分為三大類：**A.**趨向補語表示方向；**B.**趨向補語表示結果；**C.** 趨向補語表示狀態。本課只講第一類，即表示方向的趨向補語。

　　(1) 你回家去吧。（去）

(2) 張天明想最好搬出學校。（出）（第六課）

(3) 我明天搬進宿舍來。（進...來）

(4) 請你們拿出一張紙來。（出...來）

(5) 我帶回來了一個客人。（回來）

在用這類趨向補語時，應該注意賓語的位置。如果"來、去"做補語，表示人或事物的賓語可以放在"來、去"的前邊或後邊：

(6) 他搬來了一把椅子。（動作多已經發生）

(7) 請搬一把椅子來。

(8) 他從家裏搬了一把椅子來。

特別要注意的是，如果賓語表示一個處所，它只能位於"來、去"前：

(9) 我九月回北京去。

(10) 你快一點進房間來。

"上、下、進、出"等做補語時，只能在動詞後賓語前，如例(2)。

"上來、下去"等做補語時，如果賓語表示處所，它只能在"上來、下去"等的中間，如例(3)，這一點也是需要特別注意的；如果賓語是一般名詞，可以位於"上來、下去"等的中間，也可以位於"上來、下去"等的後邊或前邊，如例(4)(5)。

"上"和"上來"、"上去"表示的方向一樣，不同的是，"上來"表示人或物體通過動作向說話人趨近；"上去"表示人或物體通過動作離開說話人。如：

他把椅子搬上樓來了。（說話人在樓上，椅子現在也
　　　　　　在樓上）

他把椅子搬下樓去了。（說話人在樓上，椅子現在在樓下）

"下"和"下來"、"下去"；"進"和"進來"、"進去"等等情況相同。

6. 中文的數字按由大到小排列：

1997年10月25日　　　　　October 25, 1996

中國北京中山路25號1樓2門3號

#3 Gate 2 1st flr., 25 Zhongshan Rd., Beijing, China

第七課 男朋友

1. " ... ，才" :

在 " 張天明問了好幾次，妹妹才告訴他... " 這個句子裏，" 張天明問了好幾次 " 是 " 妹妹告訴他 " 的條件，即 " 才 " 可以用於表示在什麼條件下，才做某事。又如：

(1) 你先給我錢，我才能給你東西。

(2) 你得把你的看法告訴我，我才把我的看法告訴你。

(3) 爸爸對我說：" 你今年能畢業，我才給你錢去中國旅行。"

2. " (先...)再..." :

用 " (先)...，再... " 時，意思是 " 現在不想做(不是不能做)某事，以後做 "。例如：

(1) 老師，我今天不想考試，準備好了以後再考，可以嗎？

(2) A：咱們今年夏天去台灣旅行好嗎？

　　B：我今年不想去，畢業以後再去。

(3) 你先吃飯吧，我寫完這封信再吃。

比較：

(1) 你寫完功課才能吃飯。(意思是：現在不能吃飯)

(2) 我寫完功課再吃飯。(意思是：不想現在吃飯)

注意，" 再 " 的後面不能用 " 能 " 之類的能願動詞。

3. "...上":

"...上" 可以用在抽象名詞的後面，表示 "在...方面" 的意思。如 "性格上、興趣上、學習上、工作上" 等等。

(1) 在興趣上，湯姆跟天華不太一樣。（第七課）

(2) 小林學習上，工作上都很不錯。

(3) 在性格上，她以前的男朋友比現在的男朋友好多了。

4. "V來V去":

"V來V去" 表示同一動作反復進行。例如 "走來走去、飛來飛去、想來想去、說來說去、討論來討論去、研究來研究去"。

5. 趨向補語（二）：表示結果

表示結果意義的趨向補語就像結果補語一樣。不是所有的趨向補語都有結果意義。我們學過的如：

(1) 先生，加上稅一共是三百八十六塊四。（加上，第四課）

(2) 其他的課......也學到了不少東西。（學到，第五課）

(3) 把房租跟飯錢省下來。（省下來，第五課）

每個趨向補語的結果意義不同，有的結果意義還不止一個。趨向補語的結果意義是很抽象的，而且哪個動詞和哪個補語可以一起用也不是隨便的，所有雖然我們可以一個一個地解釋，但是我們認為學習趨向補語結果意義時，最好連同前面的動詞一起記。我們在生詞裏也把它們放在一起。

6. "V+出(來)" 表示結果：

"V+出來" 的意思是：由無到有、由隱蔽到公開、由不清楚到清楚。後面有賓語的時候，多半用 "V+出"；如在句尾，一定要用 "V+出來"。如：

(1) 我想出來一個好辦法。

(2) 這兩本書有什麼不同，我沒看出來。

(3) 從電話裏我聽出來是姐姐的聲音。

7. "...以後"和"...以來"比較：

"...以後"的意思是從某一時間以後，如：

(1) 上大學以後，我們一直沒有見過她。

(2) 她跟我吵架以後，我就不喜歡她了。

(3) 95年我們住在一個宿舍，96年以後我搬走了。

"以來"的意思是從某一時間開始一直到現在。如：

(1) 上大學以來，我一直沒有見過她。

(2) 1995年以來，我沒有搬過家。

(3) 自從我認識她以來，沒有看見她哭過。

(4) 他們結婚以來，一直相處得很好。

(5) 三天以來，他一直在考試。

有時"以來"可以用"以後"替換，如"...以來"的例(1)--(4)，但表示的意思並不完全一樣，像前面說過的，"以來"的意思是從某一時間開始一直到現在，"...以後"的意思是從某一時間以後與現在無關。如果"以後/以來"前是一個表示時段的詞語，"以後"不能替換"以來"，如"以來"的例(5)。

第八課　電影和電視的影響

1. "的、地、得" 的分別：

A. "的" 用在定語後邊，"的" 的後邊一般是名詞，有時也可以是動詞或形容詞；"的" 的前面可以是代詞、名詞、形容詞、動詞等等，但不可能是副詞。例如：

(1) 我的專業是統計學，妹妹的專業是文學。

(2) 小張買的衣服不太好看。

(3) 我喜歡跟性格開朗的人交朋友。

(4) 你的建議不錯。

B. "地" 是狀語的標誌，用在動詞的前面；"地" 的前面常常是形容詞、副詞或固定詞組，不可能是名詞、代詞。例如：

(1) 老師慢慢地走進教室來。

(2) 孩子們很快地跑了出去。

(3) 學生們正在努力地學習中文。

C. "得" 是補語的標誌，用在動詞或形容詞的後面，"得" 的後面，一般是形容詞、動詞短語或副詞。例如：

(1) 妹妹跑得很快。

(2) 李明聽說不考試了，高興得跳了起來。

(3) 今天熱得很。

2. "一邊...，一邊..."：

"一邊...，一邊..." 用於表示同時進行兩個動作的句子，通常後一個動作是主要動作，前一個是伴隨動作。例如：

(1) 我喜歡一邊吃飯一邊看電視。

(2) 他一邊聽古典音樂一邊給他家人寫信。

(3) 你不要一邊走路一邊看書。

4. "就是...，也..." (even if... still...)：

連詞 "就是...，也..." 表示假設，有兩種用法：

A: 前後兩個分句或兩個短語分別指有關係的兩件事，前面的表示一種假設的情況，後面的表示結果或結論不受這種情況的影響。例如：

(1) 南加州的天氣很好，就是冬天也很暖和。

(2) A：外邊很黑，他要是不來，你就不要去看電影了。

　　B：我不怕，他就是不來，我一個人也要去。

(3) A：明天要是天氣不好，我們還去波士頓嗎？

　　B：這件事已經說定了，就是天氣不好，也要去。

假設的情況常常是很極端的：

(4) 你就是給我一百萬塊錢，我也不跟你結婚。

(5) 他眼睛很好，就是芝麻大的字，他都看得見。

"就是...，" 後邊也可以是一個名詞，"也..." 後面是前面的名詞的謂語。例如：

(6) 我餓得很，誰有吃的，就是一小塊糖也可以。

(7) 別說是你，就是指導教授我也不怕。

(8) 這兒很暖和，就是冬天也不用穿毛衣。

B: 前後兩部分指同一個事物，後面表示退一步的估計：

(1) A：這個音樂會聽說很不錯，現在還有票嗎？

　　B：我想，就是有也不多了。

(2) 明天的晚會我可能去不了，就是去也得很晚。

4. "反而"：

"反而" 表示轉折，"反而" 後的句子的意思與前面相反，或表示出乎意料。例如：

(1) 難的字他都會寫，容易的字他反而不會寫。

(2) 他很奇怪，這次考試考得很好，好像反而不高興了。

(3) 他每天都是第一個來，今天有這麼重要的事，反而來晚了。

注意，"反而"是副詞，如果第二個句子有主語，應該放在主語後邊。

5. " 難免 " ：

"難免"的意思是"很難避免"。例如：

(1) 兒童難免會受電視的影響。

(2) 第一次教課，緊張總是難免的。

(3) 你在女同學面前說難聽話，難免讓人不高興。

(4) 就是兩個好朋友，有時也難免意見不同。

6. 反問句 (Rhetorical Questions)：

有些句子形式上是疑問句，但不是真的在問問題，而是加強肯定或否定的語氣。例如：

(1) 這麼簡單的道理，難道你都不懂嗎？
   （意思是：你應該懂）

(2) A：小明，你剛才拿我的東西了吧？
   B：誰拿你的東西了？你別亂說。（意思是：我沒動）

(3) 這麼貴的衣服，我怎麼買得起呢？（意思是：我買不起）

(4) 小孩能學好嗎？（意思是：小孩不能學好）（第八課）

(5) 我每天工作得換三次車，你說麻煩不麻煩？
   （意思是：麻煩）

(6) 你說我應該給你錢，我是你的媽媽還是你的爸爸？
   （意思是：我不是你的媽媽，也不是你的爸爸）

從上面的例句可以看出，肯定形式的反問句表示否定的意思；否定形式的，表示肯定的意思。反問句比非反問句的語氣要強得多。

第九課 旅行

1. "過"（表示經驗）：

動態助詞 "過" 的意思是 "曾經有某種經驗"。和 "了" 不同的是：

A. "了" 是敘述性的，即用 "了" 時常常是敘述動作、事件的發生。

例如：

(1) 八點鐘了，上課了，同學們都進了教室。

(2) 第二天早晨，我很早就起來了，起床後就去體育場跑步。

(3) 客人們進來以後，找到了自己的位子，坐了下來。

第(3)個句子沒有時間詞語，句子表示的時間就是正在敘述事情發生的時間就是正在敘述事情發生的時間。而 "過" 是說明性的。用 "過" 時，要說明的事實往往不在 "過" 所在的分句裏，而在另一個分句裏。例如：

(1) (以前)我們在一起學過英文，我知道他英文很好。

   (因為我們在一起學過英文，所以我知道他英文很好。)

(2) A：你去過中國，給我們建議一下，去哪兒旅行最好。

       (因為你去過中國，所以給我們建議一下，去哪兒旅

   B：誰說我去過中國？對不起，我不能給你們什麼建議。

(3) 他學過好幾年中文，都能看中文電影了。

   (因為他學過好幾年中文，所以都能看中文電影了。)

在這幾個句子裏，包含 "過" 的句子都說明後一個句子所說的事情的原因。

B. 與其功能相聯繫，用 "了" 時，句子裏往往有一個表示確定時間的時間詞語。用 "過" 時，句子裏常常沒有表示確定時間的詞語，句子所表示的時間是 "以前，從前" 等等，只有特別要說明某個時間發生過某事時，才用時間詞語。

2. "過"（表示完結）：

本課還出現了一個"過"："我已經打過電話了。"這個"過"表示完結意思。例如：

(1) 你叫我看的那本書我看過了，很不錯。

(2) A：今天我們去看這個電影好嗎？

　　B：這個電影我看過了。

(3) A：你在我們這兒吃飯吧。

　　B：不，我吃過了。

用這個"過"時，前邊的動詞所表示的動作必須是已知信息，即是聽話人已經知道的，或人們熟悉的，不言而喻的。

這個"過"的意思與表示實現、發生意思的"了"類似，可以用"了"替換，後邊也可以用"了"。

3. "除非"：

"除非"是連詞，提出唯一的先決條件。後面的分句要用"才"。

(1) 明天除非你來接我，我才去。

(2) A：今天的討論會你去嗎？

　　B：除非做完了功課，我才會去。

(3) A：今天去看電影好不好？

　　B：除非看外國電影我才去。

在"除非...，才..."還可用"(要)不然/否則..."：

(1) A：今天去看電影好不好？

　　B：除非看外國電影，我才去，否則我就不去。

有時中間一句也可省略不說。

(2) A：明天我的生日晚會她會來嗎？

　　B：除非你自己去請她，否則她不會來。

(3) 除非天氣特別好，否則我是不會出去散步的。

也可以先說出結論，然後再說出先決條件，如 "... ，除非..." 。例如：

(1) 這本書這個星期我一定要看完，除非我女朋友來看我。

(2) 明天我們一定去打籃球，除非下大雨。

(3) 他一般十點鐘就睡了，除非第二天有考試。

4. "哪兒... ，哪兒... " :

疑問代詞有時並不表示疑問的用法，本課出現的是同一個疑問代詞，出現在兩個分句中，第一個疑問代詞是虛指的，即不代表確定的人、事物、時間、處所等等，第二個疑問代詞以第一個疑問代詞為轉移，即與第一個疑問代詞所指代的相同。例如：

(1) A：咱們點菜吧。你想吃什麼？

　　 B：什麼都可以，你喜歡吃什麼，我就吃什麼。

(2) 每天姐姐去哪兒，她去哪兒。

(3) 你什麼時候有時間，什麼時候來。

(4) 這個問題，誰會請誰回答。

(5) A：咱們怎麼走？

　　 B：怎麼近怎麼走。

注意，疑問代詞這樣用時，其位置與一般句子相同。如例(1) "你喜歡吃什麼，我就吃什麼。" "什麼" 都是賓語，所以在賓語的位置上；例(3) "你什麼時候有時間，什麼時候來。" "什麼時候" 都做狀語，所以都在狀語的位置上；本課課文中的 "哪兒好玩兒就去哪兒" ，"哪兒" 在第一個分句中是主語，在第二個分句中是賓語，所以分別出現在主語和賓語的位置上。

5. "既然，...就..." :

"既然" 提出一個事實或情況，這個事實或情況是後邊的分句所表示的事情的原因；或者說後一分句表示的是由前一分句的事實或情況所推出的結論。例如：

(1) A：老師，這本書我看過了。

　　 B：既然你看過了，那麼就不必再看了。

(2) A：我很不喜歡這兒的天氣。

　　 B：既然你不喜歡這兒的天氣，就應該搬家。

(3) 既然你同意了，咱們就決定了吧。

注意，"既然"後邊的事實或情況一定是已知的，這一點與"因為"不同。請比較：

(4) A：為什麼中國人一家只能生一個孩子？

　　 B：因為中國的人口太多了，所以不得不這麼做。

　　 B：*既然中國的人口太多了，所以不得不這麼做。(incorrect)

(5) A：老師，我有一點不舒服。

　　 B：*既然你不舒服，就回去休息吧。

　　 B：因為你不舒服，就回去休息吧。(incorrect)

6. "然後"：

"然後"表示在做了一件事情之後，接著再(或又做了)另一件事，多用於尚未發生的事情，也可以用於已經發生的事情。例如：

(1) 你們先復習這一課的語法，然後預習下一課的生詞。

(2) 在這個學校，你得先念碩士，然後才能念博士。

(3) 昨天他們先去看了一場電影，然後又去一家中國餐館
　　 吃了一頓飯，很晚才回家。

注意，"然後"與"後來"不同：

A. "後來"只能用於過去，不能用於將來。

B. 用於過去時，"然後"連接的是兩個很具體的動作或事情，而且是緊接著發生的，"後來"沒有這個限制。比較：

(4) 他們認識了一年多，後來就結婚了。

　　 *他們認識了一年多，然後就結婚了。(incorrect)

(5) 我們學了兩年日文，後來就不學了。

*我們學了兩年日文，然後就不學了。(incorrect)

7. 中文的詞序（二）：按時間順序排列

中文的詞序遵循時間先後的原則：先發生的先說，後發生的後說。例如：

(1) 我還得去郵局辦護照呢。（先去郵局，才能辦護照）

(2) 一條路線是從芝加哥到上海，再從上海坐火車到南京。
（先在芝加哥，然後在上海；在上海先坐上火車才能到南京）

(3) 他在香港做生意，可以讓他開車到機場接我們。
（先開車才能到機場，才能接我們）

這條原則很重要，請注意運用。

第十課　在　郵　局

1. "Ｖ著Ｖ著..." :

　　"Ｖ著Ｖ著..." 後面一定有一個動詞短語，表示在進行第一個動作的同時，第二個動作不知不覺出現了。例如：

　　(1) 那個孩子哭著哭著睡著了。

　　(2) 老人走著走著迷路了。

　　(3) 弟弟想著想著笑起來了。

2. 結果補語（二）(Resultative Complements II) :

　　一個動詞或形容詞後可以有另一個形容詞或動詞，後一個動詞或形容詞表示前一個動詞或形容詞的結果，叫結果補語。我們學過以下幾種結果補語：

　　A.補語說明動作或狀態：

　　　　睡著了

　　B.補語說明主語：

　　　　他喝醉了

　　　　我聽懂了

　　　　書放在桌子上

　　　　信寄給哥哥

　　　　我走到學校

　　C.補語說明賓語：

　　　　打破了鏡子

　　　　寄丟了明信片

　　　　寫錯了一個字

做完了功課

洗乾淨衣服

D. 補語表示程度：

有的補語，用在形容詞和表示心理活動的動詞後，表示程度，例如：

好極了

壞透了

高興極了

急死了

注意，結果補語與前面的動詞或形容詞雖然在意義上有密切關係，但是它們互相有選擇性，即它們的結合不是自由的，哪個補語可以用在哪個動詞或形容詞的後面，或哪個動詞或形容詞可以用哪個補語，不是自由的，需要一個一個去記。因此，應該像學一個詞那樣去學動(詞)結(果補語)短語。

3. "把"字句 ("把" structure)：

要說某人或某事物，通過（或命令一個人進行）一個動作，使(或想使)另一個事物或人受到影響或發生變化時，就用"把"字句。例如：

(1) 請把那個杯子給我。

(2) 他一出門，就把媽媽剛才說的話忘了。

(3) 考試的時候，我把"人"字寫成了"入"字。

用"把"字句時應該注意：

A. "把"後邊的名詞，在句子中為一主要出現，可以說是一個話題，所以一般應該是一個已知確定的事物。有時可以是一個泛指的。把字前邊的主語可以不出現。

B. 動詞後不能沒有其他詞語。動詞後最常見的是補語（如例(3)），也可以是間接賓語）如例(1)），也可以是"了"。只有"了"時，"了"往往包含"消失、掉"的意思，如例（2）。在所談的事情是聽說雙方已知的情況下，"了"也可能只表示實現發生的意思。

4.定語和 " 的 " :

定語和名詞之間用不用 " 的 " 的簡單規則如下:

A. 名詞修飾名詞:

如果前面的名詞表示領屬關係,要用 " 的 " :

> 媽媽的衣服
> 老師的筆
> 學校的名字
> 商店的東西

如果前面的名詞不表示領屬關係,而是修飾後面的名詞則不用 " 的 " :

> 中文老師
> 體育節目
> 兒童用品
> 電影藝術
> 汽車廣告

所謂修飾關係,主要表示職業、質料等。領屬關係與修飾關係不同,請比較:

> 中國的城市一定在中國。
> 中國城不在中國。

B. 形容詞修飾名詞:

單音節形容詞通常不用 " 的 " :

> 紅花
> 小桌子
> 白紙
> 新書
> 舊報紙

雙音節形容詞通常用"的"：

> 漂亮的衣服
>
> 可愛的孩子
>
> 重要的事情
>
> 聰明的學生

有些常用的形容詞名詞短語，通常不用"的"：

> 客氣話
>
> 重要人物
>
> 新鮮水果

形容詞短語等後要用"的"：

> 很小的桌子
>
> 非常新的房子
>
> 大大的眼睛
>
> 深藍色的襯衫

C. 代詞修飾名詞，表示領屬關係，要用"的"：

> 我的書
>
> 他們的問題
>
> 你的事情
>
> 我們的朋友
>
> 你們的時間

D. 動詞、動詞短語、主謂短語修飾名詞一般要用"的"：

> 吃的東西
>
> 買的書
>
> 寫信用的紙
>
> 剛照的照片
>
> 打破的杯子
>
> 我看的書

　　　　你説的事情

　　　　妹妹穿的衣服

　　　　老師給的功課

　E. 數量詞修飾名詞，不用 " 的 " ：

　　　　一本書

　　　　兩雙鞋

　　　　三件衣服

　　　　四棟大樓

　　　　五張照片

經常在一起用的短語，成爲一個詞的，也不用 " 的 " ：

　　　　拿手菜

　　　　知識份子

　　　　清蒸魚

　　　　指導教授

5. " 一向 " 和 " 一直 " ：

　　 " 一向 " 表示從過去某一時間一直到現在動作結果或情況不變，後邊常常出現表示習慣、愛好的詞語。如：

　　(1) 我姐姐一向不喜歡看電影。

　　(2) 我一向早睡早起，從來不睡懶覺。

　　(3) 她的男朋友一向不吸煙、不喝酒。

　　(4) 他跟朋友一向相處得很好，很少有矛盾。

　　 " 一直 " 表示在一段時間內動作不間斷或狀態不改變，通常比 " 一向 " 所表示的時間要短。例如：

　　(1) 昨天一直下雨，我沒有出去跑步。

　　(2) 上個星期她一直生病，沒來上課。

　　(3) 這件事過去我一直不知道，今天老師才告訴我。

第十一課　一封信

1. " 幾天來 " ：

" 幾天來 " 中的 " 來 " 跟 " 以來 " 的意思一樣，也表示從某個時間一直到現在，但只用在一個表示時段的詞語後：三年來(意思是：從三年前開始到現在)，一年來(意思是：從一年前開始到現在)，五個月來(意思是：從五個月以前開始到現在)。前面不能用 " 自、自從 " 等等，也不能用在其他詞語後。(參見第七課 " 以來 ")

2. " 才 " 與 " 就 " 比較：

副詞 " 才 " 表示動作或事情發生的晚或慢， " 就 " 則相反，表示動作或事情發生的早或快。比較：

(1) 八點上課，她八點一刻才來。

八點上課，她七點半就來了。

(2) 我過一個鐘頭才能去。

我馬上就去。

(3) 她念了六年才大學畢業。

他念了三年半就大學畢業了。

注意：用 " 就 " 時，如果動作已經發生，句末要用 " 了 " 。

3. " 好不容易 " ：

" 好不容易 " 的意思是 " 很不容易 " ， " 好容易 " 的意思也是 " 很不容易 " ：

(1) 這本書很難買，我好容易(好不容易)才在香港買到一本。

(2) 今天的功課真多，我好不容易(好容易)才做完。

(3) 這個生詞昨天我好容易記住了，可是今天又忘了。

4. " 再三 " ：

" 再三 " 的意思是 " 一次又一次地 " 做某個動作，一般是與 " 說話 "
" 思考 " 有關係的動作。例如：

(1) 我再三向他說明我給他打電話只是想聊聊天，沒有別
的事，可是他不相信。

(2) 那個導遊幫了我很多忙，我再三向他表示感謝。

(3) 我離開家的時候，媽媽再三告訴我要注意身體，要常
常打電話。

" 再三 " 也可以用在 " 考慮、斟酌 " 之後，後面不能再用其他詞語：

(4) 爸爸讓我考醫學院，我考慮再三，選了統計學。

5. 介詞 " 跟／向／對 " 比較 ：

" 跟 " 、 " 向 " 、 " 對 " 在 " 面對 " ， " 引進動作的對象 " 上有相似
之處。

(1) 我在走廊裏看見他的時候，他跟我笑了笑。
(" 我 " 是 " (他)笑 " 的對象)

(2) 在中國，在路上遇到一個認識的人，跟他點點頭就可以
了，不必說什麼。

(3) 我把我的想法跟他說了說，他沒說什麼。

(1a) 我在走廊裏看見他的時候，他對我笑了笑。

(2a) 在中國，在路上遇到一個認識的人，對他點點頭就可以
了，不必說什麼。

(3a) 我把我的想法對他說了說，他沒說什麼。

(1c) 我在走廊裏看見他的時候，他向我笑了笑。

(2c) 在中國，在路上遇到一個認識的人，向他點點頭就可以了，不必説什麼。

(3c) 我把我的想法向他説了説，他沒説什麼。

但 "跟" 和 "向" 都有 "從...那裏" 的意思，這也是引進一個動作的對象，例如：

(4) 剛才我跟/向一個同學借了一本書，那本書很有意思。

(5) 我跟/向你打聽一件事，不知道你知道不知道。

但 "對" 不能這樣用。

這幾個介詞還有其他意思，它們不能互相替換。

6. "了" 用於動詞後與用於句末的不同：

"了" 用在句末在語義上通常表示一個句子結束，在語音上表示一個較大的停頓。例如：

(1) A：昨天上午你去哪兒了？

　　B：昨天上午我進城了。

(2) 做完功課以後我就睡覺了。

而 "了" 用在動詞後則不同。比較：

(3) 昨天我先在一個飯館吃了飯，然後又去買了一些東西，後來就回家了。

因此，如果句子沒有完，或者後邊的句子接得很緊，一般就把 "了" 放在動詞後，如果句子結束了，在語義正確的情況下，就把 "了" 放在句末。

第十二課 中國的節日

1. 可能補語：

在動詞和結果補語或趨向補語之間可以插入"得/不"，表示有沒有能力或客觀條件是否容許實現某種結果或趨向。例如：

(1) 今天的功課太多了，我做不完。（我沒有能力做完）

(2) 這是誰的聲音？我怎麼聽不出來？（我沒有聽出來的能力）

(3) 這個房間太小，擺不下三張床。（房間不容許擺三張床）

(4) A：他說的話你聽得懂聽不懂？

    B：我聽得懂。

應該注意，趨向補語多用否定形式，即它通常表示沒有能力或沒有條件實現某種結果或趨向。而且當表示這個意義時，往往必須用可能補語，而不能用"能/不能+動詞+結果補語/趨向補語"這種形式。例如，下面的句子是不對的：

(1)*今天的功課太多了，我不能做完。

(2)*這是誰的聲音？我怎麼不能聽出來？

(3)*這個房間太小，不能擺下三張床。

在問話中可以用肯定形式，也可以用否定形式，回答有肯定形式的可能補語的問話時，可以用肯定形式的可能補語來回答，如例(4)。

有時"不能+動詞+結果補語/趨向補語"表示的意思與可能補語不同。例如：

(5) 你給我的飯太多了，我吃不完。（沒有能力吃完）

(6) 飯你不能吃完，給你哥哥留一點。（不准(許)吃完）

可能補語是漢語中一種重要的表達方式，應該注意使用。

2. "戴著玩"：

"戴著玩"有兩部分，第一部分是一個動詞加上一個"著"，第二部分是動詞或形容詞短語。這種結構的第二部分表示第一部分的目的。例如課文"帶著玩"中，"玩"是"戴（荷包）"的目的。又如：

(1) 你別生氣，他是跟你說著玩呢。

(2) 媽媽：你怎麼剛吃完飯，又在吃？

    女兒：您看，這是餅乾，我吃著玩。

(3) A：你看什麼書呢，是電腦書嗎？

    B：不是，我在看閑書，看著玩。

(4) A：你怎麼買那麼多明信片？要寄給誰？

    B：不寄給誰，買著玩兒。

3. 疑問代詞"什麼"的不定用法：

疑問代詞"什麼"可以表示不肯定的人或事物。例如：

(1) A：你為什麼問我這個問題？

    B：我只是問問，並沒有什麼特別的目的。

(2) 別念了，這本書沒什麼意思。

(3) A：你馬上就要畢業了，有什麼打算？

    B：我還沒有什麼打算。

上述句子中的"什麼"後都有一個名詞，在這種句子裏 省去"什麼"，句子的意思不變，用上"什麼"，句子的語氣要緩一些。

疑問代詞還有一種不定用法，這種用法不限於"什麼"，代詞後不用名詞。例如：

(4) 我餓了，想吃點什麼。

(5) 今天下午沒事，我想找誰聊聊。

(6) 今年夏天我想去哪兒旅行幾天。

4. 敘述句的連接：

在我們說出連串的句子時，要把一個一個獨立的句子連接起來。

在連接中文句子時，可以分以下幾步：

第一步，加上起連接作用的詞語，中文連接句子的詞語有以下幾種：

    1)表示時間的詞語。如 " 今天、1998年、星期五，後來、然後、這時侯...以後，突然、立刻 " 等等；

    2)表示處所的詞語。如 " 在那兒、房間裏、前面、街上 " 等等；

    3)關聯詞。如 " 因為、所以，不但、而且，就、也 " 等等。

如下面的句子：

鄭人買履

_____，鄭國有個人想買一雙鞋。他_____在家里拿一根繩子比著自己的腳量好了尺寸，他_____高高興興地到集市上去了。

_____他找到了賣鞋的地方，他挑選了一雙，他想比比合適不合適。他往身上一摸，他_____發現忘了把良好的尺寸帶來了。他很著急，他心想： " 自己真是太粗心了，白跑了一趟。 "

_____他急急忙忙跑回家去拿。_____等他回到集市來的_____，天已經很晚，賣鞋的早就

走了。他的鞋沒有買成。

別人知道了這件事_____，_____問他： " 你給你自己買鞋，你在腳上試試不就可以了嗎？你怎麼還要跑回去拿尺寸呢？ " 他回答說：*
" 我只相信量好的尺寸，我不相信自己的腳。 "

    1)古時候，...時候，...以後，先

    2)在集市上

    3)可是，于是，就，就，才

第二步刪去多餘的名詞或代詞。在一個包含幾個分句的句子中，通常只有第一個分句出現主語，後邊的分句不要再用主語，這是要特別注意的。

第三步，在語流中，漢語的詞序需要調整。比如要把已知信息放在前面作為話題，把新信息放在賓語的位置上等等。在上面的句子中， " 尺寸 " 第一次出現時，因為是新信息，所以在賓語的位置上： " 量好了尺寸 " ，第二次出現時，因為它已經是已知信息，所以要用在 " 把 " 字後；再如， " 鞋 " 第一次出現時是新信息，所以在賓語的位置上： " 想買一雙鞋 " ，第二次則出現在主語的位置上： " 他的鞋沒買成 " ，因為它已經是已知信息。那麼為什麼同樣是已知信息的 " 這件事 " 卻出現在賓語的位置上呢？這是因為作為施事者的 " 別人 " 也是已知信息，而且又處于另一段的開頭，所以可以出現在主語的位置上。這樣用時，這一段

換了敘述的角度：由 " 鄭人 " 換成 " 別的人 " 。如果不想改變敘述的角度，那麼這個句子也可以改為 " 這件事別的人知道了，…… " 。

下面是連接以後的句子：

鄭人買履

　　古時侯，鄭國有個人想買一雙鞋。他先在家裡拿一根繩子比著自己的腳量好了尺寸，就高高興興地到集市上去了。

　　在集市上他找到了賣鞋的地方，他挑選了一雙，想比比合適不合適。往身上一摸，才發現忘了把良好的尺寸帶來了。他很著急，心想：" 自己真是太粗心了，白跑了一趟。"

　　于是他急急忙忙跑回家去拿。可是等回到集市來的時候，天已經很晚，賣鞋的早就走了。他的鞋沒有買成。

　　別人知道了這件事以後，就問他：" 你給你自己買鞋，在腳上試試不就可以了嗎？怎麼還要跑回去拿尺寸呢？ " 他回答說：" 我只相信量好的尺寸，不相信自己的腳。"

郑人买履

　　古时侯，郑国有个人想买一双鞋。他先在家里拿一根绳子比着自己的脚量好了尺寸，就高高兴兴地到集市上去了。

　　在集市上他找到了卖鞋的地方，他挑选了一双，想比比合适不合适。往身上一摸，才发现忘了把良好的尺寸带来了。他很着急，心想：" 自己真是太粗心了，白跑了一趟。"

　　于是他急急忙忙跑回家去拿。可是等回到集市来的时候，天已经很晚，卖鞋的早就走了。他的鞋没有买成。

　　别人知道了这件事以後，就问他：" 你给你自己买鞋，在脚上试试不就可以了吗？怎么还要跑回去拿尺寸呢？ " 他回答说：" 我只相信量好的尺寸，不相信自己的脚。"

第十三課 談 體 育

1. "連...也/都..." :

"連...也/都..." 引出一件或一個程度最高的或最低的事情或事物，後面的句子表示由此得出的推論。例如：

    (1) A：他會說中文嗎？

        B：中文他連聽都沒聽過，怎麼會說呢？

    (2) 我連這個人的名字都沒聽說過，怎麼會認識他呢？

    (3) 我姐姐會很多種語言，連阿拉伯文都會。

    (4) 這兒天氣很冷，連夏天都得穿毛衣。

在例(1)中，"聽過中文"對會說中文來說是最低的條件，從一個人沒有聽過中文可以自然地得出他不會說中文的推論。例(3)從 "我姐姐" 會最難學、會的人最少的阿拉伯文，推出她會很多種語言。例(4)從這兒 "夏天都得穿毛衣" 點出這兒天氣很冷的結論。

2. "反正" :

副詞 "反正" 有兩個意思：

A. 強調在任何情況下，結果或結論都不會改變。"反正" 一般在後一個分句出現，前面常有一個表示包含兩種或多種情況的分句。例如：

    (1) 這間房子你想住就住，反正我不住。

    (2) 那個電影，你們誰想看誰看，反正我不看。

    (3) 不管你信不信，反正我不信。

B. "反正" 指明情況或原因，這個情況或原因往往是已知的，或是一種很明顯的情況。例如：

    (1) 圖書館反正也不遠，咱們走著去吧。

    (2) 這道題你別做了，反正也不會考。

(3) 我送你回去吧，反正是順路。

本課學的是第二個用法。

3. "（成千）上（萬）"：

"上" 是達到的意思，如：

(1) 上百個中學生參加了這次考試。

(2) 這件衣服上千塊錢，你買得起嗎？

(3) 他賺的錢都上百萬了。

(4) 這場決賽有成千上萬的人排隊買票。

4. "（有益）於"：

介詞 "於" 多用於書面語，有很多意思，可以用在動詞前，也可以用在動詞後。"有益於" 中的 "於"，相當於介詞 "對"。"體育運動有益於身體健康" 的意思是："體育運動對身體健康有益"。

5. 比較的方式：

表示事物之間比較時，可以用以下幾種方式：

A. 比較的結果相同時，用 "A 跟/和 B... 一樣"：

A 跟/和 B... 一樣

(1) 這本書和那本書的價錢一樣。

(2) 姐姐跟妹妹一樣高。

(3) 這兩個房間一樣大。

B. 比較的結果不同時，可以用以下幾種方式：

a. A 比 B + Adj

(1) 這本書比那本書貴。

(2) 今天比昨天冷一點。

(3) 南方比北方暖和多了。

注意：如果有表示程度、數量的詞語時，要放在形容詞的後邊，如例(2)的
"一點"，例(3)的"多"。又如：

(4) 上海的人比北京多得多。

(5) 這個教室比那個教室大多了。

(6) 他姑媽比他父親大八歲。

b. A 沒有 B ＋ Adj

(1) 日文語法沒有中文的好學。

(2) 紐約沒有華盛頓遠。

(3) 今天沒有昨天那麼冷。

應該注意，用"沒有"時，形容詞一般用"大、長、好、高、粗、漂亮、好
看"等，而不用"小、短、壞、細、醜、難看"等，但可以用"冷、熱、貴、便
宜"等。如果形容詞前加上"那麼"，各種形容詞就都可以用了。

在比較時，在不改變意義的情況下，A或B中相同的部分常常可以省略
一成分。如A之例(1)，Ba之例(4)，Bb之例(1)。

c. A 不如 B ＋ Adj *(see Lesson Sixteen)*

6. 書面語：

中文的書面和口語有所不同。書面語的特點是

a. 句子較長，定語和狀語等修飾成分較多。

b. 有一些古漢語遺留成分。比如說"有益於健康"中的"於"（意思是
對）"為此"的"此"意思是"這"。

c. 連接詞較多。比如：

> 每當中國運動員在國際比賽中取得好成績時，就有成千上萬的人上
> 街慶祝。表哥談到這些事情時很激動。<u>可是</u>張天明認為，人們<u>所以</u>
> 參加體育運動，<u>是因為</u>運動有益於身體健康，<u>不是為了</u>給國家爭榮
> 譽。<u>而且因為</u>贏了一兩塊金牌就上街慶祝，實在沒有必要。

第十四課　家　庭

1. 趨向補語（三）：表示狀態

趨向補語的狀態意義表示動作狀態的變化。有以下幾種：

A. 表示由靜態轉爲動態--動作開始並繼續進行（上、起、起來、
開）：

(1) 他……就打起電話來。（起來，第五課）

(2) 汽車開得快起來了。

(3) 打開燈，房間一下子亮起來了。

(4) 孩子從學校一回家就彈起鋼琴來。

(5) 兩個老朋友坐下以後，聊起天來了。

"起來"還可以用於由"慢"、"暗"、"涼"、"瘦"變爲"快"、
"亮"、"熱"、"胖"等等狀態變化。例如：

(1) 天氣慢慢暖和起來了。

(2) 這幾年學中文的學生多起來了。

注意：如果有賓語，賓語要放在"起"和"來"之間，如例(1)、(2)。

"上、開"也可以表示動作或狀態的開始，但"起來"可以結合的形
容詞很廣，而"上、開"可以結合的形容詞很少。

(1) 我們在上課，你怎麼唱上了？

　　我們在上課，你怎麼唱開了？

(2) 她剛才還很高興，現在怎麼哭上了。

　　她剛才還很高興，現在怎麼哭開了。

(3) 他一回家就唱上了。

(4) 他聽了我的話以後就笑開了。

B. "下來"表示由動態轉爲靜態（包括由"快"、"亮"、"熱"、

"胖"變為"慢"、"暗"、"涼"、"瘦")。

　　(4) 汽車停下來了。

　　(5) 關上燈,房間一下子暗下來了。

　　(6) 最近他瘦下來了。

　　C. "下去"表示動作或狀態繼續:

　　(1) 張天明不好意思不聽下去。(第五課)

　　(2) 說下去!

　　(3) 天再熱下去,我就受不了了。

2. 可能補語 " (V)+不/得+了 (liao3) ":

　　可能補語 " (V)+不/得+了 "的意思是 "不能/能(V)"。例如:

　　(1) 外面在下雨,比賽不了了。(不能比賽了)

　　(2) 孩子病了,上不了學了。

　　(3) 一百塊錢買不了幾本書。

　　這類可能補語也主要用否定形式,一般都可以用 "能/不能" 替換。

　　注意, " (V)+不/得+了 " 還有另外一個意思,即 " 不能/能+(V)+完 " 的意思。如 "吃不了"。比較:

　　(4)水果壞了, 吃不了了。

　　(5)飯給得太多了,我吃不了。

3. " 要 "(應該):

　　" 要 "可以表示 "應該、需要" 的意思。如:

　　(1) 中國人認為孩子要聽父母的話,幫忙帶弟弟妹妹。

　　(2) 明天早上有考試,你們要早一點起來。

　　(3) 你跟他借的錢要還給他。

否定時,用 " 不用/不必 ":

(4) 你跟我借的錢，不必還了。

(5) 明天是週末，不用早起。

4. "下來"（結果意義）：

"下來" 表示 "分離、固定" 的意思。如：撕下來、摘下來、揭下來、拿下來、住下來、待下來、決定下來、定下來。

5. 話題（二）：

在一個句子裏，如果一個名詞表示的是已知信息，而對它描寫的形容詞表示一個新的信息時，這時應該把名詞放在句首，即話題的位置上，而把形容詞放在名詞的後邊，作謂語。這是中文和英文很不同的一點，應該特別加以注意。例如本課的幾個句子：

  (1) 只是有時候中文課的功課多一點。

這個句子不能說成：

  (1)' 只是有時候有比較多的功課。

  (2) 東方人和西方人生活習慣不一樣。

這個句子不能說成：

  (2)' 東方人和西方人有不同的生活習慣。

  (3) 你看，天華和湯姆就是因為文化背景不同分手的。

這個句子不能說成：

  (3)' 你看，天華和湯姆就是因為有不同的文化背景而分手的。

第十五課　男女平等

1. "同樣"和"一樣"：

"同樣"總是出現在名詞前，即定語的位置上；而"一樣"總是出現謂語或補語的位置上。例如：

(1) A：這本字典的價錢跟那本一樣。

　　B：我想用同樣的價錢，也買一本你這樣的字典。

(2) A：我們兩個人的看法一樣。

　　B：你們常常看同樣的書，有同樣的看法一點也不奇怪。

(3) 姐姐跟妹妹長得一樣。

(4) 哥哥和弟弟在一個班，上同樣的課。

2. "隨著......"：

"隨著"出現在第一個分句，表示一種變化的情況，第二個分句表示伴隨第一個分句所表示的變化而出現的相應的變化。例如：

(1) 隨著經濟的發展，人民的生活水平也得到提高。

(2) 隨著他們交往的時間越長，兩個人相處得越好。

(3) 隨著他中文水平的提高，他看中文報的速度越來越快了。

3. "在...方面"：

"在...方面"主要表示範圍，中間可以用動詞和某些抽象的雙音節名詞：

(1) 在男女平等方面，這個國家還存在很大的問題。

(2) 在穿的方面，他不太在乎，可是在吃的方面，他非常挑剔。

(3) 在體育運動方面，中國最近幾年發展很快。

(4) MIT可以說是在工程技術方面最有名的大學了。

4. "甚至"：

連詞"甚至"的作用是突出某一點來說明說話人得一種看法：

(1) 弟弟很聰明，才五歲，不但能看書，甚至能寫詩。

（用"能寫詩"來證明"很聰明"。）

(2) 他是個中國通，甚至連氣功都懂。

（用"懂氣功"說明"中國通"。）

(3) A：你看過電影《白毛女》嗎？

B：沒有，什麼《白毛女》，我甚至都沒聽說過。

（用"沒聽說過"說明"沒看過"。）

(4) 他對中國的節日一點都不清楚，甚至連春節都不知道。

（用"不知道春節"說明"不清楚中國的節日"。）

"甚至"常常與"連...也/都..."一起用。

5. 句子的結構和順序(三)：

我們前面已經講過中文句子的順序，本課將做一個總結。
中文的句子通常的順序是：

（定語)主語--時間+處所+其他狀語--動詞--補語--(定語)賓語

這裏說的補語是指結果補語與趨向補語(趨向補語與賓語的位置問題，請看本書有關部分。)帶"得"的補語句與賓語同時出現時，要重復動詞；動詞後有表示動作持續的時間或次數的，也要重復動詞。例如：

(1) 我昨天在電影院看了一個新電影。

(2) 明天我上完課就去圖書館。

(3) 他學中文學了三年多了。

(4) 我寫字寫得很慢。

當從上文或語言環境中可以知道某人或事物是已知信息時，通常就應該把表示一致的人或事物的名詞放在句首作話題，或放在"把"的後邊：

(5) 你告訴我的那件事情我已經知道了。

(6) 請你把桌子上的地圖給我。

第十六課 健康與保險

1. 多項定語：

　　一個名詞前面可以有幾個定語，這些定語的排列是有一定的次序的。第一，描寫性的定語要放在表示領屬關係等非描寫性的定語後，數量詞、指示代詞+量詞則在這兩種定語中間。例如：

(1) 在中國，我們遊覽了北京的幾個最大的公園，以及南京的那個有名的夫子廟。

　　"北京、南京"表示處所，是非描寫性的，在前面；"最大、有名"是描寫性的，在後面；"幾個、那個"在這兩類定語的中間。又如：

(2) 媽媽昨天給妹妹講了一個非常有意思的故事。

(3) 我給姐姐買的那件襯衫很漂亮。

(4) 我從來不看電視裏撥的那些無聊的新聞。

　　在描寫性定語中，不用"的"的定語最靠近所修飾的名詞。如：好的中文老師，很新的木頭桌子。兩個定語都是形容詞時，簡單的形容詞在後，結構比較複雜的形容詞在前，如：窄窄的小河、胖胖的圓臉、很大的紅蘋果。如果兩個都是形容詞，表示顏色的在後，其他的形容詞在前，如：大紅蘋果、小白兔。

2. "是"表示肯定：

　　漢語的形容詞做謂語前面不能用"是"。可是在肯定剛剛說過的話是事實時，可以用"是"，這時"是"可以重讀。例如：

(1) A：今天天氣不錯。

　　　B：今天天氣是不錯，咱們出去玩玩吧？

(2) 你剛才說現在男女不平等。對，現在男女是還不夠平等，可是已經比從前好多了。

(3) A：這個女孩鋼琴彈得真好。

B： 她鋼琴彈得是好，連我都被她吸引住了。。。

3. "V+不／得+起"：

"V+不／得+起"的意思是：在經濟、時間上等方面是否有能力承受。例如：

(1) 戲票太貴，我買不起。

(2) 多穿點兒，別生病了。我們沒保險，看不起病。

(3) 那家飯館的菜貴得不得了，咱們吃不起。

(4) 我每天那麼忙，你讓我陪你去看電影，我可陪不起。

4. 能願動詞"會"：

能願動詞"會"有幾個意思，一個常用的意思是：通過學而有能力做某事，如："我會說漢語。""你會開車嗎？""妹妹不會游泳。"本課學的"會"意思是"將來可能"。如：

(1) A：我沒有錢了，你說我跟小王借，他會借給我嗎？

　　B：我想他會借給你。

(2) A：飛機是九點的，現在走會晚嗎？

　　B：別著急，不會晚。

5. "畢竟（到底、究竟）"：

副詞"畢竟"的意思是"歸根結底"，強調原因或特點，這樣用時，與"究竟、到底"基本相同。例如：

(1) 你畢竟在家裏常常聽父母說中文，學中文比我容易多了。

(2) 媽媽畢竟是媽媽，永遠會愛自己的孩子的。

(3) 現在畢竟是春天了，天氣無論多冷，也跟冬天不一樣。

6. 用 " 不如 " 的比較句 :

" 不如 " 可以用來比較,例如:

(1) 今天的天氣不如昨天。

(2) 他覺得美國的健康保險制度不如加拿大好。

(3) 這部電影不如昨天看的那部有意思。

注意:

　A. 用 " 不如 " 時,可以省去表示比較結果的形容詞 " 好 " ,如例 (1);

　B. 用於這種比較句的形容詞,一般是正向形容詞,如:好、大、長、厚、重、亮等,而不用壞、小、短、薄、輕、暗等。

(4) 我的功課不如他。

(5) 你的指導教授不如我的指導教授負責任。

(6) 打字機不如電腦方便。

這種比較方式與用 " 沒有 " 很接近。但用 " 不如 " 時,可以不用任何形容詞,如例 (1),意思是 " (不如...)好 " 。

我們也可以用 " 不比 " 表示比較。但應該注意:

第一,用 " 不比 " 時,通常是上文出現了用 " 比 " 的句子,說話人不同意對方的說法。例如:

(7) A : 我姐姐比你高。

　　B : 不,你姐姐不比我高。

(8) A : 日文比中文難。

　　B : 我覺得日文不比中文難。

第二, " 沒有 " 和 " 不比 " 表示的意思不完全一樣。例如:

(9) 我姐姐沒有你高。

　(意思是你比我姐姐高)

　我姐姐不比你高。

　(意思可以是:你比我姐姐高/我姐姐跟你一樣高。)

在比較時，在不影響意義的情況下，B項(有時是A項)常常可以省略一些
詞語。如 (1)，(2)，(4)等。

7. 量詞重迭：

量詞可以重迭，表示由個體組成的全體，有＂毫無例外＂的意思。＂
人、年、天＂等少數幾個名詞也可以重迭。例如：

(1) 今天過年，人人都很高興。

(2) 我們班的學生，雖然個個都很聰明，可是都很懶。

(3) 他頓頓都吃魚。

注意：

A. ＂每＂跟量詞重疊形式不同：

＂每＂既表示由個體組成的全體，也表示全體中的個體。比較：

(4) 端午節的時候，家家都吃粽子。（ 由個體組成全體 ）

　　端午節的時候，每家都吃粽子。（ 由個體組成全體 ）

(5) 我們姐妹三人，每個人的興趣不同。（ 全體中的個體 ）

　　*我們姐妹三人，人人的興趣不同。

B. 量詞重迭一般不出現在賓語或賓語的定語的位置上，而＂每＂
沒有這個限制。比較：

(6) 你要把信寄給班上每一個人。

　　*你要把信寄給班上人人。

(7) 請你把信送到每一家的門口。

　　*請你把信送到家家的門口。

第十七課 教育

1. "很不以為然":

"不以為然"的意思是"認為不對","很"是修飾"不以為然",所以"很不以為然"的意思就是"認為很不對"。近年來,在中國大陸,"不以為然"在有些人當中有了一個新的用法:"覺得無所謂"。例如"媽媽告訴他小孩子不應該抽煙,他卻不以為然。"本課用的是第一個意思。

2. "簡直":

"簡直"表示一種誇張的語氣,有"差不多"或"幾乎完全"的意思。例如:

(1) 他們結婚才半年就要離婚,我簡直不能相信。

(意思是"幾乎不相信,但還是相信了")

(2) 他居然做這樣的事,簡直不是一個人。

(3) 他減肥以後,我簡直認不出他來了。

3. "V+壞+了"表示程度:

"壞"用在動詞後可以表示很深的程度,如:急壞了,餓壞了,累壞了,氣壞了,樂壞了。

4. "適合(與"合適"比較)":

"適合"是動詞,後面一定要有賓語:

(1) 這件衣服不適合你穿,你媽媽穿可能合適。

(2) 這種家俱適合家裏用,放在辦公室不合適。

(3) 你跟父母這樣說話很不合適,應該向他們道歉。

(4) 這個專業不適合你,你還是選別的專業吧。

5. " 被 " 字句 :

中文表示被動意義時，常常不用任何表示被動意義的詞。例如：

(1) 水果都吃完了，該去買了。

(2) 功課做錯了，他只好再做一次。

(3) 房子租好了，明天就可以搬家了。

在上面的句子裏，" 水果、功課、房子 " 等都是動作的受事，整個句子具有被動意義，但沒有用 " 被、叫、讓 " 等表示被動意義的詞。在這些句子裏，" 水果 " 等是話題(topic)。在這些句子裏不能用 " 被、叫、讓 " 等介詞。

" 被、叫、讓 " 時，句子通常表示對受事者(主語)來說是不愉快的事，或者失去了什麼，例如：

(1) 屈原被楚國國王趕到南方去了。

(2) 書叫郵局寄丟了。

(3) 他讓爸爸打了一頓。

但是也可以說：

(4) 王朋被同學選為班長。

(5) 哥哥被派到國外去了。

能這樣用的動詞很有限。

6. " 從來 " :

" 從來 " 的意思是 " 從過去到現在一直... "，語氣肯定，常用於否定句：

(1) A : 我的作業是不是你拿去了？

　　B : 沒有啊，我從來不拿你的東西。

(2) 這件事情我從來沒聽説過。

(3) 我跟我的哥哥從來沒有在一起打過球。

" 從來 " 也可以用於肯定句，後邊常常跟著 " 都是、是 " :

(1) 這個人從來都是這樣，見到人不愛打招呼。

(2) 他從來是看別人怎麼做，他就怎麼做。

第十八課 槍枝與犯罪

1. " 槍走了火 ... " :

在口語中，中文常常不用連詞，分句與分句之間的關係，只能從上下文來判斷。比如 " 我們這兒進進出出的人那麼多，萬一不小心，槍走了火怎麼辦？" 這個句子，在 " 萬一不小心，槍走了火 " 前實際上有 " 如果/要是 " 之類的連詞。所以，在理解中文的句子時，要注意這種沒有連詞的句子表示的究竟是什麼關係。

" 走火 " 在詞匯上是一個詞，但在語法上是兩個詞，中間可以加上 " 了、過 " 之類的詞，如 " 槍走了火 "。類似的詞語還有 " 睡覺、洗澡、鞠躬、跳舞、唱歌、見面 " 等等。注意不要在這類詞語後再用賓語、補語等，如不能說：*我昨天見面他。*今天晚上我要跳舞一會兒。

2. 副詞 " 正 " :

副詞 " 正 " 可以表示 " 恰巧、正好 " 的意思。如：

(1) 學生：老師，這個題我不會做，可以不做嗎？

老師：正因為你不會做，才更應該做。不懂的地方可以問我。

(2) 今天正好我沒有事，我們出去看電影好嗎？

(3) A：這本書借我看看可以嗎？

B：對不起，這本書我正在看，我看完了你再看吧。

3. 連詞 " 並 " :

連詞 " 並 " 表示進一層的意思，與 " 並且 " 的意思一樣，可以連接兩個動詞(詞組)或兩個分句，多用於書面語。例如：

(1) 昨天上課，老師帶我們念課文並講解了語法。

(2) 最近報上報導中國的文章很多，其中有一篇介紹了
中國經濟發展很快的原因，並指出了現有的問題。

(3) 學校昨天開會，聽取學生提出的意見，並研究了解決的
辦法。

注意，在上述句子裏，不能用"和"。

4. "等(等)"：

用於表示列舉的並列關係詞語之後，例如：

(1) 參加討論會的有中國、美國、法國等三個國家。

(2) 奧林匹克運動會今天的比賽有籃球、游泳、跳水等等。

(3) 上半年我去了北京、上海、南京等五個城市。

"等"之前可以列出所列舉的全部項目，如例(1)，也可以列出部分項
目，如例(3)；"等"和"等等"的用法一樣。

第十九課 動物與人

1. " 為了 " 和 " 因為 " :

" 為了 " 表示目的, " 因為 " 表示原因:

(1) 為了學習中文,我明年要去中國。

(2) 為了解決人口問題,中國政府只讓每個家庭生一個孩子。

(3) 我買槍是為了保護自己。

(4) 因為在美國學中文太貴,所以我去中國學。

(5) 因為中國的人口太多,所以中國政府只讓一家生一個孩子。

(6) 因為這兒不安全,所以我買了一枝槍。

(7) 因為這個學校很有名,所以我申請。

(8) 我申請這個學校,是為了能跟我的女朋友在一起。

2. 表示語氣的 " 可 "(你可別後悔):

在祈使句中, " 可 " 有勸導、告誡的意思,後面常常有 " 要、能、應該 " 一類能願動詞,句末一般有語氣詞:

(1) 那兒很危險,你可要注意啊!

(2) 明天的會特別重要,你可不能忘了。

(3) 這件事你答應了,可別後悔呀。

3. " (死)於 " :

(1) 每年不少人死於艾滋病。

(2) 最近我忙於寫論文,沒有時間給你打電話。

4. "其中" :

"其中"的意思"在那些中間",一般指"範圍"。例如:

(1)三年級有十五個學生,其中有三個是日本人,三個是韓國人,其他的是美國人。

(2)學校附近有很多中國餐館,其中有一家是從紐約搬來的。

(3)老師問了我不少問題,其中只有一個很容易,我會回答,別的我都不會。

注意,用"其中"時,前面必須有另外一個句子,在那個句子裏,要有包含表示"多數不止一個(人或事物)"的詞語。如例(1)的"十五學生",例(2)的"很多中國餐館",例(3)的"不少問題","其中"正是接在這些詞語的後邊,表示"在那些當中"。

5. "而" :

"而"可以把表示目的、原因的詞語連接到動詞上,前面常常有"由於、因為"等詞語,是書面語。例如:

(1) 我們為國家而工作。

　("為國家"是目的,動詞是"工作")

(2) 他們因為贏得金牌而驕傲起來。

　("贏得金牌"是原因,動詞和結果是"驕傲起來")

第二十課 環境保護

1. " 怎麼 " 和 " 為什麼 " :

" 怎麼 " 是一個詢問方式的疑問代詞,如 " 那個字怎麼寫? " " 怎麼 " 也可以用來詢問原因。例: " 怎麼這幾天沒見到你? " 這樣用的 " 怎麼 " 與 " 為甚麼 " 有什麼不同呢?

用 " 怎麼 " 問問題時,總有一些表示奇怪、詫異的成分。例:

(1)三點了,他應該來了,怎麼還沒來?

(2)明天考試?我怎麼不知道?

(3)怎麼?他沒來上課?

用 " 為什麼 " 時,主要是問原因,不一定有奇怪的成分。上述句子,例(1)的 " 怎麼 " 可以用 " 為什麼 " 替換,替換後奇怪的成分減輕了,指責的成分加重了。例(2)不宜用 " 為什麼 " 替換,如果用 " 為什麼 " 好像在質問誰,與原句意思相差很遠。用 " 為什麼 " 時,顯然詢問的成分比 " 怎麼 " 重:

(4)這麼重要的事情,你為什麼不告訴我?

(5)飛機為什麼會飛?

(6)他為什麼不來?為什麼?為什麼?

例(4)可以用 " 怎麼 " 替換,替換後,奇怪的成分增加了,質問的語氣減弱了。例(5)不能用 " 怎麼 " 來替換,這可能是物理教科書中的句子,只為了提問,沒有一點奇怪的成分。例(6)的兩個 " 為什麼 " 都不宜用 " 怎麼 " 替換,因為這是一個語氣很重的表示質問的句子。因此,當詢問中包含奇怪、詫異的成分時,最好用 " 怎麼 " ;當詢問的成分大於奇怪時,最好用 " 為甚麼 " ;當只表示奇怪、詫異時,應該用 " 怎麼 " ;當只表示詢問時,應該用 " 為什麼 " 。此外 " 怎麼 " 不能用於句末,如例(6)中的 " 為什麼 " ;而 " 為什麼 " 不能在一個始發句的開頭單獨成句,如例(3)中的 " 怎麼 " 。

2. "(好)多了" 與 "(好)得多" :

在表示比較時，形容詞後邊可以用 "多了、得多" 表示程度。例如：

(1) 這兒的天氣比東岸熱多了。

這兒的天氣比東岸熱得多。

(2) 中國的人口比美國多多了。

中國的人口比美國多得多。

(3) A：你姐姐的病好一點了嗎？

(意思是：比以前好一點了嗎？)

B：好多了。

注意：

A. 在比較句裏，形容詞前不能用任何表示程度的詞語，例如，不能說：*他比我很好。*他比我一點兒好。但可以在形容詞的後邊用 "一點兒、得很、得多、多了、很多" 等等，但不能把上述詞語混在一起用，例如不能說：*他比我好得多了：

B. 句子中沒有 "比" 等表示比較的詞語時，形容詞後面只能用 "一點兒、多了"，見例(3)。

3. "...吧，...吧...，" :

連用兩個用 "吧" 的句子，表示交替假設，有左右為難或猶豫不決的意思。例如：

(1) 我的車買了好幾年了，最近老有問題。修理吧，得花不少錢，不修理吧，不能開，買新的吧，又沒有錢，真難辦。

(2) 晚上有一個電影，聽說不錯，可是今天作業很多。去看電影吧，怕回來作業做不完，不看吧，又覺得很可惜。

(3) 他的女朋友的妹妹明天舉行生日晚會。他想，去吧，沒有錢買禮物，不去吧，又怕女朋友生氣。怎麼辦呢？

4. "往往" 與 "常常" :

"往往" 與 "常常" 都表示動作或情況經常出現。但二者有所不同：

A. "往往" 一般來說比 "常常" 表示的頻率更高，即 "往往" 相對地表示更加經常；

B. "往往" 用於到目前為止的一種有規律的現象，不能跟表示主觀願望的動詞一起用。在動詞前 "常常" 只表示重復出現，一般沒有什麼規律，也可以用於表示主觀願望。例如：

(1) 過去我常常希望他來，現在怕他來。

　*過去我往往希望他來，現在怕他來。

(2) 我希望你以後常常來。

　*我希望你以後往往來。

(3) 週末他往往不在家。

　週末他常常不在家。

這兩個句子意思不同。

C. "往往" 只能用於過去或沒有時間性的情況，不能用於將來，"常常" 沒有這個限制。例如：

我以後星期六會常常來。

*我以後星期六會往往來。